Sample freedom from bottle-washing

With Steri-bottle®, when you're taking a break from the daily grind, you can take a break from bottle-washing too.

Because it's pre-sterilised, Steri-bottle® takes all the hassle out of bottle preparation! Simply open the top, put in the feed (the wide mouth makes it suitable for expressed breastmilk too), and click shut.

When you've finished feeding, you simply dispose of it. Being made from one safe plastic, it's easily recyclable.

For your free sample simply cut out the coupon and we'll send you a free sample. It could just be the break you need!

Ready, steri...go!®

Available from most major **Supermarkets, Boots and wellbeing.com,** and most good chemists. Packs of 4 at just £1.99. In 125ml and 250ml sizes with medium-flow and fast-flow teats.

Terms and Conditions

Free Steri-bottle offer is open to all UK residents aged 16 or over. Only one application per household. **Closing date 31st August 2003.** No photocopies of coupons accepted. Please send your free coupon to: Free Steri-bottle offer, **PO Box 39307 London SE13 7WE.** On receipt of a fully completed Free Steri-bottle coupon, a single 250ml medium flow Steri-bottle sample will be sent out. Please allow 28 days for delivery. In the event of no stock being available, a voucher of equal or greater value to the cost of a 250ml Steri-bottle will be sent out. Promoter: Steri-bottle Ltd, London EC4 4BN.

✂

Sample freedom from bottle washing here!

Name _____

Address _____

_____ Postcode _____

Tel (day): _____ Tel (evening): _____

☐ Please tick this box if you do not wish to receive further information from Steri-bottle or its associated companies.

3

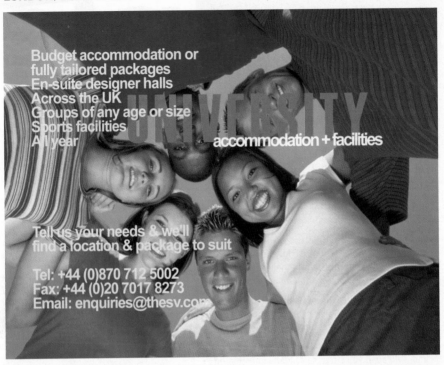

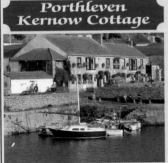

FHG

Self-Catering Holidays

in Britain 2003

Including
Caravan & Camping

England, Scotland, Wales, Ireland and The Channel Islands

For Contents see Page 44/45

For Index of towns/counties see back of book

FHG Publications
Paisley

Part of IPC Country and Leisure Media

ENGLAND and WALES Counties

NORTH WALES
1. Denbighshire
2. Flintshire
3. Wrexham

SOUTH WALES
4. Swansea
5. Neath and Port Talbot
6. Bridgend
7. Rhondda Cynon Taff
8. Merthyr Tydfil
9. Vale of Glamorgan
10. Cardiff
11. Caerphilly
12. Blaenau Gwent
13. Torfaen
14. Newport
15. Monmouthshire

NORTHUMBERLAND

TYNE & WEAR

DURHAM

CUMBRIA

ISLE OF MAN

NORTH YORKSHIRE

LANCASHIRE

EAST RIDING OF YORKSHIRE

WEST YORKSHIRE

GREATER MANCHESTER

MERSEYSIDE

SOUTH YORKSHIRE

ISLE OF ANGLESEY

CONWY

CHESHIRE

DERBYSHIRE

LINCOLNSHIRE

NOTTINGHAMSHIRE

GWYNEDD

STAFFORDSHIRE

SHROPSHIRE

LEICESTERSHIRE

RUTLAND

NORFOLK

WEST MIDLANDS

POWYS

CAMBRIDGESHIRE

NORTHAMPTONSHIRE

CEREDIGION

WARWICKSHIRE

WORCESTERSHIRE

SUFFOLK

HEREFORDSHIRE

BEDFORDSHIRE

PEMBROKESHIRE

CARMARTHENSHIRE

GLOUCESTERSHIRE

BUCKINGHAMSHIRE

HERTFORDSHIRE

ESSEX

OXFORDSHIRE

BRISTOL

BERKSHIRE

GREATER LONDON

WILTSHIRE

SURREY

KENT

SOMERSET

HAMPSHIRE

WEST SUSSEX

E. SUSSEX

DEVON

DORSET

ISLE OF WIGHT

CORNWALL

SCILLY ISLES

©MAPS IN MINUTES™ 2001

Mini bungalow (sleeps two) within the grounds of an old country house. Lovely garden, rural district. Lounge/diner/cooking area, bedroom, shower room, conservatory. Bed linen provided. Parking within grounds. No children or pets. Central for touring South West Peninsula. Sea two miles. Available all year. Terms from £130 (including heating).

Mrs Catherine Wall, Relubbus Lane, St Hilary, Penzance TR20 9EA • 01736 762308

Bamham Farm Cottages
ETC ★★★ & ★★★★

Eight individually designed cottages, ideally situated in beautiful countryside one mile from the ancient capital of Cornwall, Launceston, which is dominated by its Norman castle. The North and South coasts are easily accessible, as are both Dartmoor and Bodmin Moor.

◆ Heated indoor swimming pool ◆ Sauna ◆ Solarium
◆ Video recorders ◆ Children's play area ◆ Games room
◆ Trout fishing ◆ Open all year
◆ Short breaks available out of season

Jackie Chapman, Higher Bamham Farm,
Launceston, Cornwall PL15 9LD
Tel: 01566 772141 • jackie@bamhamfarm.co.uk
www.bamhamfarm.co.uk

◆◆ Coombe Farm Holiday Cottages ◆◆

Within easy reach of the coast, Bodmin Moor and the Eden Project, Coombe Farm offers a superb base for holidays and out-of-season short breaks. Converted barns offer simple but comfortable accommodation finished to a high standard. The cottages have very well-equipped kitchens, Sky TV, CD players and shared use of a washing machine and tumble dryer. All cottages tastefully furnished with local hand-made pine furniture. All linen, towels, fuel and power included. The games room offers table tennis, snooker and darts, and there is a lovely walk around the pond. **SHORT BREAKS:** Between January and the end of April and from October to December (excluding Easter, Whit, October half term and Christmas/New Year) – minimum stay 3 nights. **DISCOUNTS:** Bookings of 14 nights + receive a 10% discount. **NEW:** From Spring 2002 freshly prepared local food delivered straight to your cottage.

Coombe Farm Holiday Cottages, Herodsfoot, Liskeard, Cornwall PL14 4RS
01579 320548 • www.coombe.farm.co.uk   we welcome well-behaved dogs

Fiona and Ian welcome you to Hilton Farm

Where coast meets countryside, in an Area of Outstanding Natural Beauty. The ideal place to make the most of Devon & Cornwall. Superb setting in 25 acres of ground. Self-catering cottages open all year, with farmhouse B&B available from October to June, from £18pp.

★ 16th century Farmhouse, sleeps 10 ★ 3 new luxury cottages
★ 6 fully equipped converted barn cottages ★ Superb heated outdoor swimming pool
★ Activity area/play area/BBQ and picnic area ★ Laundry facilities
★ Just 2 miles from sandy beaches ★ World-famous Eden Project 45 minutes' drive.

Whether you want a quiet, relaxing holiday, or a fun-packed leisure and sporting activity holiday, Hilton Farm House & Holiday Cottages are the ideal spot to make the most of your holiday in the West Country.

Hilton Farm & Cottages, Marhamchurch, Bude EX23 0HE • Tel/Fax: 01288 361521
www.hiltonfarmhouse.co.uk • ian@hiltonfarmhouse.freeserve.co.uk

Trenannick Cottages

Five delightful cottages converted from 18th century farm buildings, standing at the end of a private, tree-lined drive, in a quiet rural setting. All cottages have small private gardens, and access to barbecue area, children's playing field, and small copse. Ideal touring base for North Cornish coast, two miles from A39, with Crackington Haven, Bude, and Boscastle all nearby. Accommodation varies from two to six persons per cottage, with wheelchair access in the Roundhouse. Open throughout the year, with log fires for those colder evenings. Short Breaks available. Pets welcome in certain cottages. Rates from £130 to £475 per week.

Details from **Mrs L. Harrison, Trenannick Farmhouse, Warbstow, Launceston PL15 8RP** • Tel: **01566 781443**
e-mail: **lorraine.trenannick@il2.com** • website: **www.trenannickcottages.co.uk**

Penrose Burden Holiday Cottages

St Breward, Bodmin, Cornwall PL30 4LZ
Tel: 01208 850277 / 850617; Fax: 01208 850915

Situated within easy reach of both coasts and Bodmin Moor on a large farm overlooking a wooded valley with own salmon and trout fishing. These stone cottages with exposed beams and quarry tiled floors have been featured on TV and are award winners. Home-made meals can be delivered daily. All are suitable for wheelchair users and dogs are welcomed. Our cottages sleep from two to seven and are open all year.
Please write or telephone for a colour brochure. — *Nancy Hall*

Close to The Eden Project

Duchy Holidays — A selection of seaside and countryside holiday homes located throughout Cornwall. A luxury bungalow with a private swimming pool, farmhouse with fishing lake, beachside cottages, lodges and villas with swimming pools and entertainment. All properties are inspected and personally supervised. Short breaks and long weekends available from £85 (excluding school holidays).

**Duchy Holidays, 14 St Georges Hill,
Perranporth, Cornwall TR6 0DZ
Tel & Fax: 01872 572971
e-mail: duchy.holidays@virgin.net
website: www.duchyholidays.co.uk**

Greenhowe
Caravan Park
Great Langdale, English Lakeland.

VERY GOOD

Greenhowe is a permanent Caravan Park with Self Contained Holiday Accommodation. Subject to availability Holiday Homes may be rented for short or long periods from 1st March until mid-November. The Park is situated in the heart of the Lake District some half a mile from Dungeon Ghyll at the foot of the Langdale Pikes. It is an ideal centre for Climbing, Fell Walking, Riding, Swimming, Water Skiing or just a lazy holiday. **Please ask about Short Breaks.**

Winners of the Rose Award 1983-2000.
ETC Grading "Very Good".

Greenhowe Caravan Park
Great Langdale, Ambleside
Cumbria LA22 9JU

For free colour brochure
Telephone: (015394) 37231
Fax: (015394) 37464
Freephone: 0800 0717231

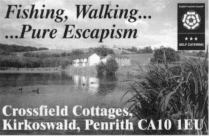

CUDDY'S HALL HOLIDAY COTTAGE

A peaceful rural retreat set amidst forest and winding streams in the beautiful Cumbrian/Scottish Borders. Perfect for the great outdoors – Walking, cycling, pony trekking. Also a good base to explore – Scotland, the Roman Wall, Kielder Water, the Solway Coast and the Lake District, to name but a few...

• A good value Quality Country Cottage • Highly Commended by the English Tourist Council •
• Open all Year • Sleeps up to 5 guests • See also advertisement in main section under Cumbria •
For further details please telephone Mrs Joanna Furness: 016977 48160
Or visit our website: www.cuddys-hall.co.uk

Kirkstone Foot

Kirkstone Pass Road
Ambleside, Cumbria LA22 9EH

★★★★ SELF CATERING

A 17th Century converted Country House with self-catering cottages and apartments for 2 to 6 persons. Set in peaceful gardens adjoining the magnificent Lakeland Fells, and yet only 4 minutes' walk from the centre of Ambleside.

Dogs are very welcome in most self-catering cottages and apartments, which have fully equipped kitchens, bathrooms with bath and shower, colour TV/video. All Linen, Towels and electricity supplied.

Open all year. Bookings taken for three or more nights.

Colour brochure: Please telephone (015394) 32232 or fax (015394) 32805
e-mail: kirkstone@breathemail.net • website:www.kirkstonefoot.co.uk

Birthwaite Edge, Windermere

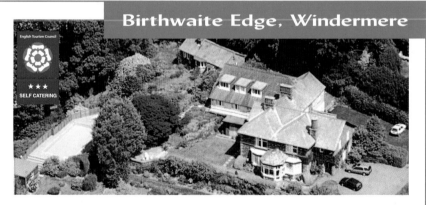

★★★ SELF CATERING

10 minutes' walk from lake or village. Open all year. 10 fully equipped spacious apartments, sleep two-six.

For brochure contact resident owners or visit our website for pictures:
Marsha Dodsworth, Birthwaite Edge, Birthwaite Road,
Windermere LA23 1BS
Telephone/Fax: 015394 42861
e-mail: fhg@lakedge.com website: www.lakedge.com

Regret, no smoking and no pets

NOTE

All the information in this guide is given in good faith in the belief that it is correct. However, the publishers cannot guarantee the facts given in these pages, neither are they responsible for changes in ownership or facilities that may take place after the date of going to press. Readers should always satisfy themselves that the facilities they require are available and that the terms, if quoted, still apply.

Hall Lane, Walton-on-the-Naze, Essex CO14 8HL
Fax: 01255 682 427 • E-mail: nazemarine@gbholidayparks.co.uk
web: www.gbholidayparks.co.uk

...lazy days at the Naze

The Essex coast is dotted with colourful seaside resorts and Naze Marine sits alongside one of these. Walton on the Naze boasts golden beaches, a nature reserve and pier. Take time to explore the many shops selling seaside specialities and when you're ready head back to the park where the emphasis is on relaxation. This delightful park offers a friendly, country club together with superb heated outdoor pool complex.

* Outdoor swimming pool • Sea fishing trips • Adjacent Nature Reserve
* Children's amusements and play area • Well stocked convenience store • Naze Armada Country Club
* Golf, horse riding and fishing locally • Crabbing off the jetty
* Attractive Marina close-by • Café/take-away • Sandy beaches

HOLIDAY BOOKING LINE: 0870 442 9292

Main Road, St. Lawrence Bay, Near Southminster, Essex CM0 7LY
Fax: 01621 778 106 • E-mail: waterside@gbholidayparks.co.uk
web: www.gbholidayparks.co.uk

Leisurely pursuits in an idyllic countryside setting

Waterside is an attractive park with leafy, tree-lined avenues. Situated by the River Blackwater, the park enjoys fine estuary views towards Mersea Island. With a modern, quality fleet of hire caravans and excellent facilities that include an indoor pool, sauna and jacuzzi the park is well equipped for holidaymakers. The surrounding district has varied attractions and several nature reserves and footpaths, or for shopping there's Maldon, an attractive riverside town.

* Indoor leisure pool with adjacent children's splash pool and slide • Relaxing sauna and jacuzzi
* Amusement Centre • Outdoor Play Area • Sheltered beach nearby • Waterside Country Club
* Lovely tree-lined walks • Golf (9 & 18-hole) and fishing nearby
* Café/take-away • Horse riding available locally
* Well-stocked mini-market • Lake feature

HOLIDAY BOOKING LINE: 0870 442 9298

London Road, Clacton-on-Sea, Essex CO16 9QY
Fax: 01255 689 805 • E-mail: highfield@gbholidayparks.co.uk
web: www.gbholidayparks.co.uk

...the ultimate in holiday venues

Highfield enjoys high levels of repeat business and being located on the famous Essex sunshine coast it's easy to see why. Within easy reach of golden beaches and bustling, colourful promenades on the one hand and gentle Essex countryside on the other, it's a region of contrasts. Enjoy the superb entertainment and range of facilities on offer at Highfield and enjoy a drink at the pool's edge whilst your children amuse themselves for hours on the new flume and slide.

* Large outdoor pools with amazing new flume and slide • Outdoor adventure play area
* Children's entertainment with Dylan the Dinosaur • Well-stocked convenience store • Solarium
* Wide-screen satellite TV • Amusement centre featuring some of the latest electronic games
* Organised outdoor games (football, rounders, baseball)
* Fantastic beaches nearby • Pony trekking available locally
* Pool-side bar for snacks and beverages.

HOLIDAY BOOKING LINE: 0870 442 9287

East Mersea, Mersea Island, Nr Colchester, Essex CO5 8TN
Fax: 01206 385 483 • E-mail: coopersbeach@gbholidayparks.co.uk
web: www.gbholidayparks.co.uk

Discover an island that will capture your imagination

Coopers Beach is located on Mersea Island, whose only link with the mainland is an ancient causeway known as The Strood. West Mersea is a small resort and sailing centre. At East Mersea, beautiful leafy lanes wind their way towards the seafront, where you will find the park. Here the clubhouse with adjacent pool is an ideal place to relax, and offers great sea views. We think you will agree, this park has it all.

* Popular outdoor heated pool (open May-Sept) • Beach access • Adventure playground
* Dylan the Dinosaur's Children's Club • Golf courses nearby • Pony trekking nearby (7 miles)
* Fast food takeaway • Adult beach club • Fishing trips nearby • Nightlife Countryside walks
* Multi-sports centre • Tennis court • Launderette
* Family clubroom (suitable for children) with outdoor beach terrace and fantastic sea views.

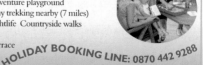

HOLIDAY BOOKING LINE: 0870 442 9288

THE LODGE

The Lodge, being the former Verger's cottage, can be found in a tranquil setting just eight miles north of the historic cathedral town of Hereford. Peacefully located next to the Parish Church. Guests can enjoy the pleasure of the gardens of Felton House, the stone-built former Rectory, now a guest house. The Lodge has been completely renovated and restored to its Victorian character but with the convenience of central heating, a modern kitchen. two shower rooms, a diningroom and a sittingroom with TV. There are three bedrooms with accommodation for five people (one double room, one twin, one single), and in addition a cot is available. Linen may he hired. Children, and pets with responsible owners, are most welcome. Private parking, patio and garden. The Lodge is a cosy, restful cottage, spotlessly clean. Short Breaks catered for and weekly terms range from £150 to £275 per week, exclusive of electricity. Brochure available.

Marjorie and Brian Roby, Felton House, Felton HR1 3PH   Tel/Fax: (01432) 820366
e-mail: bandb@creal.net   website: www.SmoothHound.co.uk/hotels/felton.html

Mainoaks Farm Cottages
Goodrich, Ross-on-Wye

Six units sleeping two, four, six and seven. Set in 80 acres of pasture and woodland beside the River Wye in an area of outstanding natural beauty with an abundance of wildlife, this 15th century Listed farm has recently been converted to form six cottages of different size and individual character. All with exposed beams, pine furniture, heating, fully-equipped kitchens with microwaves, washer/dryers, colour TV. Private gardens and barbecue area. Linen and towels provided. An ideal base for touring the local area, beautiful walks including Forestry Commission, fishing, canoeing, pony trekking, bird-watching or just relaxing in this beautiful tranquil spot. Short Breaks available. Open throughout the year. Pets by arrangement.

Mrs P. Unwin, Hill House, Chase End, Bromsberrow, Ledbury, Herefordshire HR8 1SE
Telephone 01531 650448   ETC ★★★ to ★★★★ Highly Commended

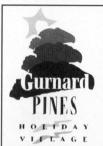

Cowes, Isle of Wight PO31 8QE

Gurnard Pines is ideally set in a countryside location, minutes' drive away from the world-famous yachting haven of Cowes. It offers the ideal setting for the perfect holiday and a base for exploring the beautiful Isle of Wight. The accommodation within the grounds consists of pine lodges sleeping 2, 4 or 6, each overlooking a pond area, also caravans and bungalows sleeping 4 or 6. Gurnard Pines prides itself on the large range of leisure facilities for your enjoyment, with indoor and outdoor heated pools, hi-tech gymnasium, health suite with pine sauna, steam rooms and solarium. We can even arrange some professional tennis coaching on one of our all-weather floodlit tennis courts. There is a health and beauty salon, where you may relax and indulge yourself with a pampering hair and beauty treatment.

With a seasonal entertainment programme with visiting cabaret and Syril the Squirrel's children's club for 5 to 12 year olds, a play fort, crazy golf – and not forgetting the patio chess – a holiday for you and your family will be more than complete.

Catering facilities within the centre include a top quality restaurant serving evening meals and Sunday lunches, and a coffee shop open during the day and early evening, serving hot and cold food, home-baked daily specials and takeaways.
Open all year (please note that some facilities are seasonal only).

Tel: 01983 292395 • Fax: 01983 299415
info@gurnardpines.co.uk • www.gurnardpines.co.uk

Reach Road, St. Margaret's at Cliffe, Near Dover, Kent CT15 6AE
Fax: 01304 853 434 • E-mail: stmargarets@gbholidayparks.co.uk
web: www.gbholidayparks.co.uk

...a breath of fresh air!

St. Margaret's is an exclusive 4 star park perched high on the white cliffs and close to the bustling port of Dover. There are spectacular views over the English channel towards the hazy distant shores of France and the gentle rolling countryside is typical of rural Kent.
The park itself has well manicured lawns and houses a superb leisure complex with indoor pools, gymnasium, reflexology and massage clinic, sauna, spa pool and solarium.
* Two indoor heated pools • Alternative therapy clinic • Fully equipped gymnasium
* Dylan the Dinosaur Children's Club at peak times • Outdoor Play Area
* Spa pool, sauna and solarium • Garden restaurant and Bistro bar
* Horse riding nearby • **Superb walking** opportunities
* Quality golf courses nearby (incl. Royal St. George's at Sandwich)

HOLIDAY BOOKING LINE: 0870 442 9286

The Parade, Greatstone-on-Sea, New Romney, Kent TN28 8RN
Fax: 01797 367 497 • E-mail: romneysands@gbholidayparks.co.uk
web: www.gbholidayparks.co.uk

...a park designed for families

Romney Sands is a popular 4-star park that sits opposite one of the finest sandy beaches on the Kent coast and is surrounded by the mysterious Romney Marsh, past haunt of smugglers. Straddling the Sussex/Kent border there's lush countryside, pretty villages, colourful seaside resorts and a legacy of historic castles and stately homes. All this and a park offering fabulous facilities and quality entertainment makes for a memorable holiday experience.

* Bistro restaurant • Well-conditioned, outdoor bowling green • Celebrities Club **for live entertainment**
* Dylan the Dinosaur Children's Club and outdoor play area • Large indoor pool complex
* Ideal area for cycling • Tennis courts • Pool and darts
* **Karting and** Golf nearby • Well-stocked mini-market • Crazy golf
* Pub snacks in Tavern bar • Nearest town one mile

HOLIDAY BOOKING LINE: 0870 442 9285

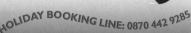

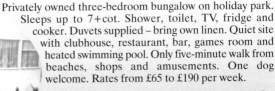

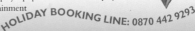

WOODTHORPE HALL COUNTRY COTTAGES

Very well appointed luxury one and three bedroomed cottages, overlooking the golf course, all with central heating, colour TV, microwave, washer, dryer, dishwasher and fridge freezer. Woodthorpe is situated approximately six miles from the coastal resort of Mablethorpe and offers easy access to the picturesque Lincolnshire Wolds. Adjacent facilities include golf, fishing, garden centre, aquatic centre, snooker, pool and restaurant with bar and family room. ETC ★★★★. For further details contact:

Woodthorpe Hall, Woodthorpe, Near Alford, Lincs LN13 0DD • Tel: 01507 450294
• Fax: 01507 450885 • E-mail: enquiries@woodthorpehall.com • www.woodthorpehall.com

LOWE CARAVAN PARK
SMALL FRIENDLY COUNTRY PARK

Primarily a touring park, we now have four luxury holiday homes for hire in peaceful surroundings ideal for touring East Anglia or quiet relaxing break. More suited to over 50s but children are welcome. Touring caravans also for hire.

Tel: 01953 881051
May Lowe, Ashdale Hills Road, Saham Hills (Near Watton), Thetford, Norfolk IP25 7EZ

THE OLD MILL

The Old Mill in the heart of Norfolk has been tastefully converted to provide peaceful holidays, away from the rush of modern living. Standing in the owners' delightful grounds, it has one round Victorian style double bedroom with French doors overlooking the paddock. Lounge/diner with TV, kitchen, bathroom, scullery with fridge and microwave. Linen and towels provided. Electricity with £1 coin meter. Village has a surgery, chemist, bakery, butcher, P.O. etc. Market town of Dereham four miles, Norwich 12. Convenient for Sandringham and the Broads. Your privacy respected. Warm welcome. Sorry no smoking or pets. Open all year. Terms on request.

Margaret & Don Fisher, Ivydene,
Mill Road, Mattishall, Dereham NR20 3RL
Tel: 01362 850312

Cresswell, Near Morpeth, Northumberland NE61 5JT
Fax: 01670 860 226 • E-mail: cresswelltowers@gbholidayparks.co.uk
web: www.gbholidayparks.co.uk

GREAT BRITISH
Holiday Parks

...total relaxation in a natural setting

Cresswell Towers is a highly attractive park in a natural woodland setting that lends the park much of its charm. You cannot help but be taken by the lush leafy lanes. This area does have spectacular beaches, and Druidge Bay with its huge sand dunes is worth a visit.

On the park the emphasis is on relaxation, and a friendly bar, welcoming holiday caravans, pleasant walks and attractive outdoor pool make this easy to achieve.

• Sun terrace • Popular golf courses nearby • Café offering meals throughout the day
• Watersport opportunities locally • Well-stocked shop • Sandy beaches with amazing sand dunes
• Multi-sports court • Children's amusement arcade and play area
• Sea fishing locally • Outdoor heated pool • Norseman Club

HOLIDAY BOOKING LINE: 0870 442 9311

Pensford, Near Bristol BS39 4BA
Telephone or Fax: 01761 490281

Leigh Farm is situated in the old mining village of Pensford. 7 miles to Bristol and 8 miles to Bath. Overlooking the floodlit pool; a 3-bedroomed cottage sleeping 6 plus baby. Terraced bungalow conversion built tastefully in natural stone with original oak beams. One or two bedroomed, with shower room, WC and basin. TV. Night storage heating. Bed linen is not supplied but can be hired. Cot and high chair available. Wander round the ponds where duck and moorhen nest. Park and Ride for both cities near, and plenty of tourist information for your use. Safe floodlit car park. Open all year. No pets. £170-£400 weekly. B&B available. *For brochure contact Josephine Smart.*

KNOWLE FARM (ETC ★★★

Four cottages superbly converted from old barns and furnished to a high standard. Pretty gardens to relax in and separate play area for children. Two cottages have kitchen/diner, separate lounge, colour TV, the other two have kitchen, lounge/diner, colour TV. Cot, highchair by prior arrangement. Bed linen supplied, towels by request. Situated in quiet secluded countryside yet close to Wells, Glastonbury, Bath, etc. Area also has a wide selection of family attractions. Sorry, no pets. Terms: high season £180 to £450. Car essential, ample parking. Payphone for guests. Open all year. Cottages sleep two/five/six/eight.

West Compton, Shepton Mallet BA4 4PD • **Tel: 01749 890482** • **Fax: 01749 890405**

Withy Grove Farm

Come and enjoy a relaxing and friendly holiday "Down on the Farm" set in beautiful Somerset countryside. Peaceful rural setting adjoining River Huntspill, famed for its coarse fishing. The farm is ideally situated for visiting the many local attractions including Cheddar Gorge, Glastonbury, Weston-super-Mare and the lovely sandy beach of Burnham-on-Sea. Self-catering cottages tastefully converted, sleeping 4-5. Fully equipped with colour TV.

★ *Heated Swimming Pool* ★ *Games Room*
★ *Licensed Bar and Entertainment (in high season)*
★ *Skittle Alley* ★ *Laundry*

For more information please contact: Mrs Wendy Baker, Withy Grove Farm, East Huntspill, Near Burnham-on-Sea, Somerset TA9 3NP • Telephone: 01278 784471

CHEDDAR - SUNGATE HOLIDAY APARTMENTS
Church Street, Cheddar, Somerset BS27 3RA

Delightful apartments in Cheddar village, each fully equipped. Sleep two/four. Laundry facilities. Private parking. Family, disabled, and pet friendly.

Contact: Mrs. M. M. Fieldhouse for brochure

Tel: 01934 742264 • Fax: 01934 741411

Further details in classified section under Somerset

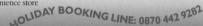

Publisher's Note

While every effort is made to ensure accuracy, we regret that FHG Publications cannot accept responsibility for errors, omissions or misrepresentations in our entries or any consequences thereof. Prices in particular should be checked because we go to press early. We will follow up complaints but cannot act as arbiters or agents for either party.

Ratings You Can Trust

ENGLAND

The *English Tourism Council* (formerly the English Tourist Board) has joined with the *AA* and *RAC* to create a new, easily understood quality rating for serviced accommodation, giving a clear guide of what to expect.

HOTELS are given a rating from One to Five *Stars* – the more Stars, the higher the quality and the greater the range of facilities and level of services provided.

GUEST ACCOMMODATION, which includes guest houses, bed and breakfasts, inns and farmhouses, is rated from One to Five *Diamonds*. Progressively higher levels of quality and customer care must be provided for each one of the One to Five Diamond ratings.

HOLIDAY PARKS, TOURING PARKS and CAMPING PARKS are now also assessed using *Stars*. Standards of quality range from a One Star (acceptable) to a Five Star (exceptional) park.

Look out also for the new *SELF-CATERING* Star ratings. The more *Stars* (from One to Five) awarded to an establishment, the higher the levels of quality you can expect. Establishments at higher rating levels also have to meet some additional requirements for facilities.

SCOTLAND

Star Quality Grades will reflect the most important aspects of a visit, such as the warmth of welcome, efficiency and friendliness of service, the quality of the food and the cleanliness and condition of the furnishings, fittings and decor.

THE MORE STARS, THE HIGHER THE STANDARDS.

The description, such as Hotel, Guest House, Bed and Breakfast, Lodge, Holiday Park, Self-catering etc tells you the type of property and style of operation.

WALES

Places which score highly will have an especially welcoming atmosphere and pleasing ambience, high levels of comfort and guest care, and attractive surroundings enhanced by thoughtful design and attention to detail

STAR QUALITY GUIDE FOR

HOTELS, GUEST HOUSES AND FARMHOUSES

SELF-CATERING ACCOMMODATION
(Cottages, Apartments, Houses)

CARAVAN HOLIDAY HOME PARKS
(Holiday Parks, Touring Parks, Camping Parks)

★★★★★ *Exceptional quality*
★★★★ *Excellent quality*
★★★ *Very good quality*
★★ *Good quality*
★ *Fair to good quality*

In England, Scotland and Wales, all graded properties are inspected annually by Tourist Authority trained Assessors.

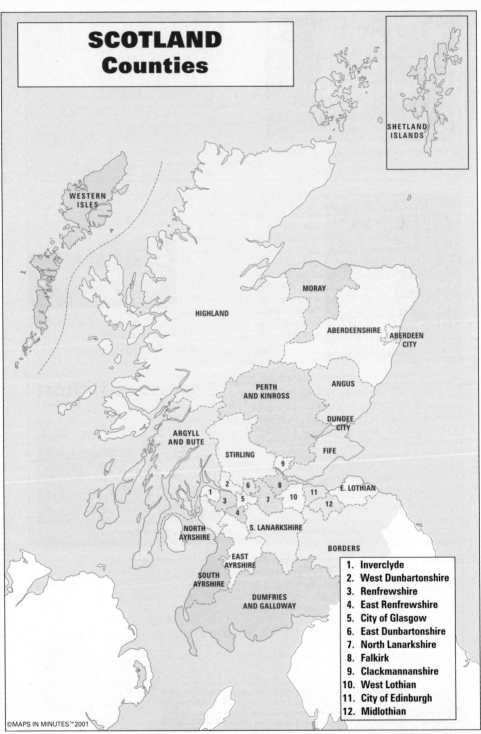

SCOTLAND
Counties

SHETLAND ISLANDS

WESTERN ISLES

HIGHLAND

MORAY

ABERDEENSHIRE

ABERDEEN CITY

PERTH AND KINROSS

ANGUS

DUNDEE CITY

ARGYLL AND BUTE

STIRLING

FIFE

9

2 6 8

1 11 E. LOTHIAN

3 5 7 10

4 12

NORTH AYRSHIRE

S. LANARKSHIRE

BORDERS

EAST AYRSHIRE

SOUTH AYRSHIRE

DUMFRIES AND GALLOWAY

1. Inverclyde
2. West Dunbartonshire
3. Renfrewshire
4. East Renfrewshire
5. City of Glasgow
6. East Dunbartonshire
7. North Lanarkshire
8. Falkirk
9. Clackmannanshire
10. West Lothian
11. City of Edinburgh
12. Midlothian

©MAPS IN MINUTES™ 2001

Please mention Self-Catering Holidays in Britain when enquiring

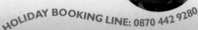

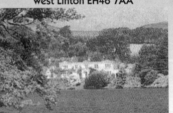

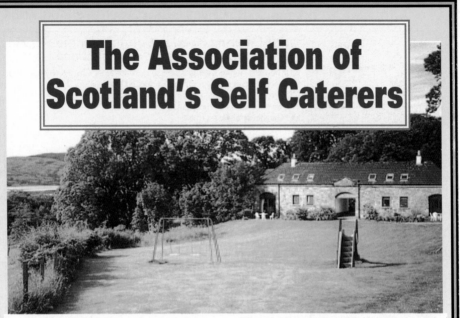

The Association of Scotland's Self Caterers

Selected Self-Catering Holidays in Scotland

Members of the ASSC are committed to high and consistant standards in self catering.
Contact your choice direct and be assured of an excellent holiday.

Brochures: 0990 168 571 • Web site: www.assc.co.uk

Owner-Operators ready to match our standards and interested in joining are requested to
contact our Secretary for information – 0990 168 571

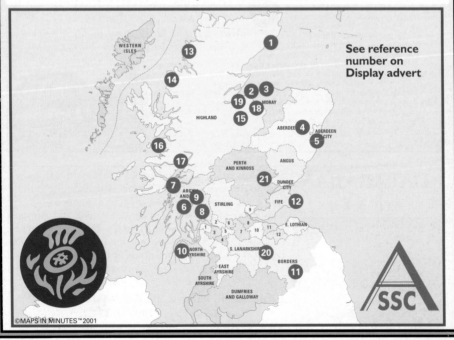

See reference
number on
Display advert

©MAPS IN MINUTES™ 2001

Please mention Self-Catering Holidays in Britain when enquiring

ABERDEEN • Holiday Flat to suit couple or small family. Clean, comfortable and conveniently located for Aberdeen city centre and attractions. Lounge, double bedroom, bathroom with shower, fully equipped galley kitchen. Heating, lighting and all bedding included. Regular bus service to city centre. No smoking and no pets. STB ★★★

WICK – *A Quality Home for Your Quality Time* Sleeps up to 6. Close to airport, bus and rail stations. Lounge with DVD, SKY TV, Playstation; dining kitchen, bathroom, en suite double bedroom, twin/double and single/twin; ground floor single. Fully equipped.

Details of both properties from **Donald Campbell, The Old Schoolhouse, Ulbster, Lybster, Caithness KW2 6AA** (Tel & Fax: 01955 651297) • e-mail: ulbster@ntlworld.com • www.visit.ourflat.co.uk • www.assc.co.uk

---

Tulloch Lodges • *Peace, Relaxation and Comfort in Beautiful Natural Surroundings* One of the loveliest self-catering sites in Scotland. Modern, spacious, attractive and beautifully equipped Scandinavian lodges for up to 6 in glorious woodland/water setting. Perfect for the Highlands and Historic Grampian, especially the Golden Moray Coast and the Golf, Castle and Malt Whisky Trails. £235-£675 per week. Brochure: **Tulloch Lodges, Rafford, Forres, Moray IV36 2RU** • Tel: **01309 673311** Fax: **01309 671515** • web: www.tullochlodges.co.uk • STB ★★★★ *Self-Catering*

Sheriffston Farm Chalet *Near Elgin*

One 'A' frame chalet on working farm. 'Habitat' furnished, fully equipped for two – six people, colour TV, bed linen, duvets. Beautiful rural location in Moray – famous for flowers – district of lowlands, highlands, rivers, forests, lovely beaches, historic towns, welcoming people. Excellent local facilities. Moray golf tickets available. *From £180-£300 (January-December)* Contact: **Mrs. J. M. Shaw, Sheriffston, Elgin, Moray IV30 8LA** Tel & Fax: **01343 842695** • e-mail: jennifer_m_shaw@hotmail.com

---

THE GREENKNOWE

A comfortable, detached, renovated cottage in a quiet location at the southern edge of the village of Kintore. Ideally situated for touring castles and pre-historic sites or for walking, fishing and golfing. The cottage is on one level with large sittingroom facing south and the garden. Sleeps four.

• Walkers Welcome Scheme •

Terms £275–£475 per week including electricity and linen.

Mr & Mrs P. A. Lumsden, Kingsfield House, Kingsfield Road, Kintore, Aberdeenshire AB51 OUD Tel: **01467 632366** • Fax **01467 632399** • e-mail: kfield@clara.net

---

The Robert Gordon University in the heart of Aberdeen offers a variety of accommodation in the city centre to visitors from June through to August. Aberdeen is ideal for visiting Royal Deeside, castles and historic buildings, playing golf or touring the Malt Whisky Trail. The city itself is a place to discover, and Aberdonians are friendly and welcoming people. We offer Two Star self-catering accommodation for individuals or groups at superb rates, in either en suite or shared facility flats. Each party has exclusive use of their own flat during their stay. The flats are self-contained, centrally heated, fully furnished and suitable for children and disabled guests. All flats have colour TV, microwave, bed linen, towels, all cooking utensils, and a complimentary 'welcome pack' of basic groceries. There are laundry and telephone facilities on site as well as ample car parking spaces.

Contact: **The Robert Gordon University, Business & Vacation Accommodation, Schoolhill, Aberdeen AB10 1FR** • Tel: **01224 262134** • Fax: **01224 262144** e-mail: p.macinnes@rgu.ac.uk • website: www.scotland2000.com/rgu

---

When making postal enquiries, remember that a stamped, addressed envelope is always appreciated

---

Please mention Self-Catering Holidays in Britain when enquiring

6 BRALECKAN HOUSE. A mid19th century stone building carefully restored to provide two comfortable houses. Situated on private upland farm. Each comprises sitting room, fully fitted kitchen, two bedrooms, bathroom and shower room. Both are completely private, or suitable for two families wishing to holiday together. Large parking area and garden. Children most welcome, but regretfully no pets. Contact Mr & Mrs Crawford, Brenchoille Farm, Inveraray, Argyll PA23 8XN • Tel: 01499 500662

7

Cologin
Country Chalets
Oban
All Scottish Glens have their secrets: let us share ours with you – and your pets !

Call now for our colour brochure and find out more
Open all year round. Rates from £160 to £495 per week.
Autumn Gold breaks and mid-week deals also available
MRS LINDA BATTISON, COLOGIN FARMHOUSE, LERAGS GLEN,
BY OBAN, ARGYLL PA34 4SE Tel: (01631) 564501 • Fax: (01631) 566925
e-mail: cologin@west-highland-holidays.co.uk
web: www.west-highland-holidays.co.uk

STB
★★★
to
★★★★
Self
Catering

8

WEST LOCH TARBERT, ARGYLL – DUNMORE COURT

Five cottages in architect design conversion of home farm on the estate of Dunmore House. Spacious accommodation for 2-8 persons. All have stone fireplaces for log fires. Bird-watching, fishing and walking. Easy access to island ferries. Pets welcome. Open all year. Colour brochure. From £175-£490. STB ★★

Telephone: 01880 820654
e-mail: dunmorecourtsc@aol.com
www.dunmorecourt.com

Contact: Amanda Minshall,
Dunmore Court, Kilberry Road,
Near Tarbert, Argyll PA29 6XZ

9

Mr & Mrs E. Crawford

Blarghour Farm

Loch Awe-side, by Dalmally, Argyll PA33 1BW
Tel: 01866 833246 • Fax: 01866 833338
e-mail: blarghour@aol.com
www.self-catering-argyll.co.uk

At Blarghour Farm one may choose from four centrally heated and double glazed holiday homes sleeping from two to six people, all enjoying splendid views of lovely Loch Awe. Kitchens are well appointed, lounges tastefully decorated and furnished with payphone, TV and gas fire, beds are made up and towels supplied while the two larger houses have shower rooms in addition to bathrooms, all with shaver point. The two larger houses are suitable for children and have cots and high chairs. No pets are allowed. Open all year. Centrally situated for touring. Illustrated brochure on request.

Recommended
Short Break Holidays in Britain 2003

Specifically designed to cater for the most rapidly growing sector of the holiday market in the UK. Illustrated details of hotels offering special "Bargain Breaks" throughout the year.

Available from bookshops and larger newsagents for £5.99

FHG PUBLICATIONS LTD
Abbey Mill Business Centre, Seedhill, Paisley, Scotland PA1 1TJ
www.holidayguides.com

SUMMER WATERSPORTS AND WINTER SKIING

Just six miles south of Aviemore these superb log chalets are set in 14 acres of woodland in the magnificent Spey Valley, surrounded on three sides by forest and rolling fields with the fourth side being half a mile of beach frontage. Free watersports hire for guests, 8.30-10am/4-5.30pm daily. Sailing, windsurfing, canoeing, salmon fishing, archery, dry ski slope skiing. Hire/instruction available by the hour, day or week mid April to end October. Boathouse Restaurant on the shore of Loch Insh offering coffee, home-made soup, fresh salads, bar meals, children's meals and evening à la carte. Large gift shop and bar. New Children's Adventure Areas, 3km Lochside/Woodland Walk/Interpretation Trail, Ski Slope, Mountain Bike Hire and Stocked Trout Lochan are open all year round. Ski, snowboard hire, and instruction available December-April.

Loch Insh Log Chalets, Kincraig,
Inverness-shire PH21 1NU
Tel: 01540 651272
e-mail: office@lochinsh.com
website: www.lochinsh.com

SSC

Arisaig House Cottages – *luxurious secluded accommodation in mature woodland*

Achnahanat

• ACHNAHANAT in the grounds of Arisaig House, sleeps up to 8
• THE BOTHY set at the end of the walled gardens, sleeps up to 8
• THE COURTYARD self-contained apartment on first floor, sleeps 2
• FAGUS LODGE set in mature gardens, sleeps up to 6
• GARDENER'S COTTAGE set in gardens off small courtyard, sleeps up to 3
• ROSHVEN overlooks walled gardens of Arisaig House, sleeps up to 4

SSC

Set in an area of breathtaking coastal and hill scenery, and wonderful sandy beaches. Mountain bike hire, clay pigeon shooting, and fishing on Loch Morar can be arranged. Golf 7 miles, swimming pool 13 miles. Day trips to the Small Isles and to Skye.

Details from: **Andrew Smither, Arisaig House, Beasdale, Arisaig, Inverness-shire PH39 4NR**
Tel/Fax: 01687 450399
e-mail: enquiries@arisaighouse-cottages.co.uk • www.arisaighouse-cottages.co.uk

---

Cuilcheanna Cottages
Onich, Fort William
Inverness-shire PH33 6SD

A small peaceful site for self catering with three cottages and eight caravans (6 x 2003 models). Situated in the village of Onich, 400 yards off the main road. An excellent centre for touring and hill walking in the West Highlands.

For further details please phone
01855 821526 or 01855 821310

SSC

BLACKPARK FARM Westhill, Inverness IV2 5BP

This newly built holiday home is located one mile from Culloden Battlefield with panoramic views over Inverness and beyond. Fully equipped with many extras to make your holiday special, including oil fired central heating to ensure warmth on the coldest of winter days. Ideally based for touring the Highlands including Loch Ness, Skye etc. Extensive information is available on our website. A Highland welcome awaits you.

Tel: 01463 790620 • Fax: 01463 794262 • e-mail: i.alexander@blackpark.co.uk • website: www.blackpark.co.uk

SSC

Visit the FHG website www.holidayguides.com
for details of accommodation featured
in the full range of FHG titles

Other FHG Holiday Guides

ONLY £5.99

Recommended
Country Hotels
of Britain 2003

A quality selection of country hotels and country houses which offer the best of traditional hospitality and comfort.

This is a guide for those who appreciate good living with the high standards of food, wine, accommodation and service which that entails.

Mainly independent, with a resident proprietor. and often historic or with unique character, these hotels are ideal for quiet holidays in pampered surroundings.

Quick reference sections for Hotels with Leisure and Hotels with Conference Facilities

Recommended
Wayside & Country Inns
of Britain 2002

This guide lists a large selection of inns, pubs and small hotels in every part of the country, all offering the same high-quality service, accommodation and, especially, cuisine as many of the bigger hotels, yet managing to retain that sense of history and the warm, friendly atmosphere for which the traditional inn is renowned. With separate supplements for Pet-Friendly and Family-Friendly Pubs to ensure that every member of the party receives a warm welcome when they stop for refreshment, the guide is an invaluable and informative source.

ONLY £5.99

Both guides available from most bookshops and larger newsagents

Only £5.99 each

SELF-CATERING
HOLIDAYS IN
BRITAIN 2003

**Farms, Cottages, Houses, Chalets,
Flats and Caravans throughout Britain**

FHG

Other FHG Publications

Recommended Country Hotels of Britain
Recommended Wayside & Country Inns of Britain
Recommended Short Break Holidays in Britain
Pets Welcome!
The Golf Guide: Where to Play/Where to Stay
Farm Holiday Guide to Coast & Country Holidays
in England/Scotland/Wales/Ireland
Britain's Best Holidays
Guide to Caravan and Camping Holidays
Bed and Breakfast Stops
Children Welcome! Family Holiday and Days Out Guide

ISBN 185055 344 0
© IPC Media Ltd 2003
Cover photographs:
Topham Picturepoint
Cover design: Focus Network
No part of this publication may be reproduced by any means or
transmitted without the permission of the Publishers.

Maps: ©MAPS IN MINUTES™ 2001. ©Crown Copyright, Ordnance Survey 2001.

Typeset by FHG Publications Ltd. Paisley.
Printed and bound in Great Britain by Polestar Wheatons Ltd, Exeter, Devon

Distribution. Book Trade: Plymbridge House, Estover Road, Plymouth PL6 7PY
Tel: 01752 202300; Fax: 01752 202333
News Trade: Market Force (UK) Ltd, 5th Floor Low Rise, King's Reach Tower,
Stamford Street, London SE1 9LS
Tel: 0207 633 3450; Fax: 0207 633 3572

Published by FHG Publications Ltd., Abbey Mill Business Centre,
Seedhill, Paisley PA1 ITJ (Tel: 0141-887 0428 Fax: 0141-889 7204).
e-mail: fhg@ipcmedia.com

Self Catering Holidays in Britain is an FHG publication, published by
IPC Country & Leisure Media Ltd, part of IPC Media Group of Companies.

Ratings You Can Trust

ENGLAND

The **English Tourism Council** (formerly the English Tourist Board) has joined with the **AA** and **RAC** to create a new, easily understood quality rating for serviced accommodation, giving a clear guide of what to expect.

HOTELS are given a rating from One to Five **Stars** – the more Stars, the higher the quality and the greater the range of facilities and level of services provided.

GUEST ACCOMMODATION, which includes guest houses, bed and breakfasts, inns and farmhouses, is rated from One to Five **Diamonds**. Progressively higher levels of quality and customer care must be provided for each one of the One to Five Diamond ratings.

HOLIDAY PARKS, TOURING PARKS and CAMPING PARKS are now also assessed using **Stars**. Standards of quality range from a One Star (acceptable) to a Five Star (exceptional) park.

Look out also for the new **SELF-CATERING** Star ratings. The more **Stars** (from One to Five) awarded to an establishment, the higher the levels of quality you can expect. Establishments at higher rating levels also have to meet some additional requirements for facilities.

SCOTLAND

Star Quality Grades will reflect the most important aspects of a visit, such as the warmth of welcome, efficiency and friendliness of service, the quality of the food and the cleanliness and condition of the furnishings, fittings and decor.

THE MORE STARS,
THE HIGHER THE STANDARDS.

The description, such as Hotel, Guest House, Bed and Breakfast, Lodge, Holiday Park, Self-catering etc tells you the type of property and style of operation.

WALES

Places which score highly will have an especially welcoming atmosphere and pleasing ambience, high levels of comfort and guest care, and attractive surroundings enhanced by thoughtful design and attention to detail

STAR QUALITY GUIDE FOR

HOTELS, GUEST HOUSES AND FARMHOUSES

SELF-CATERING ACCOMMODATION
(Cottages, Apartments, Houses)

CARAVAN HOLIDAY HOME PARKS
(Holiday Parks, Touring Parks, Camping Parks)

★★★★★ *Exceptional quality*
★★★★ *Excellent quality*
★★★ *Very good quality*
★★ *Good quality*
★ *Fair to good quality*

In England, Scotland and Wales, all graded properties are inspected annually by Tourist Authority trained Assessors.

CONTENTS

ENGLAND

CONTENTS

SCOTLAND

WALES

SELF-CATERING HOLIDAYS IN BRITAIN 2003

We are pleased to present once again a large range of self-catering choices for your holiday planning in 2003. There are a number of new entries, as well as some old friends, and readers can choose from commercial holiday centres; country and seaside properties, well restored and fully equipped with all the comforts of home; traditional cottages, holiday apartments and flats to suit all tastes and pockets; and a small selection of caravans. There are full contact details, a good description of the facilities available, and often features of interest nearby, such as restaurants, pubs and visits.

The following points of guidance should help you make the most of the huge selection available in the 2003 edition of *SELF-CATERING HOLIDAYS IN BRITAIN*.

ENQUIRIES AND BOOKINGS. Give full details of dates (with an alternative), numbers and any special requirements. Ask about any points in the holiday description which are not clear and make sure that prices and conditions are clearly explained. You should receive confirmation in writing and a receipt for any deposit or advance payment. If you book your holiday well in advance, especially self-catering, confirm your arrival details nearer the time. Some proprietors, especially for self-catering, request full payment in advance but a reasonable deposit is more normal.

CANCELLATIONS. A holiday booking is a form of contract with obligations on both sides. If you have to cancel, give as much notice as possible. The longer the notice the better the chance that your host can replace your booking and therefore refund any payments. If the proprietor cancels in such away that causes serious, inconvenience, he may have obligations to you which have not been properly honoured. Take advice if necessary from such organisations as the Citizen's Advice Bureau, Consumer's Association, Trading standards Office, Local Tourist Office, etc., or your own solicitor. It is possible to insure against holiday cancellation. Brokers and insurance companies can advise you about this.

COMPLAINTS. It's best if any problems can be sorted out at the start of your holiday. If the problem is not. solved, you can contact the organisations mentioned above. You can also write to us. We will follow up the complaint with the advertiser – but we cannot act as intermediaries or accept responsibility for holiday arrangements.

FHG Publications Ltd. do not inspect accommodation and an entry in our guides does not imply a recommendation. However our advertisers have signed their agreement to work for the holidaymaker's best interests and as their customer, you have the right to expect appropriate attention and service.

THE FHG DIPLOMA. Every year we award a small number of Diplomas to holiday proprietors who have been specially recommended to us by readers. The names of our 2002 Diploma winners are listed in this book and we will be happy to receive your recommendations for 2003.

Please mention *SELF-CATERING HOLIDAYS IN BRITAIN* when you are making enquiries or bookings and don't forget to use our Readers' Offer Voucher/Coupons if you're near any of the attractions which are kindly participating.

Anne Cuthbertson,
Editor

FHG Diploma Winners 2002

Each year we award a small number of diplomas to holiday proprietors whose services have been specially commended by our readers. The following were our FHG Diploma Winners for 2002.

England

DEVON
Woolacombe Bay Holiday Park,
Woolacombe, North Devon
EX34 7HW (01271 870343).

LANCASHIRE
Mrs Holdsworth,
Broadwater Hotel,
356 Marine Road, East Promenade
Morecambe, Lancashire LA4 5AQ
(01524 411333).

Peter & Susan Bicker,
Kelvin Private Hotel,
Reads Avenue, Blackpool,
Lancashire FY1 4JJ
(01253 620293).

LINCOLNSHIRE
Sue Phillips & John Lister,
Cawthorpe Farm, Cawthorpe
Bourne, Lincolnshire PE10 0AB
(01778 426697).

OXFORDSHIRE
Liz Roach, The Old Bakery,
Skirmett, Nr Henley on Thames
Oxfordshire RG9 6TD
(01491 638309).

SOMERSET
Pat & Sue Weir, Slipper Cottage,
41 Bishopston, Montacute,
Somerset TA15 6UX
(01935 823073)

Scotland

ARGYLL & BUTE
David Quibell,
Rosneath Castle Caravan Park
Near Helensburgh,
Argyll & Bute G84 0QS
(01436 831208)

DUNDEE & ANGUS
Carlogie House Hotel,
Carlogie Road, Carnoustie,
Dundee DD7 6LD
(01241 853185)

EDINBURGH & LOTHIANS
Geraldine Hamilton,
Crosswoodhill Farm, West Calder
Edinburgh & Lothians EH55 8LP
(01501 785205)

FIFE
Mr Alastair Clark,
Old Manor Country House Hotel,
Lundin Links, Nr St Andrews
Fife KY8 6AJ
(01333 320368)

HIGHLANDS
N & J McCallum, The Neuk
Corpach, Fort William PH33 7LE
(01397 772244)

HELP IMPROVE BRITISH TOURISM STANDARDS

Why not write and tell us about the holiday accommodation you have chosen from one of our popular publications? Complete a nomination form giving details of why you think YOUR host or hostess should win one of our attractive framed diplomas and send it to:

FHG Publications, Abbey Mill Business Centre, Seedhill, Paisley PA1 1TJ

THE FHG DIPLOMA

HELP IMPROVE BRITISH TOURIST STANDARDS

You are choosing holiday accommodation from our very popular FHG Publications. Whether it be a hotel, guest house, farmhouse or self-catering accommodation, we think you will find it hospitable, comfortable and clean, and your host and hostess friendly and helpful.

Why not write and tell us about it?

As a recognition of the generally well-run and excellent holiday accommodation reviewed in our publications, we at FHG Publications Ltd. present a diploma to proprietors who receive the highest recommendation from their guests who are also readers of our Guides. If you care to write to us praising the holiday you have booked through FHG Publications Ltd. – whether this be board, self-catering accommodation, a sporting or a caravan holiday, what you say will be evaluated and the proprietors who reach our final list will be contacted.

The winning proprietor will receive an attractive framed diploma to display on his premises as recognition of a high standard of comfort, amenity and hospitality. FHG Publications Ltd. offer this diploma as a contribution towards the improvement of standards in tourist accommodation in Britain. Help your excellent host or hostess to win it!

FHG DIPLOMA

We nominate ....

....

Because

Name ....

Address ....

....

Telephone No..

A 65-minute journey into the lost world of the English narrow gauge light railway. Features historic steam locomotives from many countries.

PETS MUST BE KEPT UNDER CONTROL AND NOT ALLOWED ON TRACKS

Open: Sundays and Bank Holiday weekends 16 March to 29 October. Additional days in summer.

Directions: On A4146 towards Hemel Hempstead, close to roundabout junction with A505.

FHG PUBLICATIONS, ABBEY MILL BUSINESS CENTRE, PAISLEY PA1 1TJ

Be a giant in a magical miniature world of make-believe depicting rural England in the 1930's. "A little piece of history that is forever England."

Open: 10am to 5pm daily 15th February to 26th October.

Directions: Junction 16 M25, Junction 2 M40.

FHG PUBLICATIONS, ABBEY MILL BUSINESS CENTRE, PAISLEY PA1 1TJ

A working steam railway centre. Steam train rides, miniature railway rides, large collection of historic preserved steam locomotives, carriages and wagons.

Open: Sundays and Bank Holidays April to October, plus Wednesdays in June, July and August 10.30am to 5.30pm.

Directions: off A41 Aylesbury to Bicester Road, 6 miles north west of Aylesbury.

FHG PUBLICATIONS, ABBEY MILL BUSINESS CENTRE, PAISLEY PA1 1TJ

Cornwall's only Donkey Sanctuary set in 14 acres overlooking the beautiful Tamar Valley. Donkey rides, rabbit warren, goat hill, children's playgrounds, cafe and picnic area.

Open: Easter to end of October and February half-term - daily from 10am to 5.30pm. November to March open weekends. Closed January.

Directions: Just off A390 between Callington and Gunnislake at St Ann's Chapel.

FHG PUBLICATIONS, ABBEY MILL BUSINESS CENTRE, PAISLEY PA1 1TJ

A collection of cars from film and TV, including Chitty Chitty Bang Bang, James Bond cars, Del Boy's van, Fab1 and many more.

PETS MUST BE KEPT ON LEAD

Open: Daily 10am-5pm. Closed February half term. Weekends only in December.

Directions: In centre of Keswick close to car park.

FHG PUBLICATIONS, ABBEY MILL BUSINESS CENTRE, PAISLEY PA1 1TJ

England's oldest working watermill, milling oatmeal daily

DOGS ON LEADS

Open: 11am to 5pm April to September (may be closed Mondays).

Directions: Near inland terminus of Ravenglass & Eskdale Railway or over Hardknott Pass.

World's finest steamboat collection and premier all-weather attraction. Swallows and Amazons exhibition, model boat pond, tea shop, souvenir shop. Free guided tours. Model boat exhibition.

Open: 10am to 5pm 3rd weekend in March to last weekend October.

Directions: on A592 half-a-mile north of Bowness-on-Windermere.

Large range of natural water-worn caverns featuring mining equipment, stalactites and stalagmites, and fine deposits of Blue-John stone, Britain's rarest semi-precious stone.

DOGS MUST BE KEPT ON LEAD

Open: 9.30am to 5.30pm.

Directions: Situated 2 miles west of Castleton; follow brown tourist signs.

A superb family day out in the atmosphere of a bygone era. Explore the recreated period street and fascinating exhibitions. Unlimited tram rides are free with entry. Play areas, shops, tea rooms, pub, restaurant and lots more.

Open: daily April to October 10 am to 5.30pm, weekends in winter.

Directions: Eight miles from M1 Junction 28, follow brown and white signs for "Tramway Museum".

An underground wonderland of stalactites, stalagmites, rocks, minerals and fossils. Home of the unique Blue John stone – see the largest single piece ever found. Suitable for all ages.

Open: Opens 10am. Enquire for last tour of day and closed days.

Directions: Half-a-mile west of Castleton on A6187 (old A625)

A picturesque 200-year old woollen mill with machinery that spins yarn and weaves cloth. Mill machinery, restaurant, shop and gardens in a waterside setting and the largest stiched embroidery in the world.

Open: March to December daily 10.30am to 5pm.

Directions: Two miles from Junction 27 M5; follow signs to Willand (B3181) then brown tourist signs to Museum

---

Visit 1000+ gnomes and pixies in two acre beech wood. Gnome hats are loaned free of charge - so the gnomes think you are one of them - don't forget your camera! Also 2-acre wild flower garden with 250 labelled species.

Open: Daily 10am to 6pm 21st March to 31st October.

Directions: Between Bideford and Bude; follow brown tourist signs from A39/A388/A386.

Themed exhibition, changed annually, based in a Tudor house. Collection contains items of dress for women, men and children from 17th century to 1980s, from high fashion to everyday wear.

Open: Open from May 27th to end of September. 11am to 5pm Monday to Friday.

Directions: Centre of town, opposite Market Square. Mini bus up High Street stops outside.

Britain's best preserved lead mining site – and a great day out for all the family, with lots to see and do. Underground Experience – Park Level Mine now open.

Open: April 1st to September 30th 10.30am to 5pm daily. Weekends and half term in October

Directions: Alongside A689, midway between Stanhope and Alston in the heart of the North Pennines.

Farm Centre with animals, museum, blacksmith, glassblowing, miniature railway (Sundays and August), craft shops, tea room and licensed restaurant.

DOGS MUST BE KEPT ON LEAD

Open: 1st March to 31st October.

Directions: M25, A127 towards Southend. Take A176 junction off A127, 3rd exit Wash Road, 2nd left Barleylands Road.

Discover the fascinating history of cider making. There is a programme of temporary exhibitions and events plus free samples of Hereford cider brandy.

Open: April to Oct
10am to 5.30pm (daily)
Nov to Dec 11pm to 3pm (daily)
Jan to Mar 11am to 3pm (Tues to Sun)
Directions: situated west of Hereford off the A438
Hereford to Brecon road.

The museum of everyday life in Roman Britain. An award-winning museum with re-created Roman rooms, hands-on discovery areas, and some of the best mosaics outside the Mediterranean.

Open: Monday to Saturday
10am-5.30pm
Sunday 2pm-5.30pm.

Directions: St Albans.

Kent's award-winning open air museum is home to a collection of historic buildings which house interactive exhibitions on life over the last 150 years.

Open: Seven days a week from March to November.
10am to 5.30pm.

Directions: Junction 6 off M20, follow signs to Aylesford.

We are a working farm, with lots of animals to see and touch. Enjoy a walk round the Nature Trail or refreshments in the tearoom. Lots of activities during school holidays.

Open: Summer: daily
10.30am to 5pm
Winter: daily except Tuesdays
10.30am to 4pm.
Directions: Junction 35 off M6, take B6254 towards Kirkby Lonsdale, then follow the brown signs.

The world's largest collection of Grand Prix racing cars – over 130 exhibits within five halls, including McLaren Formula One cars.

Open: Daily 10am to 5pm
(last admission 4pm).
Closed Christmas/New Year.

Directions: 2 miles from M1 (J23a/24) and M42/A42; to north-west via A50.

Located in 100 acres of landscaped grounds, Snibston is a unique mixture, with historic mine buildings, outdoor science play areas, wildlife habitats and an exhibition hall housing five hands-on galleries. Cafe and gift shop.

Open: Seven days a week 10am to 5pm.

Directions: Junction 22 from M1, Junction 13 from M42. Follow Brown Heritage signs.

FHG PUBLICATIONS, ABBEY MILL BUSINESS CENTRE, PAISLEY PA1 1TJ

Large wildlife park with Reptile Land, Tropical House, Insectarium, Birds of Prey Centre, farm animals, wallaby enclosure, llamas; adventure playground, tea room and gift shop.

Open: Daily from 10am April to 28th October 2003

Directions: Off A17 at Long Sutton.

FHG PUBLICATIONS, ABBEY MILL BUSINESS CENTRE, PAISLEY PA1 1TJ

Well known for rescuing and rehabilitating orphaned and injured seal pups found washed ashore on Lincolnshire beaches. Also: penguins, aquarium, pets' corner, reptiles, Floral Palace (tropical birds and butterflies etc).

Open: Daily from 10am. Closed Christmas/Boxing/New Year's Days.

Directions: At the north end of Skegness seafront.

FHG PUBLICATIONS, ABBEY MILL BUSINESS CENTRE, PAISLEY PA1 1TJ

Over 100 rides and attractions, including the Traumatizer - the UK's tallest, fastest suspended looping coaster and the new Lucozade Space Shot.

Open: March to November, times vary.

FHG PUBLICATIONS, ABBEY MILL BUSINESS CENTRE, PAISLEY PA1 1TJ

Lions, snow leopards, chimpanzees, otters, reptiles, aquarium and lots more, set amidst landscaped gardens. Gift shop, cafe and picnic areas.

Open: all year round from 10am

Directions: on the coast 16 miles north of Liverpool; follow the brown and white tourist signs

FHG PUBLICATIONS, ABBEY MILL BUSINESS CENTRE, PAISLEY PA1 1TJ

Farm animals, 18th century watermill and farmhouse, farm artifacts, caravan and camping, children's play area. Restaurant and gift shop.

Open: all year 9.30am to 5pm.

Directions: signposted off both A47 and A1.

Beautiful walled garden with famous collections of herbs and herbaceous plants, including Roman Garden, National Thyme and Marjoram Collections. There is also a woodland walk. Gift shop.

Open: From Easter to the end of October 10am to 5pm daily.

Directions: Six miles north of Hexham off B6318 next to Chesters Roman Fort.

Europe's largest indoor family funfair, with exciting rides like the new rollercoaster, disco dodgems and swashbuckling pirate ship. There's something for everyone whatever the weather!

Open: Open daily except Christmas Day. 10am to 8pm Monday to Saturday, 11am to 6pm Sunday. (Open from 12 noon Monday to Friday during term time).

Directions: Signposted from the A1

750-year old man-made cave system beneath a modern day shopping centre. Discover how the caves were used with a unique 40-minute audio tour.

Open: Daily Mon-Sat 10am to 4.15pm, Sundays 11am to 4pm

Directions: In Nottingham city centre, inside Broadmarsh Shopping Centre on upper level

---

Journey with us through 300 years of Crime and Punishment on this unique atmospheric site. Witness a real trial in the authentic Victorian courtroom. Prisoners and gaolers act as guides as you becomepart of history.

Open: Tuesday to Sunday 10am to 5pm peak season 10am to 4pm off-peak.

Directions: from Nottingham city centre follow the brown tourist signs.

A collection of 61 aircraft and cockpit sections from across the history of aviation. Extensive aero engine and artefact displays.

Open: Daily from 10am (closed Christmas period).

Directions: Follow brown and white signs from A1, A46, A17 and A1133.

A modern working farm with displays indoors and outdoors designed to help visitors listen, feel and learn whilst having fun. Daily baby animal holding sessions plus a large indoor play barn.

Open: Daily 10am to 5pm.

Directions: 12 miles from Nottingham on A614 or follow Robin Hood signs from J27 of M1.

Travel back in time to the dark and romantic world of intrigue and adventure of Medieval England's most endearing outlaw - Robin Hood. Story boards, exhibitions and a film show all add interest to the story.

Open: 10am -6pm, last admission 4.30pm.

Directions: Follow the brown and white tourist information signs whilst heading towards the city centre.

Historic manor house and farm with traditional animals. Baking in the Victorian kitchen every afternoon.

Open: April to 2nd December: Tuesday to Friday 10.30am to 5.30pm. Saturday and Sunday 12-5.30pm.

Directions: Just off A40 Oxford to Cheltenham road at Witney.

The Avon Valley Railway offers a whole new experience for some, and a nostalgic memory for others. Steam trains operate every Sunday May to September, plus Bank Holidays and Christmas.
PETS MUST BE KEPT ON LEADS AND OFF TRAIN SEATS

Open: Steam trains operate every Sunday May to Sept plus Bank Holidays and Christmas

Directions: On the A431 midway between Bristol and Bath at Bitton

FHG READERS' OFFER 2003

The Helicopter Museum

The Heliport, Locking Moor Road, Weston-Super-Mare BS24 8PP

Tel: 01934 635227• Fax: 01934 645230

e-mail: office@helimuseum.fsnet.co.uk • website: www.helicoptermuseum.co.uk

| One child FREE with each full-paying adult |

valid from April to October 2003

NOT TO BE USED IN CONJUNCTION WITH ANY OTHER OFFER

FHG READERS' OFFER 2003

Wookey Hole Caves & Papermill

Wookey Hole, Wells, Somerset BA5 1BB

Tel: 01749 672243

e-mail: witch@wookey.co.uk • website: www.wookey.co.uk

| £1 per person OFF full admission price (up to max. 5 persons) |

valid during 2003

NOT TO BE USED IN CONJUNCTION WITH ANY OTHER OFFER

FHG READERS' OFFER 2003

Royal Doulton Visitor Centre

Nile Street, Burslem, Stoke-on-Trent, Staffs ST6 2AJ

Tel: 01782 292434 • Fax: 01782 292424

e-mail: visitor@royal-doulton.com • website: www.royal-doulton.com

| Two admissions for the price of one – does not apply to factory tours |

valid during 2003

NOT TO BE USED IN CONJUNCTION WITH ANY OTHER OFFER

FHG READERS' OFFER 2003

Easton Farm Park

Easton, Near Wickham Market, Ipswich, Suffolk IP13 0EQ

Tel: 01728 746475 • e-mail: easton@eastonfarmpark.co.uk

website: www.eastonfarmpark.co.uk

| £1 per person off for up to 4 full paying admissions |

Valid until end 2003

NOT TO BE USED IN CONJUNCTION WITH ANY OTHER OFFER

FHG READERS' OFFER 2003

New Pleasurewood Hills

Leisure Way, Corton, Lowestoft, Suffolk NR32 5DZ

Tel: 01502 508200 • Fax: 01603 567393

e-mail: info@pleasurewoodhills.com • website: www.pleasurewoodhills.com

| '3 for 2' One FREE adult/child with two full paying adults |

valid during 2003, except special events and at Christmas

NOT TO BE USED IN CONJUNCTION WITH ANY OTHER OFFER

The world's largest helicopter collection - over 60 exhibits, includes two royal helicopters, Russian Gunship and Vietnam veterans plus many award-winning exhibits. Cafe, shop. Flights.

PETS MUST BE KEPT UNDER CONTROL

Open: Wednesday to Sunday 10am to 6pm.
Daily during school and public holidays.
(10am to 4pm November to March)
Directions: Junction 21 off M5 then follow the propellor signs.

---

* Britain's most spectacular caves
* Traditional paper-making
* Penny Arcade
* Magical Mirror Maze *

Open: Summer 10am to 5pm last tour;
Winter 10.30am to 4.30pm last tour.
Closed 17-25 Dec.
Directions: From M5 J22 follow brown-and-white signs via A38 and A371. Two miles from Wells.

Extensive displays of Royal Doulton products both past and present including figures, giftware, tableware and crystal. Live demonstrations, museum area, restaurant and shop. Factory Tours by prior booking weekdays only.

Open: Monday to Saturday 9.30am to 5pm; Sundays 10.30am to 4.30pm
Closed Christmas/New Year period.

Directions: From M6 Junction 15/16; follow A500 to exit for A527. Follow signs for about one mile.

Lots of baby animals. FREE pony rides, face painting, green trail, 'pat-a-pet', indoor children's soft play area; gift shop, tearoom, pets' paddocks

DOGS MUST BE KEPT ON LEADS

Open: March to October 10.30am to 6pm

Directions: Follow brown tourist signs off A12 and other roads

---

With over forty rides, shows and attractions set in fifty acres of parkland - you'll have everything you need for a brilliant day out. The mixture of old favourites and exciting new introductions are an unbeatable combination.

Open: From 10am.
Closing time varies depending on season.

Directions: Off A12 between Great Yarmouth and Lowestoft.

The past is brought to life at the top attraction in the South East 2002 (England for Excellence Awards). Step back in time and wonder through over 30 shop and room settings.

PETS NOT ALLOWED IN CHILDREN'S PLAY AREA

Open: 9.30am to 6pm (last admission 4.45pm, one hour earlier in winter).

Directions: Just off A21 in Battle High Street opposite the Abbey.

A plant lover's paradise with outstanding themed gardens and extensive Museum of Natural History. Conservatory gardens contain a large and varied collection of the world's flora. Sussex History Trail. Dinosaur Museum. Rides and amusements.

Open: Open daily, except Christmas Day and Boxing Day.

Directions: Signposted off A26 and A259.

Wilderness Wood is a unique family-run working woodland in the Sussex High Weald. Explore trails and footpaths, enjoy local cakes and ices, try the adventure playground. Many special events and activities. Parties catered for.

Open: daily 10am to 5.30pm or dusk if earlier.

Directions: On the south side of the A272 in the village of Hadlow Down. Signposted with a brown tourist sign.

---

100 acres of parkland, home to hundreds of duck, geese, swans and flamingos. Discovery centre, cafe, gift shop; play area.

Open: Every day except Christmas Day

Directions: Signposted from A19, A195, A1231 and A182.

Shire horses and rare breeds, country village exhibition, indoor and outdoor playground, snackbar and gift shop, tours or parades at 11.15am and 2pm.

DOGS MUST BE KEPT ON LEADS AT ALL TIMES

Open: Easter to Early Sept 10am to 5pm Saturday to Wednesday, except school holidays when open every day.

Lovely rural farm with 50 breeds of rabbit, and several breeds of poultry, pig, sheep, goat, horses and ponies. Cafe, craft shop, events throughout holidays, famous pig races, nature trail, indoor and outdoor play.

Open: 10.30am to 6pm in season, weekends 10am to 4pm in winter.

Directions: Near Stonehenge, just off the A303 at the intersection with A338 Salisbury/Swindon Road.

A fascinating world of historic buildings covering seven centuries, rescued and rebuilt on an open-air site in the heart of the Worcestershire countryside.

Directions: A38 south of Bromsgrove, near Junction 1 of M42, Junction 5 of M5.

A fascinating display of railway carriages and a wide range of railway items telling the story of rail travel over the years.

ALL PETS MUST BE KEPT ON LEADS

Open: Daily 11am to 4.30pm

Directions: Approximately one mile from Keighley on A629 Halifax road. Follow brown tourist signs

---

Visitor centre dedicated to the much-loved Scottish writer Lewis Grassic Gibbon. Exhibition, cafe, gift shop. Outdoor children's play area. Disabled access throughout.

Open: Daily April to October 10am to 4.30pm. Groups by appointment including evenings.

Directions: On the B967, accessible and signposted from both A90 and A92.

45-acre natural wildlife park, with nature trails. On view are fallow deer, raccoons, wallabies, Scottish wild cats, foxes, monkeys, birds of prey, deer and much more. Small cafe and gift shop.

Open: Easter weekend to October 31st. Open 10am, last admission 5pm.

Directions: A82 Glasgow-Tarbet, then A83 Campbeltown. One mile south of Inveraray village.

Rare breeds of farm animals,
pets' corner, conservation groups,
tea room, woodland walk
in beautiful location

Open: 10am to 6pm
mid-March to end October

Directions: two-and-a-half miles
from Oban along Glencruitten road

Set in the rolling hills of Ayrshire,
Europe's best preserved ironworks.
Guided tours, audio-visuals,
walks with electronic wands.
Restaurant/coffee shop.

Open: April to October
daily 10am to 5pm.

Directions: A713 Ayr to Castle
Douglas road, 12 miles from Ayr,
3 miles from Dalmellington.

The historic home of the Earls of Glasgow.
Waterfalls, gardens, famous Glen, unusual
trees. Riding school, Falconry Centre
stockade, play areas, exhibitions, shop,
cafe and The Secret Forest.

PETS MUST BE KEPT ON LEAD

Open: daily 10am to 6pm
Easter to October.

Directions: On A78 between
Largs and Fairlie,
45 mins drive from Glasgow.

Scotland's seafaring heritage is
among the world's richest and you
can relive the heyday of Scottish
shipping at the Maritime Museum.

Open: all year except Christmas and
New Year Holidays.
10am - 5pm
Directions: Situated on Irvine
harbourside and only a 10 minute
walk from Irvine train station.

Worldwide collection of gems,
minerals, crystals and fossils
•Erupting Volcano•Audio Visual•
•Crystal Cave•Unique Giftshop•
•Relax in our themed tea room•
•Internet Cafe

Open: Open daily Easter to 30th
November; December to February –
weekends only.

Directions: 7 miles from Newton Stewart,
11 miles from Gatehouse of Fleet; just off
A75 Carlisle to Stranraer road.

An innovative museum exploring the history and environment of West Lothian on a 20-acre site packed full of things to see and do, indoors and out.

Open: Daily (except Christmas and New Year) 10am to 5pm.

Directions: 15 miles from Edinburgh, follow "Heritage Centre" signs from A899.

Watch the craftsmen, feel the passion and discover the history of the UK's favourite crystal on tours of the glasshouse. Plus great shopping.

Open: Monday to Saturday 10am to 5pm, Sundays 11am to 5pm. Closed Christmas and New Year fortnight

Directions: 30 minutes south of Edinburgh city centre. From city bypass, take A701 to Peebles, following the signs for Penicuik.

On show is a large collection, from 1899, of cars, bicycles, motor cycles and commercials. There is also a large collection of period advertising, posters and enamel signs.

Open: Daily Easter to September 11am to 4pm; October to Easter: Sundays 1pm to 3pm or by special appointment.

Directions: Off A198 near Aberlady. Two miles from A1.

Scotland's award-winning aquarium where you can enjoy a spectacular diver's eye view of our marine environment through the world's longest underwater safari. New 'Amazing Amphibians' display, (Cayman crocodile), behind the scenes tours. Aquamazing entertainment for all the family

Open: Daily except Christmas Day.

Directions: From Edinburgh follow signs for Forth Road Bridge, then signs through North Queensferry. From North, follow signs through Inverkeithing and North Queensferry.

Highland croft open to visitors for "hands-on" experience with over 30 different breeds of farm animals "stroke the goats and scratch the pigs". Farm information centre and old farm implements. For all ages, cloud or shine!

Open: July and August 10am to 5pm.

Directions: On A835 15 miles north of Ullapool

300 years of history has been recreated in a thriving township from the 1700s, a working Highland farm with old breed horses, cattle, ducks, farm machinery and and an old tin school where the teacher rules!

Open: Mid-April to October. Check for opening times.

Directions: Follow signs from A9 to Newtonmore. North end of Newtonmore on A86.

FHG PUBLICATIONS, ABBEY MILL BUSINESS CENTRE, PAISLEY PA1 1TJ

Great day out for all the family. Wild Water Coaster, Microworld exhibition, Forest Trails, Viewing Tower, Climbing Wall*, Tree Top Trail, Steam powered Sawmill*, Clydesdale Horse*. Shop, restaurant and snackbar.
(* Easter to October)*
DOGS MUST BE KEPT ON LEADS

Open: Daily except Christmas Day.

Directions: 20 miles south of Inverness at Carrbridge, just off the A9.

FHG PUBLICATIONS, ABBEY MILL BUSINESS CENTRE, PAISLEY PA1 1TJ

Award-winning attraction with unique 'Heather Story' exhibition, extensive giftshop. Large garden centre selling 300 different heathers, antique shop, children's play area and famous Clootie Dumpling restaurant.

Open: All year except Christmas Day.

Directions: Just off A95 between Aviemore and Grantown-on-Spey.

FHG PUBLICATIONS, ABBEY MILL BUSINESS CENTRE, PAISLEY PA1 1TJ

A beautifully restored cotton mill village close to the Falls of Clyde. Explore the fascinating history of the village, try the 'New Millennium Experience', a magical chair ride which takes you back in time to discover what life used to be like.

Open: 11am to 5pm daily. Closed Christmas and New Year.

FHG PUBLICATIONS, ABBEY MILL BUSINESS CENTRE, PAISLEY PA1 1TJ

Colourful gardens, imaginative woodland play areas and tumbling waterfalls. The Estate combines history with adventure in a fun day out for the family, where your dog can run freely. Step back in time and uncover its secrets.

Open: Daily
10.30am to 5pm

Directions: Off A8 west of Langbank

FHG PUBLICATIONS, ABBEY MILL BUSINESS CENTRE, PAISLEY PA1 1TJ

Take a trip along this narrow gauge steam railway, passing by the largest natural lake in Wales.

Open: Easter to the end of September, except some Mondays and Fridays.

Directions: Off the A494 at Llanuwchllyn.

A 40-minute ride along the shores of beautiful Padarn Lake behind a quaint historic steam engine. Magnificent views of the mountains from lakeside picnic spots.

DOGS MUST BE KEPT ON LEAD AT ALL TIMES ON TRAIN

Open: Most days Easter to October. Free timetable leaflet on request.

Directions: Just off A4086 Caernarfon to Capel Curig road at Llanberis; follow 'Country Park' signs.

Walk through the Rabbit Hole to the colourful scenes of Lewis Carroll's classic story set in beautiful life-size displays. Recorded commentaries and transcripts available in several languages.

Open: 10am to 5pm daily (closed Sundays Easter to November); closed Christmas/Boxing/New Year's Days.

Directions: situated just off the main street, 250 yards from coach and rail stations.

Journey through the lanes of cycle history and see bicycles from Boneshakers and Penny Farthings up to modern Raleigh cycles. Over 250 machines on display

PETS MUST BE KEPT ON LEADS

Open: 1st March to 1st November daily 10am onwards.

Directions: AA signs to car park. Town centre attraction.

Make a pit stop whatever the weather! Join an ex-miner on a tour of discovery, ride the cage to pit bottom and take a thrilling ride back to the surface. Multi-media presentations, period village street, children's adventure play area, restaurant and gift shop. Full disabled access.

Open: Open daily 10am to 6pm (last tour 4.30pm). Closed Mondays October to Easter, also Christmas/Boxing days.

Directions: Exit Junction 32 M4, signposted from A470 Pontypridd. Trehafod is located between Pontypridd and Porth.

UNIVERSITY ACCOMMODATION & FACILITIES
Budget accommodation or fully tailored packages (0870 712 5002; Fax: 020 7017 8273). En suite designer halls across the UK. Groups of any age or size. Sports facilities all year. Tell us your needs and we'll find a location and package to suit.
e-mail: enquiries@thesv.com

BUCKINGHAMSHIRE

BUCKINGHAM

Chris and Fiona Hilsdon, Huntsmill Farm, Shalstone, Buckingham MK18 5ND (Tel & Fax: 01280 704852; mobile: 07973 386756). Situated midway between the market towns of Buckingham and Brackley, close to Stowe Gardens and the Silverstone Circuit; an ideal touring base for Oxford and the Cotswolds. The farm courtyard is a delightfully peaceful spot, overlooking rolling countryside. Three imaginatively converted traditional stone, timber and slate properties offer the very best in holiday accommodation amidst the peace of the English countryside. Huntsmill is a working, mainly arable farm, with many nature trails and walks. **ETC ★★★★,** *MEMBER FARMSTAY UK.* **website: www.huntsmill.com**

CAMBRIDGESHIRE

Cathedral House

17 ST MARY'S STREET, ELY CAMBRIDGESHIRE CB7 4ER

TEL: 01353 662124

The Coach House has been imaginatively converted into a delightful abode full of character and charm, situated close to Ely Cathedral. Arranged on two floors, the accommodation downstairs comprises a sitting room and country-style kitchen with a cooker, fridge etc. Upstairs there are two charming double rooms (one has a view of the Cathedral), and a cosy single room. All have an en suite bathroom, with a toilet, wash hand basin and a half-size bath with shower taps. Gas central heating. Linen, towels, toilet soap, cleaning materials and some basic provisions are provided. Prices range from £200 - £1000 depending on season and length of stay. B&B From £40 per person per night (Subject to availablity). Sleeps 4/5.
farndale@cathedralhouse.co.uk   www.cathedralhouse.co.uk

A useful index of towns and counties appears at the back of this book on pages 273 – 276. Refer also to Contents Pages 44/45.

ENGLAND

CORNWALL

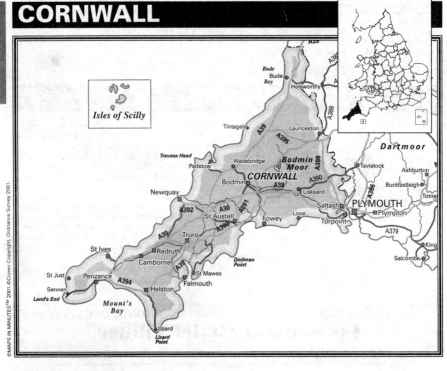

FHG PUBLICATIONS

publish a large range of well-known accommodation
guides. We will be happy to send you details or you
can use the order form at the back of this book.

Penrose Burden Holiday Cottages

St Breward, Bodmin, Cornwall PL30 4LZ
Tel: 01208 850277 & 850617; Fax: 01208 850915

Situated within easy reach of both coasts and Bodmin Moor on a large farm overlooking a beautiful wooded valley with own salmon and trout fishing. These stone cottages with exposed beams and quarry tiled floors have been featured on TV and are award-winners. Home-made meals can be delivered daily. All are suitable for wheelchair users and dogs are welcomed. Our cottages sleep from two to seven and are open all year. Please write or telephone for a colour brochure. Close to The Eden Project.

See also Colour Advertisement

BODMIN

Ruthern Valley Holidays, Ruthernbridge, Near Bodmin PL30 5LU (01208 831395; Fax: 01208 832324). An 'oasis' of tranquillity, colour and space in the heart of Cornwall. No bar, no bingo, no disco, just eight acres of high quality, mature, landscaped grounds. Ideal for the outdoor family – walking, riding, fishing and the 'Camel Cycle Trail' all nearby. Centrally based for a range of fine beaches, Eden Project, Lost Gardens of Heligan, etc. A unique choice of eight timber lodges, four Cedarwood Bungalows and six holiday caravans to suit all family budgets. All two-bedroomed, sleeping up to six. Fully self contained and well equipped including bathroom with shower, colour TV etc. Site shop, children's play area. Listen to the wildlife, not the traffic. **ETC ★★★★** *HOLIDAY PARK, DAVID BELLAMY GOLD AWARD,* **AA** *THREE PENNANTS.*
website: www.self-catering-ruthern.co.uk

BOSCASTLE

Jackie and Robin Haddy, Home Farm, Minster, Boscastle PL35 0BN (01840 250195). Sleeps 4. Home Farm Cottage is a traditional Cornish Cottage, situated on the National Trust property of Home Farm, a mixed working farm of 145 acres consisting of beef suckler cows, sheep and corn. The farm lies in an Area of Outstanding Natural Beauty, with picturesque views of the heritage coast and the historic village of Boscastle with its pretty harbour. The cottage is tastefully furnished to a very high standard, whilst retaining charm and character. It benefits from modern conveniences including dishwasher, washing machine, tumble dryer, colour TV, video, bathroom, separate shower room and equipped utility/laundry room. One double bedroom and one twin room, with optional sofa bed in lounge. The cottage also has its own safe, secluded garden. Please telephone for further details. **ETC ★★★★**
e-mail: jackie.haddy@btclick.com   website: www.homefarm-boscastle.co.uk

BOSCASTLE

Mrs V.M. Seldon, Tregatherall Farm, Boscastle PL35 0EQ (01840 250277). Two new self-catering cottages on a warm, friendly Cornish farm, midway between Boscastle and Tintagel. Fully equipped en suite bedrooms, luxuriously furnished, sleeping four and six respectively. Oil-fired central heating and own parking. We offer out-of-season, spring and autumn short breaks. Please contact us for special offers and availablility. Brochure on request.

BUDE

Fiona & Ian Goodwin, Hilton Farm Holiday Cottages, Marhamchurch, Bude EX23 0HE (Tel & Fax: 01288 361521). Where coast meets countryside, in an Area of Outstanding Natural Beauty, the ideal place to make the most of Devon & Cornwall. Superb setting in 25 acres of ground. 16th century Farmhouse, sleeps 10; three new luxury cottages and six fully equipped converted barn cottages. Superb heated outdoor swimming pool, activity area/play area/BBQ and picnic area; laundry facilities. Just two miles from sandy beaches; world-famous Eden Project 45 minutes' drive. Self-catering cottages open all year, with farmhouse B&B available from October to June, from £18pp.
ETC ★★★/★★★★
e-mail: ian@hiltonfarmhouse.freeserve.co.uk
website: www.hiltonfarmhouse.co.uk

CORNWALL

Duchy Holidays, Cornwall. A selection of seaside and countryside holiday homes located throughout Cornwall. A luxury bungalow with a private swimming pool, farmhouse with lake fishing, beachside cottages, lodges and villas with swimming pools and entertainment. All properties are inspected and personally supervised. Short Breaks and long weekends available from £85 (excluding school holidays). Telephone or fax on **01872 572971** or visit our website for more information.
e-mail: duchy.holidays@virgin.net
website: www.duchyholidays.co.uk

COVERACK

Polcoverack Farm Cottages, Coverack, Helston TR12 6SP (01326 281021; Fax: 01326 280683). A cluster of delightful stone built cottages approached via a private lane and set within a coastal farm providing a glorious rural setting. Coverack, one of Cornwall's most picturesque fishing villages, is within a ten minute walk. Here you will find a sandy beach, inn, general stores and restaurants. Each cottage offers comfortable, well-equipped accommodation sleeping two to six. They include colour television, video recorder, microwave oven, full-sized cooker, refrigerator, cafetiere, hairdryer and all bed linen. Cot and high chair if required. We also provide a laundry room, plus large games room, and ample parking. Phone for a free colour brochure.
website: www.polcoverack.co.uk

CUSGARNE (Near Truro)

Sleeps 2. Dogs welcome. A cosy single-storey, clean, detached dwelling with own garden, within grounds of Saffron Meadow, in quiet hamlet five miles west of Truro. Secluded and surrounded by wooded pastureland. Bedroom (double bed) with twin vanity unit. Fully tiled shower/WC and LB. Comprehensively equipped kitchen/diner. Compact TV room. Storage room. Hot water galore and gas included. Metered electricity. Automatic external safety lighting. Your own ample parking space in drive. Shop, Post Office and Inn a short walk. Central to Truro, Falmouth and North and South coasts. £140 to £210 per week. **Joyce and George Clench, Saffron Meadow, Cusgarne, Truro TR4 8RW (01872 863171).**

FALMOUTH

Mrs J. Matthews, Boskensoe Farm Holiday Bungalow, Mawnan Smith, Falmouth TR11 5JP (01326 250257). Sleeps 6/8. Bungalow overlooking farm on edge of village. Three bedrooms. Colour TV. Electric cooker, fridge/freezer, washing machine and microwave. Fitted with storage heaters and electric fires. Spacious garden and ample parking for cars and boats. Situated in the picturesque village of Mawnan Smith, Falmouth five miles, one-and-a-half miles from lovely Helford River famous for beautiful coastal walks, gardens and scenery. Several quiet safe beaches for bathing. Also excellent sailing and fishing facilities. Terms from £150 to £425. Apply for brochure.

FALMOUTH

Mrs Newing, Glengarth, Burnthouse, St Gluvias, Penryn, Cornwall TR10 9AS (01872 863209). Ideally situated for touring Cornwall and furnished to a high standard. Centrally heated first-floor apartment in a delightful detached house four miles from Falmouth. Two double bedrooms and one with full-size bunk beds, all with washbasins; comfortable lounge with colour TV and video; fully-equipped kitchen/diner; bathroom; shower room with toilet. Hot water, electricity, bed linen, duvets and towels included in tariff. Cot and high chair available. Garden and ample parking. Open all year. Low season £155, High Season £332. Short breaks available in low season. Member of Cornwall Tourist Board. Pets welcome. Families and couples only please. Brochure available.

FALMOUTH

Mrs Kathleen Terry, 'Shasta', Carwinion Road, Mawnan Smith, Falmouth TR11 5JD (01326 250775). 'Shasta Annex' Sleeps 2. A short walk from Mawnan Smith, with thatched pub, Italian restaurant, shops. Maenporth's sandy beach, the beautiful Helford river, tropical gardens are a short drive away. Ideal for coastal walking, Falmouth approximately four miles. Well equipped comfortable ground floor flat, with patio overlooking lovely mature garden. Cooker, fridge, washing machine, microwave etc. TV and video. Garden furniture, night storage heaters. Towels and linen provided. Electricity included in price. Parking. Welcome pack on arrival. Tourist Board Approved. Terms from £160–£290. Brochure available.
e-mail: katerry@btopenworld.com

FOWEY

Fowey Harbour Cottages. Sleep 2/6. We are a small Agency offering a selection of cottages and flats situated around the beautiful Fowey Harbour on the South Cornish Coast. Different properties accommodate from two to six persons and vary in their decor and facilities so that hopefully there will be something we can offer to suit anyone. All properties are registered with the English Tourism Council and are personally vetted by us. Short Breaks and weekend bookings accepted subject to availability (mainly out of peak season but sometimes available at "last minute" in season). Brochure and details from **W. J. B. Hill & Son, 3 Fore Street, Fowey PL23 1PH (01726 832211; Fax: 01726 832901).**
e-mail: hillandson@talk21.com

HAYLE TOWANS

Sleeps 6. Detached three-bedroom bungalow with sea views across St Ives Bay. Beach 100 yards, three miles of soft golden sand, backed by rolling sand dunes. Located in an area of Cornwall noted for its scenery and attractions. Local supermarket, or Hayle town shops five minutes by car. Accommodation comprises kitchen, lounge/dining room with colour TV, three bedrooms sleeping six. Bathroom with shower. Storage heating. Off-road parking for two cars. Available all year. **Mrs Langford, 1 Fleetway, Thorpe, Surrey TW20 8UA (Tel & Fax: 01932 560503).**

See also Colour Display Advertisement

HELFORD ESTUARY

**Mrs S. Trewhella, Mudgeon Vean Farm, St Martin, Helston
TR12 6DB (01326 231341).** Leave the hustle and bustle of
town life. Come and enjoy the peace and tranquillity of the Helford
Estuary. Three homely cottages sleep two/six, equipped to a high
standard. Open all year for cosy winter breaks. Open fires/heating.
Set amidst a small 18th century organic working farm with
magnificent views across an extensive valley area, surrounded by
fields and woodland – a walk through the woods takes you to the
Helford River. A superb location in an area of outstanding natural
beauty with the rugged coastline of the Lizard Peninsula and
beaches only a short drive away. Children and pets welcome.
From £115 to £390 per week

LAUNCESTON

**Mrs Kathryn Broad, Lower Dutson Farm, Launceston
PL15 9SP (Tel & Fax: 01566 776456). Working farm.
Sleeps 2/6.** Enjoy a holiday on our traditional working farm. A
warm welcome awaits you at our 17th century farmhouse.
Historic Launceston with its Norman Castle (even Tescos!) is two
miles away. Centrally situated for visiting National Trust houses
and gardens, Dartmoor, Bodmin Moor and the beaches and
harbours of Devon and Cornwall. Walk or fish along our stretch
of the River Tamar for salmon and trout or try your skills at our
coarse fishing lake. Well-equipped cottage with three bedrooms,
two bathrooms. Enjoy the 'suntrap' just outside the front door.
Children welcome. Terms £140 to £480. **ETC ★★★**
**e-mail: francis.broad@btclick.com
website: www.farm-cottage.co.uk**

LAUNCESTON

Jackie Chapman, Bamham Farm Cottages, Higher Bamham, Launceston PL15 9LD. Eight individually designed cottages, situated in beautiful countryside one mile from Launceston, ancient capital town of Cornwall. The north and south coasts are easily accessible as are Dartmoor and Bodmin moor. The cottages are equipped to high standard, some having open fires, microwaves and dishwashers. Facilities include heated indoor swimming pool, sauna, games room, laundry room, video recorders and trout fishing. The cottages and facilities are open all year and available for short breaks before the middle of May and after the end of September (excluding school holidays). Colour brochure available. **(01566 772141; Fax: 01566 775266). ETC ★★★/★★★★**
e-mail: jackie@bamhamfarm.co.uk
website: www.bamhamfarm.co.uk

LISKEARD

Mrs C. Hutchinson, Caradon Country Cottages, East Taphouse, Near Liskeard PL14 4NH (Tel & Fax: 01579 320355). Luxury cottages located in magnificent countryside between Bodmin Moor and Looe. Ideal location for exploring Cornwall and Devon, coast and countryside, National Trust properties and the Eden Project. Five acre grounds of gardens, lawned play area, sun trap patios and nature trail around the unspoilt hedgerows of our meadow and pony paddock. Children and pets welcome. Central heating and woodburners for Winter Breaks.
website: www.caradoncottages.co.uk

LISKEARD

Mr & Mrs Trevelyan, Coombe Farm Holiday Cottages, Herodsfoot, Liskeard PL14 4RS (01579 320548). Within easy reach of the coast, Bodmin Moor and the Eden Project, Coombe Farm offers a superb base for holidays and out-of-season short breaks. Converted barns offer simple but comfortable accommodation finished to a high standard. The cottages have very well-equipped kitchens, colour TV, CD players and use of a washing machine and tumble dryer. All linen, towels, fuel and power included. The games room offers table tennis, snooker and darts. Freshly prepared local food delivered straight to your cottage. Well-behaved dogs welcome.
website: www.coombe.farm.co.uk

LISKEARD

Trewalla Farm Cottages, Trewalla Farm, Minions, Liskeard PL14 6ED (Tel & Fax: 01579 342385). Sleeps 3/4 plus cot. Our small, traditionally run farm near the ancient Hurlers on Bodmin Moor has rare breed pigs, sheep, hens and some geese. The three cottages are very comfortably furnished and extremely well equipped. Their moorland setting offers perfect peace, wonderful views, ideal walking country and a good base for visiting the Eden Project or exploring both coastlines – if you can tear yourself away! Linen and electricity included. Open March to December and New Year. **ETC ★★★★**
e-mail: cotter.trewalla@virgin.net

The FHG Directory of Website Addresses

on pages 243-272 is a useful quick reference guide for holiday accommodation with e-mail and/or website details

Cottages for Romantics

Old world charm, log fires, antiques, beautifully furnished with the comforts of home. Private gardens, spectacular views, peace ~ for families, friends and couples to enjoy. Nestling on a south- facing hillside, near coast ~ heated pool, tennis, badminton, lake, shire horses, etc. Enchanting 70-acre estate with bluebell wood, walking and wildlife. Delicious fare also available by candlelight 'at home' or in our tiny inn.

A Country Lover's Paradise ~ with an abundance of country walks from your garden gate and coastal walks only 4 miles away.

S. Slaughter, Trefanny Hill, Duloe, Near Liskeard, Cornwall PL14 4QF • Tel: 01503 220 622
enq@trefanny.co.uk • website: www.trefanny.co.uk

See also Colour Advertisement

LISKEARD

Lametton Barton, St Keyne, Liskeard PL14 4SQ. Lametton Barton is a working farm set in the very heart of Cornwall, an ideal base from which to visit the Cornish coast. Local attractions include the Lost Gardens of Heligan, the Eden Project and the historic port of Looe. On the first floor there is one double and one twin-bedded room, and a bathroom. There is also a smaller room containing a single bed/optional bunk bed conversion. Cot can be provided. Ground floor comprises sitting room with beamed ceiling, kitchen and dining room. Fully equipped with cooker, fridge, microwave and washing machine etc. Well-behaved dogs are welcome. Prices include electricity, bed linen, duvets and tea towels. Terms from £300 per week. Spring and Autumn weekend rates available. Contact: **Peter & Sharon Clemens (01579 343434).**

LOOE

Raven Rock and Spindrift, Looe. Two bungalows adjacent to Plaidy Beach. Spindrift has en suite bedroom, sleeps two; Raven Rock has two bedrooms and sleeps four. Own parking spaces, central heating, wheelchair accessible. Semi-detached bungalows are fully furnished, well equipped and have sea views. Set in peaceful surroundings at Plaidy. Open plan lounge-diner-kitchen. Colour TV. Patio garden. Electricity and gas included in rent. Pets by arrangement. Personally supervised. Looe is a fishing port with a variety of shops and restaurants and is only a few minutes by car or a 15 to 20 minute walk. Weekly terms: Spindrift from £170 to £280; Raven Rock from £200 to £375. Apartment in centre of town also available (sleeps 6/8). Short breaks (three days minimum) before Easter and after middle of October. Contact: **Mrs S. Gill, Bodrigy, Plaidy, Looe PL13 1LF (01503 263122).**

LOOE VALLEY

Mr & Mrs R. A. Brown, Badham Farm, St Keyne, Liskeard PL14 4RW (Tel & Fax: 01579 343572). Sleeps 2-8 plus 2 children. Once part of a Duchy of Cornwall working farm, now farmhouse and farm buildings converted to a high standard to form a six cottage complex around former farmyard. Sleeping from two to ten. All cottages are well furnished and equipped and prices include electricity, bed linen and towels. Most cottages have a garden. Five acre grounds, set in delightful wooded valley, with tennis, putting, children's play area, fishing lake, animal paddock, games room with pool and table tennis. Separate bar. Laundry. Barbecue. Railcar from Liskeard to Looe stops at end of picnic area. Have a 'car free' day out. Children and well behaved dogs welcome (no dogs in high season, please). Prices from £120 per week. **ETC ★★★**, *GREEN TOURISM AWARD.*
website: www.looedirectory.co.uk/badhamcottages.htm

ENGLAND

MARAZION (Near)

Mrs W. Boase, Trebarvah Farm, Trebarvah Lane, Perranuthnoe, Penzance TR20 9NG (01736 710361) Trebarvah Farm Cottages. Three cottages, two sleeping four people, one sleeping six people, with magnificent views across Mount's Bay and St Michael's Mount. Just east of Marazion, Perranuthnoe is easily accessible on foot or by car and has a sandy beach. Accommodation – TUE BROOK: one double and two twin-bedded rooms, one en suite, kitchen/diner, lounge and large conservatory. TAIRUA: one double and one twin-bedded room and a livingroom. KERIKERI COTTAGE: one twin room and a double sofa bed in the livingroom. All properties include duvets, pillows and blankets but no linen or towels. Kitchens are electric and power is through a pre-payment £1 coin meter. Colour TV. Rates from £140 to £450 per week. Short breaks available out of summer season.
e-mail: jaybee@trebarvah.freeserve.co.uk   website: www.trebarvahfarmcottages.co.uk

NEWQUAY

The Granary at Trewerry Mill, Newquay. Trewerry Mill nestles in a peaceful valley four miles from the north coast, central for Cornish gardens, coastal walks and The Eden Project (25 minutes). The Granary is a newly converted, centrally heated cottage sleeping 2 to 4. From an enclosed courtyard, steps lead up into the lounge with wood burning stove, dining area and fully-fitted kitchen. Off a half-landing is a large bathroom and shower. Downstairs are a double (king-size) bedroom with original fireplace and a second twin-bedded room. Available Thursdays at £225 to £600 per week, electricity, heating and linen included. One well-behaved dog welcome. Colour brochure available. Contact: **Mr D. Clark, Trewerry Mill, Trerice, St Newlyn East, Cornwall TR8 5GS (Tel & Fax: 01872 510345).**
e-mail: trewerry.mill@which.net
website: www.trewerrymill.co.uk

PADSTOW

Mr Mike Benwell, Trevorrick Farm, St Issey, near Padstow PL27 7QH (01841 540574). Sleeps 2 - 5. Working farm, join in. Well-equipped stone and slate cottages on a smallholding, set in an Area of Outstanding Natural Beauty. Beautiful location overlooking Little Petherick Creek and the Camel Estuary. Ideal for walking – easy access to Padstow, Saints Way and the Camel Trail. Great for cycling (cycle hire nearby) with the signed Cornish Way and The Camel Trail. Good pub/restaurant half a mile. Heated indoor swimming pool and games room in converted barn. Ideal for children; toys/games can be provided to suit ages of children. Safe sandy/surfing beaches nearby and some excellent coastal walking. Shorts Breaks available. Open all year. All facilities on site. Pets and children welcome. Disabled and non-smoking accommodation available. Terms from £180 to £750 linen included. **ETC ★★★**
e-mail: info@trevorrick.co.uk   website: www.trevorrick.co.uk

PENZANCE

Mrs James Curnow, Barlowenath, St Hilary, Penzance TR20 9DQ (01736 710409). Working farm. Cottages sleep 4/5. These two cottages are on a farm, in a little hamlet right beside St Hilary Church, with quiet surroundings and a good road approach. A good position for touring Cornish coast and most well-known places. Beaches are two miles away; Marazion two-and-a-half miles; Penzance six miles; St Ives eight; Land's End 16. Both cottages have fitted carpets, lounge/diner with TV/video; modern kitchen (microwave, fridge, electric cooker, toaster, iron); bathroom with shaver point. Electricity by £1 meter, night storage heaters extra. One cottage sleeps five in three bedrooms (one double, twin divans and one single). The second cottage sleeps four in two bedrooms (twin divans in both). Linen not supplied, may be hired by arrangement. Cot by arrangement. Available all year. £95 to £350 weekly, VAT exempt.

See also Colour Display Advertisement

PENZANCE

Mrs Catherine Wall, Trenow, Relubbus Lane, St Hilary, Penzance TR20 9EA (01736 762308). Sleeps 2. Mini-bungalow within the grounds of old country house. Lovely garden in rural district. Lounge/diner with cooking area, bedroom, shower room and conservatory. Bed linen provided. Parking within grounds. No children, no pets. Central for touring south west peninsula. Sea two miles. Available all year.Terms from £130 per week (including storage heaters).

PERRANPORTH

"Makhan" and "Kinsi", Liskey Hill Crescent, Perranporth, & Cradock, 7 Wainsway, Liskey Hill, Perranporth. "Makhan' and 'Kinsi" are two adjacent semi-detached houses offering basic accommodation at a budget price. Makhan sleeps 8-12 and Kinsi 6-10. They are simply furnished and suitable for a party of four or five adults with four or five children (N.B. NOT 12 adults!) "Cradock" is a detached bungalow just a stone's throw from the park, shops, pubs and the beach, sleeping 6-8. All three properties have some garden and parking, TV, etc. Perranporth itself has a fine sandy beach with rocky cliffs, caves and pools on one side and excellent surfing. There is also tennis, golf, gliding and a boating lake. Prices from £200 to £550 per house per week. Contact: **D.E. Gill-Carey, Penkerris, 3 Penwinnick Road, St Agnes, Cornwall TR5 0PA (Tel & Fax: 01872 552262).**
e-mail: info@penkerris.co.uk   website: www.penkerris.co.uk

POLPERRO

Holiday Cottages, Polperro. Sleep 2 to 8. Spectacularly situated holiday cottages in picturesque Cornish fishing village with terraced gardens and fabulous outlook over harbour encompassing 15 mile sea views. Private parking. Two minutes away are shops, beach, quay and National Trust cliff walks. Open all year, children and pets most welcome. All cottages are fully furnished and equipped, including a colour television, microwave, refrigerator, duvets and pillows. Terms from £150 to £425 per cottage per week. For more details please telephone **01579 344080.**

PORT ISAAC

The Lodge, Treharrock, Port Isaac. Sleeps 6. Pleasant south facing and convenient bungalow, set in its own small natural garden and surrounded by fields and woodland with streams. About two miles inland from Port Isaac, a sheltered, secluded spot at the end of driveway to Treharrock Manor. Rugged North Cornish cliffs with National Trust footpaths and lovely sandy coves in the vicinity. Excellent sandy, surfing beach at Polzeath (five miles), also pony trekking, golf, etc. in the area. South facing sun room leads to terrace; TV. Accommodation for six plus baby in three double bedrooms with washbasins; cot. Linen extra. Sorry, no pets. Car essential - parking. Terms from £200 to £500 per week (heating included). SAE to **Mrs E.A. Hambly, Willow Mill, St Kew, Bodmin, Cornwall PL30 3EP (01208 841806).**

ENGLAND

PORTHLEVEN

Kernow Cottage, Porthleven. Sleeps 4. Situated in the picturesque fishing village of Porthleven, one minutes' walk from the harbour, near shops and beach; this architect designed cottage with central heating is furnished to a high standard. Two bedrooms on the ground floor. First floor has a lounge with two sofas, a large bay window with seating, TV/video and CD/radio; dining area with table and six chairs; bathroom with bath/shower and WC; kitchen with electric oven/hob, dishwasher, fridge and microwave. Washing machine and tumble dryer. Travel cot. Private patio and off road parking. Non-smokers only. Sorry, no pets. Terms from £110 to £380. Bookings: **A & L Watters (Tel & Fax: 01694 781423)**
e-mail: lynnewatters@lineone.net

PORTREATH

Sunland Holiday Village, Portreath TR16 4PE (Hotline/Tel: 01209 842354; Fax: 01209 842365). Sleeps 6. Sunland Holiday Village overlooks the beautiful coastline of Portreath and virtually all of Cornwall's sights and scenes are within a short drive. The newly refurbished chalets include a lounge with TV, fully equipped kitchen with dining area, two bedrooms and bathroom. Visit our website and see the exciting new additions for 2003 or telephone the hotline now.
e-mail: info@sunlandholidays.co.uk
website: www.sunlandholidays.co.uk

PRAA SANDS

Mrs June Markham, Broom Farm, Packet Lane, Rosudgeon, Penzance TR20 9QD (01736 763738). Sleeps 2. Broom Farm Cottage, a comfortable, detached cottage converted from a granite barn and set on three-acre smallholding. Well furnished, sleeps two, pets welcome. There is a full-size cooker, fridge, colour TV. Covered car space leading to patio overlooking meadow. Shop, post office, village pub, fish and chip shop and bus stop at end of lane. Perfect for summer holidays or an out-of-season break. Two miles Praa or Perran Sands, one mile Prussia Cove. Penzance six miles. Weekly terms from £125 to £260. SAE for illustrated brochure, stating holiday period preferred.

ST BREWARD

Holiday Cottage. Sleeps 4. Warm and lovely cottage sleeping four in great comfort and utter peace. Log fires, large garden with stream. Glorious walking. Available all year. Terms from £120 to £350 per week, depending on season. Dogs welcome, £6 per week. St Breward is a picturesque village high on Bodmin Moor and within easy reach of both coasts. Situated four miles from the A30. For further details please contact **Mrs Paddy Powell (01208 850186)**
website: www.vacation-cornwall.com

ST TUDY

Chapel Cottages. Four traditional cottages in quiet farming area and ideal for spectacular north coast, Bodmin Moor and The Eden Project. These two-bedroom cottages have character and charm and are comfortable and well equipped. Garden and private parking. Rental from £120 to £388 per week. Also two smaller cottages at Blisland, suitable for couples, converted from a 17th century barn. These are situated in a peaceful farming hamlet. Rental from £110 to £288 per week. Linen is provided in all cottages. Regretfully no pets. Brochure available from **Mr and Mrs C.W. Pestell, Hockadays, Tregenna, Near Blisland PL30 4QJ (Tel & Fax: 01208 850146).**
website: www.hockadaysholidaycottages.co.uk

CHAPEL COTTAGES

TINTAGEL

Tregeath Cottage, Tregeath Lane, Tintagel. Working farm. Sleeps 4 plus cot. Tregeath is an old modernised detached cottage, built of stone and slate. With grass area and clothes line; situated beside a quiet parish road, connected to 50 acres of farmland. Two double bedrooms upstairs, one with a 4' bed, one with 4'6" bed; one single room downstairs. All with small electric fires and portable TV. Cot and high chair. Bathroom/toilet downstairs; immersion heater; airing cupboard; shaving point. Dining/sittingroom, coal grate, electric fire, five night storage heaters, colour TV, video and payphone. Kitchen, stainless steel sink, electric cooker, microwave, fridge/freezer, kettle, spin dryer; well equipped. Mains water, electricity on a £1 meter. One dog only, no cats. Parking space, car essential. No linen. Trebarwith Strand one-and-a-half miles. Cliff walks near. Shops one mile. Terms on request. **Contact: Mrs E.M. Broad, "Davina", Trevillett, Tintagel PL34 0HL (01840 770217).**

WADEBRIDGE

Peaceful farm cottages with superb views of Camel Valley. Ideal for walking, cycling, beaches and touring all Cornwall and North Devon. These fully equipped cottages have cosy log fires, private gardens and parking. Heating and linen included. Personally supervised. Sleeps 2 to 7 plus cot. Dogs by arrangement. Pets £15 per week. **Mrs Sue Zamaria, Colesent Cottages, St Tudy, Wadebridge PL30 4QX (Tel & Fax: 01208 850112).**
e-mail: welcome@Colesent.co.uk
website: www.colesent.co.uk

WADEBRIDGE/BODIEVE

Sleeps 6 plus cot. 300 year old farmhouse, converted in 1990, surrounded by sunny gardens, parking space in front of house in quiet country crescent. Only three miles from the sandy beaches at Rock and Daymer Bay, the surfing beach at Polzeath, close to the ancient fishing harbour of Padstow. Ideal for surfing, safe bathing, walking, fishing, sailing, golf, cycling (cycle hire in Wadebridge). The excellent shops, pubs, markets at Wadebridge are half-a-mile away. Wadebridge Leisure Centre with its indoor swimming pool is only a five minute walk. The house comprises lounge with wood/coal burner in fireplace, colour TV, comfortable sofa bed (double). Large, cosy, well-equipped kitchen/diner with fridge, electric cooker, dishwasher, microwave, double aspect windows; laundry room with automatic washing machine, tumble dryer, fridge/freezer. Three bedrooms - large master bedroom (double aspect windows) with king size bed, one twin bedroom and a bedroom with bunk beds. Linen and towels on request at extra charge. Bathroom, shower, toilet. Night storage heaters. Pets by arrangement. Terms from £120 to £490 per week (including electricity and cleaning). Saturday to Saturday bookings. Ring or write for further details. **Mrs Angela Holder, Roseley, Bodieve, Wadebridge PL27 6EG (01208 813024).**

Historic Cornwall

As well as having sun sea and sand, Cornwall is also home to a collection of interesting historic sites. Tintagel Castle, Pendennis Castle, St Mawes Castle, Launceston Castle, Restormel Castle and Chysauster Ancient Village are scattered throughout Cornwall and are all under English Heritage care. For more information tel: **0870 333 1181** or visit **www.english-heritage.org.uk**

Visit the FHG website
www.holidayguides.com
for details of the wide choice of accommodation
featured in the full range of FHG titles

CUMBRIA

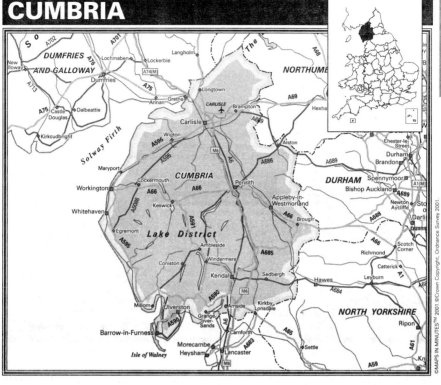

Cumbria – The Lake District

With dramatic fells and lakes, changing seas and coasts, quiet valleys, unique towns and villages plus nature that has inspired many a writer, Cumbria is an ideal area in which to spend your holiday. Quality accommodation, a reputation for good food, the best walking in England, along with a wealth of other outdoor activities ranging from sailing and canoeing to climbing and scrambling, cycling and pony trekking, all add to its appeal. If that sounds too energetic there are also plenty of attractions that celebrate Cumbrian people and history, literary and artistic life.

There is something for everyone in Cumbria!

ENGLAND

AMBLESIDE
Hole House, High Wray. HOLE HOUSE is a charming detached 17th century Lakeland cottage set in idyllic surroundings overlooking Blelham Tarn with magnificent panoramic views of the Langdale Pikes, Coniston Old Man, the Troutbeck Fells and Lake Windermere. High Wray is a quiet unspoilt hamlet set between Ambleside and Hawkshead making this an ideal base for walking or touring. This charming cottage which once belonged to Beatrix Potter has the original oak beams and feature stone staircase. Accommodation consists of one double and two twin bedrooms; bathroom with shower; large spacious lounge with Sky TV and video, log fire; fitted kitchen with microwave oven, fridge/freezer, tumble dryer, automatic washing machine and electric cooker. Storage heating included October to April. Power points via £1 coin meter. Lighting included. Play area. Ample parking. Please write, or phone, for further details: **Mrs Clare Irvine, Tock How Farm, High Wray, Ambleside, Cumbria (015394 36106).** **website: www.tock-how-farm.com**

See also Colour Display Advertisement

AMBLESIDE
Kirkstone Foot, Kirkstone Pass Road, Ambleside. A 17th century converted Country House with self-catering cottages and apartments for two to six persons. Set in peaceful gardens adjoining the magnificent Lakeland Fells, and yet only four minutes' walk from the centre of Ambleside. The cottages and apartments have fully equipped kitchens, bathrooms with bath and shower, colour TV, video. All linen, towels and electricity supplied. Pets welcome. Open all year. Booking taken for three or more nights. ETC ★★★★. For colour brochure or more information please contact: **Kirkstone Foot, Kirkstone Pass Road, Ambleside LA22 9EH (015394 32232; Fax: 015394 32805).** **e-mail: kirkstone@breathemail.net** **website: www.kirkstonefoot.co.uk**

AMBLESIDE

Mr Evans, Ramsteads Coppice, Outgate, Ambleside LA22 0NH (015394 36583). Six timber lodges of varied size and design set in 15 acres of mixed woodland with wild flowers, birds and native wild animals. There are also 11 acres of rough hill pasture. Three miles south west of Ambleside, it is an ideal centre for walkers, artists, birdwatchers, and country lovers. No pets. Children welcome. Open March to November.

See also Colour Display Advertisement

AMBLESIDE

"The Eyrie", Lake Road, Ambleside. Sleeps 6. A really delightful, characterful flat nestling under the eaves of a converted school with lovely views of the fells, high above the village. Large airy living/dining room with colour TV. Comfortably furnished as the owners' second home. Well-equipped kitchen with spacious airing cupboard; three bedrooms sleeping six; attractive bathroom (bath/WC/shower) and lots of space for boots and walking gear. Colour TV, fitted carpets, gas central heating, use of separate laundry room. Terrace garden with fine views. Sorry, but no pets. Available all year. Weekly rates £200 to £370. Also short breaks. Free parking permit provided for one car. Many recommendations. Children welcome. Brochure available. Telephone **Mrs Clark (01844 208208).**

AMBLESIDE

2 Lowfield, Old Lake Road, Ambleside. Sleeps 4/5. Ground floor garden flat situated half a mile from town centre. The accommodation comprises lounge/dining room, kitchen, bathroom/WC, two bedrooms with twin beds. Linen supplied. Children and pets welcome. Ample private parking. Bookings run from Saturday to Saturday. Terms from £130 to £200 per week. Contact: **Mr P.F. Quarmby, 3 Lowfield, Old Lake Road, Ambleside LA22 0DH (Tel & Fax: 015394 32326).**

APPLEBY-IN-WESTMORLAND

Mrs Edith Stockdale, Croft House, Bolton, Appleby-in-Westmorland CA16 6AW (Tel & Fax: 017683 61264). Sleep 2/5 and 10. Three cosy cottages recently converted from an old Westmorland style barn adjoining the owner's house. With an abundance of open stone work and oak beams and many original features. An excellent base for fell and country walking, horse-riding or as a touring base for the Lake District, beautiful Eden Valley, Scottish Borders, Hadrian's Wall and North Yorkshire Dales. Bed linen, towels, electricity and heating included in rent. Facilities include electric cooker, washing machine, fridge-freezer, microwave, colour TV, video, hi-fi and dishwasher. Stabling provided for anyone wishing to bring pony on holiday. Weekly terms from £160. Farmhouse available, sleeps 11. Brochure. **website: www.crofthouse-cottages.co.uk**

BOWNESS-ON-WINDERMERE

43A Quarry Rigg, Bowness-on-Windermere. Sleeps 4. Ideally situated in the centre of the village close to the Lake and all amenities, the flat is in a new development, fully self-contained, and furnished and equipped to a high standard for owner's own comfort and use. Lake views, ideal relaxation and touring centre. Accommodation is for two/four people. Bedroom with twin beds, lounge with TV and video; convertible settee; separate kitchen with electric cooker, microwave and fridge/freezer; bathroom with bath/shower and WC. Electric heating. Parking for residents. Sorry, no pets. Terms from £125 to £250. Weekends and Short Breaks also available. SAE, please, for details to **E. Jones, 45 West Oakhill Park, Liverpool, Merseyside L13 4BN (Tel & Fax: 0151-228 5799).**

Two children FREE with two adults at
Eskdale Historic Water Mill
See our READERS' OFFER VOUCHER for details.

BOWNESS-ON-WINDERMERE

45 Quarry Rigg, Lake Road, Bowness-on-Windermere. Sleeps 4. Very well appointed modern flat with lake views situated in a new development. Ideally placed in the centre of the village for shops, restaurants, etc. Parking for tenants. Within easy reach of tennis, boating, fishing, golf. Ideal for touring and walking. Attractive second floor flat comprising lounge/diner with newly fitted kitchenette, two bedrooms (one twin, one double), bathroom with bath and shower. Furnished, decorated and equipped to a very high standard for owner's personal use including colour TV, video, fridge, microwave, duvets. Electric heating including storage heaters. Metered electricity. No pets or children under 10 years. Non-smokers only. SAE for further details. **Mrs J. Kay, 11 Sommerville Close, The Belfry, High Legh, Near Knutsford, Cheshire WA16 6TR (01925 755612).**

BOWNESS-ON-WINDERMERE

Mrs P.M. Fanstone, Deloraine, (Dept. F), Helm Road, Bowness-on-Windermere LA23 2HS (015394 45557). Deloraine spells seclusion, space, convenience and comfort for all seasons, while exploring Lakeland heritage. Parties of two/six have choice of four apartments within an Edwardian mansion, and a detached characterful cottage. Set in one-and-a-half acres of private gardens, yet only a few minutes' walk from Bowness centre and water sports. Two units command dramatic views of the Langdale Pikes and Lake at 300 foot elevation. Ground floor flat and cottage include disabled facilities. All properties have free parking, private entrances, full equipment, colour TV, electric heaters and central heating. Double glazing. Fire Prevention systems. Payphone. Washing machine. Barbecue. Sun room. Cot hire. Linen included. Four-poster beds. FREE SWIM/SAUNA TICKETS. No pets. Resident owners. Brochure on request. Terms from £150 to £460 per week. Winter Breaks available. ETC ★★★, *NATIONAL ACCESSIBILITY SCHEME CATEGORY 2 (FIRST IN CUMBRIA).*
e-mail: gordon@deloraine.demon.co.uk   website: www.deloraine.demon.co.uk

COCKERMOUTH

Mrs M.E. Teasdale, Jenkin Farm, Embleton, Cockermouth CA13 9TN (017687 76387). Sleeps 6. Come and enjoy a peaceful away from it all holiday at our family-run working hill farm three miles from Cockermouth. Jenkin Cottage has a spectacular outlook over open countryside with views extending to the Solway Firth and the Scottish Lowlands. We are in an ideal situation for fell walking on Buttermere and the surrounding fells or for touring the Lakes by car. The cottage is personally supervised and has a homely atmosphere. We are open all year with long weekends and mid week breaks in the winter months. All linen provided. Lounge with open log fire. Fully equipped modern kitchen. Full central heating. Sorry, no pets. Children welcome. We also extend a welcome to business people. Terms from £240 to £400 per week. Brochure available. ETC ★★★★

CONISTON

Thurston House, Coniston. Flats sleep 2/6. A Lakeland stone house converted into self-contained, spacious, clean, comfortable apartments sleeping two to six. The property is carefully maintained by the owners. Open all year (storage heaters early and late season). Quiet location yet only a short walk to village centre and lake. Private parking. Children and pets welcome. Prices from £75 to £255 per week. ETC/CTB ★★. Enquiries to **Mr and Mrs Jefferson, 21 Chalegreen, Harwood, Bolton BL2 3NJ (01204 419261).**
e-mail: alan@jefferson99.freeserve.co.uk   website: www.jefferson99.freeserve.co.uk

CONISTON

Thurston View Cottage, Sleeps 4. An old stone miner's cottage located a few minutes' walk from the centre of Coniston. It commands superb panoramic views over the village and lake. Recently refurbished, it now has gas central heating, double glazing, and a living flame gas fire in the lounge. Fully tiled bathroom with bath and electric shower. A dishwasher, washer/tumble dryer, microwave, fridge/freezer, TVs and video are also provided. The garden has a patio and barbecue area and superb views. There is private parking for one car. Prices from £195 ro £350 per week. ETC ★★★★. Enquiries to **Mr and Mrs Jefferson, 21 Chalegreen, Harwood, Bolton BL2 3NJ (01204 419261).**
e-mail: alan@jefferson99.freeserve.co.uk   website: www.jefferson99.freeserve.co.uk

DENT VILLAGE

Character cottage for four
www.dentcottages.btinternet.co.uk
E-mail: dentcottages@btinternet.com

Tel: 015396 25294

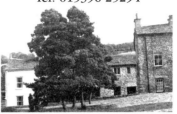

Situated in the centre of the attractive old village of Dent with its narrow cobbled streets and surrounded by marvellous scenery. This delightful 17th century cottage is a Grade ll Listed building and has been restored with care. The accommodation is comfortably furnished and is situated opposite Dent Church. This lovely holiday home enjoys an outlook over the surrounding countryside to the hills beyond and makes an ideal base for touring the Dales, or as a walking centre with open fells close at hand.

2 bedrooms - 1 double and 1 twin (with vanity unit), lounge with dining area, kitchen, and bathroom with toilet. Services: Electric fire in lounge, night storage heaters – all electricity included in the rent. Colour TV, shaver point, microwave oven. Large basement garage.

See also Colour Display Advertisement

CONISTON

The Coppermines & Lakes Cottages (015394 41765 - 24 hours). 50 unique Lakeland cottages for 2-30 of quality and character in stunning mountain scenery. Log fires, exposed beams. Weekends and Short Breaks available. Pets very welcome.
ETC ★★/★★★★★
website: www.coppermines.co.uk
website: www.lakescottages.info

See also Colour Display Advertisement

CONISTON (Near)

Mrs J. Halton, "Brookfield", Torver, Near Coniston LA21 8AY (015394 41328). Sleeps 2/4. "Brookfield" is a large attractive modern bungalow property in a rural setting with lovely outlook and extensive views of the Coniston mountains. The bungalow stands in its own half-acre of level garden and grounds. The inside is divided into two completely separate self-contained units (semi-detached). The holiday bungalow accommodation consists of large sitting/dining room, kitchen, utility room, two good bedrooms (one twin and one double), bathroom. Good parking. Well-equipped. Linen hire available. Lovely walking terrain. Two village inns with restaurant facilities approximately 300 yards. Terms from £180 to £280 weekly. Special rates for two persons. Further details on request with SAE please.

DENT

Willans, Deepdale, Dent. Come and spend a peaceful break in our cottage situated on a cattle and sheep hill farm. The farm has young calves in winter, while spring brings lambs, some looking for young helpers at feeding time. The cottage overlooks Whernside, one of the Pennines' highest peaks. Willans makes an ideal base for visiting the surrounding Dales or the Lakes. It is nicely furnished, with a well-equipped, large, family-sized kitchen. Four bedrooms – one double, two twin and one single (with washbasin). Open fire in livingroom; colour TV, washing and drying facilities. Off-road parking. For a brochure and cottage availability telephone **015396 25285** or
e-mail: KathBentham@hotmail.com

DERWENTWATER

Derwent House and Brandelhowe, Portinscale, Keswick. Sleeps up to 6. In the picturesque village of Portinscale, Keswick, Derwent House with Brandelhowe is a traditional stone Lakeland building renovated and converted to four self-contained comfortable well appointed holiday suites, each with parking. BRANDELHOWE COTTAGE SUITE on ground floor has two double bedrooms both with en suite shower/w.c. SHIRE, HUNTER AND COB SUITES have views south over Derwentwater. Central heating included. Colour TV and video. All bed linen provided. Children from age six and pets welcome. Open all year. Prices from £95 to £335 per week. Some reductions for two people. Short breaks available. **ETC ★★★.** Brochure from **Mary and Oliver Bull, Stone Heath, Hilderstone, Staffordshire ST15 8SH**

(01889 505678; Fax: 01889 505679).
e-mail: thebulls@globalnet.co.uk

website: www.dhholidays-lakes.com

ELTERWATER

Lane Ends Cottages. Three cottages are situated next to "Fellside" on the edge of Elterwater Common. Two cottages accommodate a maximum of four persons: double bedroom, twin bedded room; fully equipped kitchen/diningroom; bathroom. Third cottage sleeps five: as above plus single bedroom and separate diningroom. Electricity by meters. The cottages provide an ideal base for walking/touring holidays with Ambleside, Grasmere, Hawkshead and Coniston within a few miles. Parking for one car per cottage, additional parking opposite. Open all year; out of season long weekends available. Rates from £175 per week. Brochure on request (SAE please). **Mrs M. E. Rice, "Fellside", Elterwater, Ambleside LA22 9HN (015394 37678).**

GRANGE-OVER-SANDS

Cornerways, Field Broughton. Detached bungalow, own private garden with parking. Quiet situation with all round Lakeland views. Three miles from historic village of Cartmel, three miles from Newby Bridge, southern end of Lake Windermere. Ideal base for enjoying Lakeland holiday pursuits and countryside. The bungalow has entrance hall, living/dining room with colour TV, fitted breakfast kitchen, fridge/freezer, microwave and full electric cooker. Bathroom/WC. Double and twin-bedded bedrooms sleeping four. Duvets, linen provided. Well equipped. Electric and oil heating by meter reading. Incoming telephone. No pets or children under four years. Personal supervision. £250 to £350 per week. **ETC ★★★.** Brochure and details from: **Mrs Rigg, Prospect House, Barber Green, Grange-over-Sands LA11 6HU (015395 36329).**

GRIZEDALE FOREST

High Dale Park Barn, High Dale Park, Satterthwaite, Ulverston LA12 8LJ. Delightfully situated south-facing barn, newly converted, attached to owners' 17th century farmhouse, with wonderful views down secluded, quiet valley, surrounded by beautiful broadleaf woodland. Oak beams, log fires, full central heating, patio. Grizedale Visitor Centre (three miles) includes award-winning sculpture trails, gallery and unique sculptured playground. Grizedale Forest is one of the Lake District's richest areas of wildlife. Accommodation in two self-contained units, one sleeping six, the other two plus baby, available separately or as one unit at a reduced rate. Hawkshead three miles, Beatrix Potter's home three miles. **ETC ★★★.** Contact: **Mr P. Brown, High Dale Park Farm, High Dale Park, Satterthwaite, Ulverston LA12 8LJ (01229 860226).**

KENDAL

Dora's Cottage, Natland, Kendal. Sleeps 2/4. Adjoining farmhouse in a tranquil village south of Kendal, this delightful cottage overlooks the garden amid the Lakeland Fells. Ground floor bedrooms, TV, fridge, ironing facilities, electric cooker, microwave, central heating and linen provided to help make the most of a country holiday with the Lakes and Dales nearby. Golf, riding, inns, restaurants, leisure centre, historic visits within easy distance. Children welcome. Car parking. Terms from £180 to £350 per week. Short Breaks can be arranged. Farmhouse Bed and Breakfast also available from £24.50 to £29.50. **ETC ★★★/◆◆◆◆**. For further details apply to **Mrs Val Sunter, Higher House Farm, Oxenholme Lane, Natland, Kendal LA9 7QH (015395 61177; Fax: 015395 61520).**

KENDAL

The Barns, Field End, Patton, Kendal. Properties sleep 6/8. Two detached barns converted into five spacious architect-designed houses. The Barns are situated on 200 acres of farm, four miles north of Kendal in a quiet country area with River Mint passing through farmland, and lovely views of Cumbrian Hills. Many interesting local walks, with the Dales Way passing close by; central to Lakes and Yorkshire Dales, National Parks. Fishing is available on the river. The Barns consists of four houses each with four double bedrooms, and one house with three double bedrooms. Each house has full central heating for early/late holidays, lounge with open fire, diningroom; kitchen with cooker, microwave, fridge and washer; bathroom, downstairs shower room and toilet. Many interesting features include oak beams, pine floors and patio doors. Electricity at cost. Pets and children welcome. Terms from £140 to £415. **ETC ★★★/★★★★**. For brochure apply to **Mr and Mrs E.D. Robinson, 1 Field End, Patton, Kendal LA8 9DU (01539 824220 or 07778 596863; Fax: 01539 824464). e-mail: robinson@fieldendholidays.co.uk website: www.fieldendholidays.co.uk**

KESWICK

Barrowside & Swinside Cottages, 30 & 32 Church Street, Keswick. These converted cottages provide a perfect base for a Lakeland holiday, compact and comfortable and within easy walking distance of the centre of Keswick. The property, renovated and refurbished to a high standard is carpeted throughout and has full double glazing and gas central heating. Lounge with focal fireplace, colour TV, video recorder, radio cassette and dining area. Fully fitted kitchen. Barrowside has a double-bedded room and small twin bedded room (with limited storage). Swinside has a family room with double and single bed (extra single bed if required). All bed linen is provided and the cost of all heating is included in the tariff. For further information please contact: **Mrs Walker, 15 Acorn Street, Keswick CA12 4EA (017687 74165).**

KESWICK

Mrs M. Beaty, Birkrigg Farm, Newlands, Keswick CA12 5TS (017687 78278). Sleeps 4. The cottage adjoining the farm guest house, is extremely nice with an excellent outlook. Situated very pleasantly and peacefully amongst beautiful mountain scenery in the lovely Newlands Valley in the heart of Cumbria. Five miles from Keswick, between Braithwaite and Buttermere. Perfect base for hill walking, central for touring the Lake District. Clean and comfortable, comprising lounge, TV, kitchen, fridge freezer, cooker, microwave, one double and one twin room, shower/toilet. Linen and towels provided. Oil central heating, electric stove-type fire. Available all year. Ample parking. No dogs. No smoking. Short breaks out of season. £175 – £300 weekly. **ETC ★★★**

A useful index of towns and counties appears at the back of this book on pages 273 – 276. Refer also to Contents Pages 44/45.

ENGLAND

KESWICK

Harney Peak, Portinscale, near Keswick. We can offer you the very best in self catering accommodation in our spacious well-equipped apartments in the quiet village of Portinscale – overlooking Derwentwater yet only one mile from Keswick. Hot water and central heating included in rental. Laundry facilities. Ample off-street parking. Open all year. Dogs welcome. Various sized apartments makes this an ideal location for couples or families and short breaks are available off season. For brochure please apply to: **Mr & Mrs Smith, The Leathes Head Hotel, Borrowdale, Cumbria CA12 5UY (017687 77247).**

KESWICK

Stoney Gill, Newlands, Keswick. Situated three miles from Keswick on the Braithwaite to Buttermere Road, with the most magnificent views across Newlands Valley to Catbells, Stoney Gill flat makes an excellent base for walking directly onto the fells. Also convenient for touring in the Lake District, fishing, sailing, pony trekking and golf. Stoney Gill consists of one single and two double bedrooms, all with washbasins; bathroom; open plan lounge with dining and kitchen area. Electric meter. Central heating included in rent. Weekly terms from £170 to £270. Parking for two cars. One dog only please. Further details apply to:- **Mrs L. Edmondson, Stoney Acre, Newlands, Keswick CA12 5TS (017687 78200).**

KESWICK

16 Hewetson Court, Main Street, Keswick. Sleeps 1/4. A modern apartment with balcony, giving spectacular hill views, located in Keswick town centre. Very well equipped with all necessary amenities and central heating. Non-smoking. Children and pets are welcome. Parking is provided. Prices from £280 to £350 per week. All enquiries to **Martyn Dougherty, 23 East Murrayfield, Bannockburn, Stirling FK7 8HS (01786 814955).**

KESWICK

Lakeside Studio Apartments, Derwentwater Marina, Portinscale, Keswick. Three self-catering apartments, all with stunning views of the Lake and fells, are fully equipped for two or a couple and small child. They have en suite bath or shower, TV and stereo radio/CD, and make an extremely comfortable base for a family holiday, whether you are a sailing enthusiast, a fell walker or just want a relaxing time away from it all. Children are especially welcome, and a cot and high chair are available. The Marina is an ideal location for water or mountain-based activities, and facilities include a superb bar and family restaurant, changing rooms with showers, and a well-stocked chandlery. RYA registered sailing and windsurfing centre; tuition available. Terms on request. For details please contact: **Derwentwater Marina, Portinscale, Keswick CA12 5RF (017687 72912) or visit our website: www.derwentwatermarina.co.uk**

KESWICK/COCKERMOUTH

Midtown Cottages, High Lorton, Cockermouth CA13 9UQ. Lorton lies at the northern end of Lorton Vale, a beautiful valley which runs from Cockermouth in the west to Buttermere in the east. The fast flowing streams of the River Cocker were previously used as the motive power for flour and linen mills, some buildings surviving today, having later been used by the Jennings family as their brewery. Jennings ales are still brewed in nearby Cockermouth. Our two cottages both have electric central heating for all year round use. Built around a courtyard area, they are 'upside down' - the bedrooms (one double, one twin) being downstairs with the lounge, dining area and small but well-equipped kitchen, with dishwasher and freezer, upstairs to make the most of the views over the fells. Whilst the two cottages are not absolutely identical, they are both furnished to the same high standard. They are both non-smoking, but pets are very welcome. Cot and high chair available if required. Complete weeks from £395 (High Season), £345 (Mid Season), £220 (Low Season), Short Breaks from £145. **ETC ★★★★**. Contact: **Mr & Mrs M. Burrell (Tel & Fax: 01264 710165).**
e-mail: info@midtowncottages.co.uk   **website: www.midtowncottages.co.uk**

KIRKOSWALD

Liz Webster, Howscales, Kirkoswald, Penrith CA10 1JG (01768 898666; Fax: 01768 898710). Sleeps 2/4. COTTAGES FOR NON-SMOKERS. Howscales was originally a 17th century farm. The red sandstone buildings have been converted into five self-contained cottages, retaining many original features. Set around a cobbled courtyard, the cosy, well-equipped cottages for 2-4, are surrounded by gardens and open countryside. Shared laundry facilities. Well-behaved pets welcome by arrangement. Open all year, short breaks available. Colour brochure. Non-smoking. Cared for by resident owner. Ideal base from which to explore The Eden Valley, Lakes, Pennines and Hadrian's Wall. Please ring, write or see our website for details. **ETC ★★★★**. *NATIONAL ACCESSIBILITY SCHEME: CATEGORY 2.*
e-mail: liz@howscales.fsbusiness.co.uk   **website: www.eden-in-cumbria.co.uk/howscales**

KIRKOSWALD

Crossfield Cottages and Leisure Fishing. Accessible secluded tranquil cottages overlooking two lakes, amidst Lakeland's beautiful Eden Valley countryside, only 30 minutes' drive from Ullswater, Hadrian's Wall, North Pennines and the Scottish Borders. Your beds will be freshly made for your arrival. Exclusive resident's coarse and fly fishing on your doorstep. Tranquillity and freedom to roam. Cottages are guaranteed clean, well-maintained and equipped. Centrally located. Exceptional wildlife and walking area. Relax and escape to your 'Home" in the country. Pets very welcome. 24hr Brochure Line **Tel & Fax: 01768 898711**, bookings/availabilty 6pm to 10pm, or SAE to **Crossfield Cottages, Kirkoswald, Penrith CA10 1EU. Fax available.**
e-mail: info@crossfieldcottages.co.uk   **website: www.crossfieldcottages.co.uk**

ENGLAND

HODYOAD COTTAGES

Hodyoad stands in its own private grounds, with extensive views of the surrounding fells in peaceful rural countryside. Mid-way between the beautiful Lakes of Loweswater and Ennerdale, six miles from Cockermouth and 17 from Keswick. Fell walking, boating, pony trekking and trout fishing can all be enjoyed within a three-and-a-half mile radius. Each cottage is fully centrally heated and has two bedrooms to sleep five plus cot. All linen provided. Lounge with colour TV. Kitchen with fitted units, cooker and fridge. Bathroom with shower, washbasin, toilet, shaver point. Laundry room with washing machine and tumble dryer. Car essential, ample parking. Sea eight miles. Open all year. From £190 to £340 per week. For further details please contact:

Mrs J. A. Cook, Hodyoad House, Lamplugh, Cumbria CA14 4TT • Tel: 01946 861338

LITTLE LANGDALE

Highfold Cottage, 3 Greenbank Terrace. Sleeps 5 plus cot. Cosy, comfortable, fully equipped and recently renovated three bedroomed cottage set in magnificent mountain scenery. Excellent walking area, central for touring. Fitted kitchen with washing machine, living room with open fire, bathroom with bath/electric shower. In the double, twin and single bedrooms all beds have duvets and will be made up for you on arrival. Fitted carpets throughout. Central heating. Personally maintained. Children and pets welcome. There is a lockable outside shed for bikes etc. Parking available a few yards from cottage. Rates from £200 to £330 weekly. Winter Breaks available from November to March. **ETC ★★★**. For further information or bookings please contact **Mrs C. Blair, 8 The Glebe, Chapel Stile, Ambleside LA22 9JT (015394 37686).**

LOWESWATER

Jenkinson Place Cottage, Loweswater. Sleeps 4. Jenkinson Place is a 17th century Lakeland farmstead, but no longer a working farm. The holiday cottage has been carefully and tastefully constructed from a former stable building to provide a maximum of four guests plus infant with comfortable, modernised accommodation while retaining those traditional period features. The proprietors resident in the farmhouse are able to give guests personal help and attention if or when required. Linen not supplied. Sorry, no pets. Ideal location for a quiet, relaxing holiday away from the crowds yet within easy reach of Crummock Water, Buttermere, Ennerdale, the old market town of Cockermouth, Keswick and the lovely West Cumbrian coast. Available May to September. Weekly terms from £135. Further details on request from **Mrs E.K. Bond, Jenkinson Place, Loweswater, Cockermouth CA13 0SU (01946 861748).**
e-mail: alec.bond@virgin.net

MUNGRISDALE

Mrs Weightman, Near Howe Hotel Cottages, Mungrisdale, Penrith CA11 0SH (017687 79678; Fax: 017687 79462). Grisdale View Cottage (sleeps four) is a beautifully converted old barn, with views over the fells. Living room with kitchen, dining area, cooker, microwave, fridge/freezer, toaster. Bathroom. Double and twin bedrooms. Garden. Children and pets welcome. Weekly rates from £160 to £280. Saddleback Barn (sleeps seven) is an outstanding property with two floors. It has spectacular views and is close to the North Lakes and Caldbeck Fells. Ground floor double and family bedrooms with private facilities. Boiler/store room ideal for drying clothes. First floor has double en suite bedroom. Large open plan lounge/kitchen area; colour TV, video, music centre, electric hob, microwave, fridge freezer, etc. Bed linen and electricity inclusive. Cot and high-chair available. Weekly rates from £300 to £490. **ETC ★★★★**
website: www.nearhowe.co.uk

Terms quoted in this publication may be subject to increase if rises in costs necessitate

Birthwaite Edge, Windermere

Situated in extensive grounds in one of the most exclusive areas of Windermere, 10 minutes from village and Lake, this is the perfect all year round holiday base. 10 self catering apartments for two to six people. Resident proprietors personally ensure the highest standards of cleanliness and comfort. Swimming pool open May to September. Colour TV. Well equipped kitchens. Hot water included. Coin metered electricity for lighting, cooking and electric fires. Background central heating during winter. Duvets and linen provided. High chairs and cots extra. Ample car parking. Regret, no smoking and no pets. Terms from £205 to £505.

Brochure from: **Bruce and Marsha Dodsworth, Birthwaite Edge,**
Birthwaite Road, Windermere LA23 1BS • Tel & Fax: 015394 42861
e-mail: fhg@lakedge.com • website: www.lakedge.com.

See also Colour Advertisement

NEWCASTLETON

Cumbrian/Scottish Borders. Sleeps up to 5. A three-bedroomed country cottage. Centrally heated throughout, decorated and furnished to a high standard. Own garden, patio, seating, barbecue and lockable shed for cycles. Set amidst the beautiful Kershope Forest (part of Kielder Forest Park) with its winding streams and miles of forest walks right from your door. Pony trekking, fishing and golf are all nearby. Also a good base to explore Scotland, Cumbria (the Lake District) and Northumberland. Bed linen, towels, electricity, heating and 'Welcome food pack` inclusive. Car essential. Ample parking by door. Open all year. Terms from £225 to £330 per week. Short breaks also available. Children 7 years and over welcome. Sorry no pets. Non-smoking. Colour brochure available from: **Mrs Joanna Furness, 2 Cuddy's Hall, Bailey, Newcastleton, Roxburghshire TD9 0TP (Tel & Fax: 016977 48160). ETC ★★★ website: www.cuddys-hall.co.uk**

RAVENSTONEDALE

Mrs Sally Cannon, Coldbeck House, Ravenstonedale, Kirkby Stephen CA17 4LW (Tel & Fax: 015396 23230). Access 2. Sleeps 6 plus cot. Coldbeck Cottage provides spacious accommodation and is centrally heated throughout. The underfloor heating on the ground floor gives warmth to the old stone slabs in the hall and diningroom. The sunny sittingroom has a multifuel stove. The ground floor twin bedroom is suitable for wheelchair users, and has an en suite bathroom. Upstairs are twin and double bedrooms (en suite showers) and a bathroom. Children and pets welcome. A two acre garden is available and part is kept dog-free for ball games. The country pub opposite provides inexpensive meals. Walk the Howgills from the door or the Lakes and Dales by car. Weekly terms from £350 to £400. Brochure available. **ETC ★★★★**
e-mail: david.cannon@coldbeck.demon.co.uk

ULLSWATER

The Estate Office, Patterdale Hall Estate, Glenridding, Penrith CA11 0PJ (Tel & Fax: 017684 82308 24 hours). Our range includes three very comfortable large Coach Houses, two stone built Cottages with open fires, three three-bedroomed pine Lodges, six two-bedroomed cedar Chalets, a unique detached converted Dairy and two converted Bothies which make ideal, low cost accommodation for two people. All set in a private 300 acre estate between Lake Ullswater and Helvellyn and containing a working hill farm, a Victorian waterfall wood, private lake foreshore for guests to use for boating and fishing and 100 acres of designated ancient woodland for you to explore. Children welcome. Dogs by appointment in some of the accommodation. Colour TV, central heating, launderette, payphone; daytime electricity metered. Linen hire available. Weekly prices from £139 to £452. Please phone for full brochure.
ETC ★★ – ★★★. *NATIONAL ACCESSIBILITY SCHEME CATEGORY 3.* (Four properties.)
e-mail: welcome@phel.co.uk   **website: www.phel.co.uk**

DERBYSHIRE

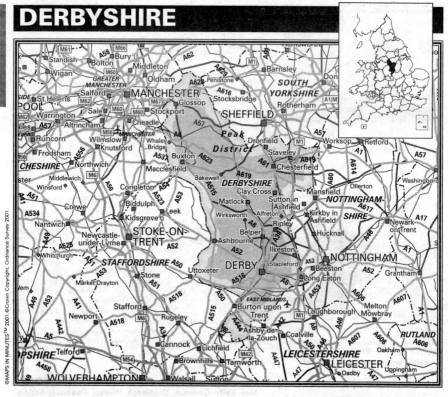

FHG PUBLICATIONS

publish a large range of well-known accommodation
guides. We will be happy to send you details or you
can use the order form at the back of this book.

ENGLAND

ASHBOURNE

Dove Cottage, Church Lane, Mayfield, Ashbourne. Sleeps 7. This modernised 200-year-old cottage in Mayfield village is ideally situated for shops, pubs, busy market towns, sporting facilities, lovely Dove Valley, Alton Towers, Peaks, Staffordshire Moorlands and many other places of interest. The cottage is comfortably furnished and well-equipped with TV, fridge, automatic washing machine, gas central heating. The fenced garden overlooks farmland. Garage and parking. Children welcome. Pets by arrangement. Available for long and short lets, also mid-week bookings. Price and brochure on request. ETC ★★★. Further details from: **Arthur Tatlow, Ashview, Ashfield Farm, Calwich, Ashbourne DE6 2EB (01335 324443/324279).**

ASHBOURNE

New House Organic Farm, Kniveton, Ashbourne DE6 1JL (01335 342429). Organic family farm in the Derbyshire Dales, near Matlock, Bakewell, Dove Dale; one mile from Carsington Watersports Centre. We serve organic, free-range and fair-traded foods; vegetarian and other diets welcome. Children's teas, babysitting and play area available; pets, horses, bicycles and children welcome. B&B or self-catering in holiday cottage, suitable for asthma/allergy sufferers; also self-catering in six-berth mobile home, gypsy caravan sleeping two/four, two small caravans sleeping two/four, space for tourers and camping. Free working holidays can be arranged. Members ECEAT and affiliated to Environmental Tourism Association. Bed and Breakfast from £10; self-catering from £80 per week.

BUXTON (Near)

Mr & Mrs C.J. Lawrenson, Grove House, Elkstones, Near Buxton SK17 0LU (01538 300487). Sleeps 2/3. Leave behind the crowds and traffic and stay in a delightful stone cottage, with original exposed beams, in the quiet Peak District village of Elkstones. Several public footpaths radiate from the village with the famous Dove Valley and Manifold Valley three to five miles away. Central for the market towns of Leek, Buxton and Ashbourne and for following the'China Trail` in the Staffordshire Potteries, numerous National Trust properties and Alton Towers. Pubs/restaurant nearby. One double bedroom. Bed linen and towels supplied. Furnished and comprehensively equipped. Patio garden with sunny aspect. Parking close to cottage. Dog by arrangement. Short Breaks out of season. Brochure. Terms from £150 to £225. **ETC ★★★**
e-mail: **elkstones@talk21.com**

HARTINGTON

Hartington Cottages. Spacious picture-postcard cottage sleeping six in three en suite bedrooms, and two further cottages in private courtyard behind sleeping two/three. All three cottages totally up-graded in 2002; fully equipped kitchen with gloss work-tops and real granite sink; fully controllable central heating (included in rental). The larger cottage is over 500 years old and of cruck construction, extensive beams, inglenook fireplace and walls over two feet thick with stone mullion windows. The village, situated in the heart of the White Peak, has tea shops, gift shops and pub; only 300 yards from the River Dove. Two cycle trails under two miles away. ETC ★★★★. Contact: **Patrick and Frances Skemp, Cotterill Farm, Liffs Road, Biggin-by-Hartington, Buxton SK17 0DJ (01298 84447).**
e-mail: **enquiries@hartingtoncottages.co.uk**   website: **www.hartingtoncottages.co.uk**

When making enquiries or bookings, a stamped addressed envelope is always appreciated

ENGLAND

MILLDALE

Old Millers Cottage, Milldale, Near Ashbourne. Sleeps 2.
Situated in the beautiful hamlet of Milldale, beside the River Dove, with its famous Packhorse Bridge, the cottage is an ideal starting point for exploring the "Peak National Park". This cosy 18th century miller's cottage has been beautifully renovated to a very high standard, to retain all its charm and character, with exposed beams and featured limestone walls. Accommodation fully furnished and equipped except for linen. Pets welcome. Colour TV, electricity for storage heating and cooking included in the rental of £180 to £200 per week. Open all year. **ETC ★★★**. Details on request from: **Mrs P.M. Hewitt, 45 Portway Drive, Tutbury, Burton-on-Trent, Staffordshire DE13 9HU (01283 815895).**

PEAK DISTRICT (Near Buxton)

Sutton, Peak District (Near Buxton). Sleep 4 plus 2.
Cottage conversions on peaceful 32 acre smallholding on the edge of the Peak District, within easy reach of Bakewell, Chatsworth Hall, Tatton Park, Jodrell Bank and the Silk Museum at Macclesfield. Ideal for a relaxing or active holiday, mountain bikes are available for hire and there are lovely walks in the surrounding countryside. Each cottage has double, bunk room and toilet upstairs with sofa bed in sitting/diningroom, TV, shower room. Excellently furnished and equipped throughout, with heating, electricity, bedlinen and towels included in the price. Two pets welcome. Terms from £180 weekly. Short Breaks available. Further details from **Greg and Sue Rowson, Lower Pethills Farm, Higher Sutton, Macclesfield, Cheshire SK11 0NJ (01260 252410).**

YOULGREAVE

April Cottage. 200-year-old traditional Derbyshire cottage offering comfortable accommodation for two/three people all year round, adjoining the owner's cottage. Situated within Peak District National Park, Youlgreave is a lively village within easy walking distance of Bradford Dale and Lathkill Dale. The Peak Park is a walker's and climber's delight. Buxton 10 miles, Matlock 8 miles and Ashbourne 12 miles, give lots of touring interest. Accommodation consists of a twin bedroom and single bedroom (linen provided), sitting/dining room and fully equipped kitchen with electric cooker, fridge and original Yorkshire range and open beamed ceiling. Automatic washing machine and tumble dryer available on request at extra cost. Gas central heating throughout – fuel costs are included in the rental. Car parking. This is a non-smoking establishment. No pets. Terms from £195 to £315. Weekend and Short Breaks available during low season. Children aged 6 years and over only please. **ETC ★★★ Mrs A. Naybour, Christmas Cottage, Church Street, Youlgreave, Bakewell DE45 1WL (Tel & Fax: 01629 636151).**

DEVON

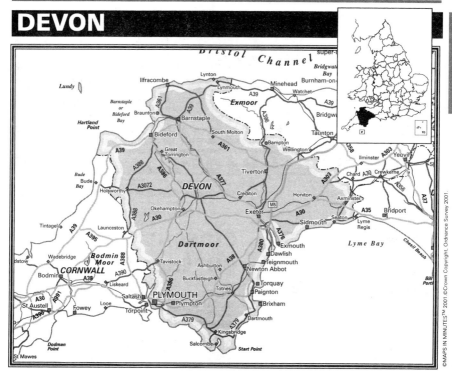

Castles of Devon

Why not visit one of the historic castles to be found in Devon? Dartmouth Castle has stood looking on to the Dart Estuary for 600 years, surrounded by exceptional beauty, an ideal place to picnic whilst watching the river. Berry Pomeroy Castle is set in beautiful woodland and is shrouded in sinister folklore and legend. Okehampton Castle is one of the country's most romantic ruins and is the medieval home of the Earls of Devon. Totnes Castle is a unique treasure, an example of a Norman motte and bailey castle.
To find out more tel: **0870 333 1181** or visit **www.english-heritage.org.uk**

See also Colour Display Advertisement

UNIVERSITY ACCOMMODATION & FACILITIES

Budget accommodation or fully tailored packages (0870 712 5002; Fax: 020 7017 8273). En suite designer halls across the UK. Groups of any age or size. Sports facilities all year. Tell us your needs and we'll find a location and package to suit.
e-mail: enquiries@thesv.com

See also Colour Display Advertisement

Devoncoast Holidays. We are a highly experienced holiday letting agency on Devon's sunny south coast. We have numerous properties on our books ranging from one-bedroom flats to large three bedroomed houses, all in sunny South Devon. We have personally inspected all of our properties and all of the accommodation is of a high standard and comes fully equipped with colour TV, microwave, full cooker and car parking. Our properties are available all year round, for mini breaks or for full week lettings. Pets and children are welcome. Many have a flat access. All of our properties are within easy reach of the coast, some have sea views. We accept all credit cards. Please telephone for a free brochure and map - 24 hour operation. **Devoncoast Holidays, P.O. Box 14. Brixham, Devon TQ5 8AB (Tel & Fax: 07050 338889).**
website: www.devoncoast.com

See also Colour Display Advertisement

North Devon Holiday Homes, 19 Cross Street, Barnstaple EX31 1BD (01271 376322 (24 hrs); Fax: 01271 346544). Easily the best choice of cottages in Devon and comfortably the best value. Contact us now for a free colour guide and unbiased recommendation service to the 400 best value cottages around Exmoor and Devon's unspoilt National Trust Coast.
e-mail: info@northdevonholidays.co.uk
website: www.northdevonholidays.co.uk

APPLEDORE

Waters Reach, West Quay, 71 Irsha Street, Appledore. Stunning uninterrupted views across the twin estuaries of the rivers Taw and Torridge. This Georgian, three storey house enjoys a fine location on West Quay. A well-fitted kitchen with breakfast room off a separate diningroom, comfortable elegant drawing room, two good bedrooms, two good sized bathrooms. Bedding can be supplied and beds made up. Book up quickly as it has ideal sheltered accommodation out of season, as well as during the summer months. Contact: **Viv or Peter Foley (01707 657644).**

e-mail: viv@vfoley.freeserve.co.uk

APPLEDORE

Sea Birds Cottage, Appledore. Sea edge, pretty Georgian cottage facing directly out to the open sea, Sea Birds is a spacious cottage with large lounge, colour TV; dining room with french windows onto garden; modern fitted kitchen with washing machine; three double bedrooms; bathroom, second WC downstairs. Lawned garden at back overlooking the sea with garden furniture. Dog welcome. Own parking. Sea views from most rooms and the garden is magnificent: views of the open sea, boats entering the estuary, sunset, sea birds. Appledore is still a fishing village - fishing trips from the quay, restaurants by the water. Area has good cliff and coastal walks, stately homes, riding, swimming, golf, surfing, excellent beaches. Off peak heating. From £95. Other sea edge cottages available. SAE or stamp for brochure to **S.S. Barnes, 140 Bay View Road, Northam, Bideford EX39 1BJ (01237 473801).**

ASHBURTON

Mrs Angela Bell, Wooder Manor, Widecombe-in-the-Moor, Near Ashburton TQ13 7TR (Tel & Fax: 01364 621391). Cottages and converted coach house, on 160-acre working family farm nestled in the picturesque valley of Widecombe, surrounded by unspoilt woodland, moors and granite tors. Half-a-mile from village with post office, general stores, inn with dining room, church and National Trust Information Centre. Excellent centre for touring Devon with a variety of places to visit and exploring Dartmoor by foot or on horseback. Accommodation is clean and well equipped with colour TV, central heating, laundry room. Children welcome. Large gardens and courtyard for easy parking. Open all year, so take advantage of off-season reduced rates. Short Breaks also available. Two properties suitable for disabled visitors. Brochure available. **ETC ★★★**

e-mail: angela@woodermanor.com   **website: www.woodermanor.com**

ASHWATER

Braddon Cottages, Ashwater, Beaworthy EX21 5EP (Tel & Fax: 01409 211350). Six secluded cottages in quiet countryside of meadow and woodland, on 500 acre site. Four barn conversions and two purpose-built houses surrounded by gardens and lawns, with views over lake to Dartmoor. All-weather tennis court; adults' snooker room and children's games room. Very comfortable, with gas central heating, wood fires, dishwashers, washing machines, clothes dryers, microwaves and payphones. Bed linen and towels supplied. Pleasant walks; large summer house with barbecue; free fishing. Licensed shop. Package holidays available for one or two weeks, including transfer to/from West Country stations and airports. Open all year. Credit cards accepted. Brochure available. Resident owners **George and Anne Ridge**. **ETC ★★★**

e-mail: holidays@braddoncottages.co.uk   **website: www.braddoncottages.co.uk**

ENGLAND

North Hill Cottages, North Devon

Surround yourself in rolling hills at **North Hill Cottages, Barnstaple** where 17th century farm buildings have been sympathetically converted into cottages with exposed beams and wood stoves. Enjoy the peace and tranquillity that North Hill offers with its abundance of wildlife ranging from squirrels and badgers to deer. North Hill is central for many activities, be it shopping, walking, cycling, visiting the local attractions or just relaxing on our vast sandy beaches at Croyde and Woolacombe. Facilities include: Indoor heated swimming pool, toddlers pool, spa, solarium, sauna, all weather tennis court, badminton/volleyball court, fitness room, games room,children's play area and BBQs.

**For a free colour brochure please telephone Nicky on
01271 850 611 or fax: 01271 850 693 or
visit our website at www.bestleisure.co.uk
or write to us at: Best Leisure, North Hill, Shirwell, Barnstaple,Devon, EX31 4LG.**

NORTH HILL COTTAGES

AXMINSTER

Cider Room Cottage, Hasland Farm, Membury, Axminster. Sleeps 4. This delightfully converted thatched cider barn, with exposed beams, adjoins main farmhouse overlooking the outstanding beauty of the orchards, pools and pastureland, and is ideally situated for touring Devon, Dorset and Somerset. Bathing, golf and tennis at Lyme Regis and many places of interest locally, including Wildlife Park, donkey sanctuary and Forde Abbey. Membury Village, with its post office and stores, trout farm, church and swimming pool is one mile away. The accommodation is of the highest standard with the emphasis on comfort. Two double rooms, cot if required; shower room and toilet; sitting/diningroom with colour TV; kitchen with electric cooker, microwave, fridge. Linen supplied if required. Pets by arrangement. Car essential. Open all year. Terms from £135 to £270. SAE, please, to **Mrs Pat Steele, Hasland Farm, Membury, Axminster EX13 7JF (01404 881558).**

BARNSTAPLE

Mr and Mrs C. L. Hartnoll, Little Bray House, Brayford, Barnstaple EX32 7QG (Tel & Fax: 01598 710295). Properties sleep 2/6. Situated nine miles east of Barnstaple, Little Bray House is ideally placed for day trips to East Devon, Somerset and Cornwall, the lovely sandy surfing beaches at Saunton Sands and Woolacombe, and many places of interest both coastal and inland. Exmoor also has great charm out of season! Lovely gardens, walks. Come and share the pace of life and fresh air straight from the open Atlantic. Able to cater for two to ten people staying in fully equipped cottages, with central heating. Linen hire available if required. Terms from £160-£230 per week. B&B also available from £20-£25.

BARNSTAPLE (Exmoor)

Hillcroft, Natsley Farm, Brayford, Barnstaple. This bungalow is an ideal holiday centre, being near the moors and within easy reach of the coasts. Hillcroft is situated beside a quiet country road in the Exmoor National Park. Lovely walks, touring, pony trekking available locally or just relax and enjoy the glorious views. Lawn at front and back of bungalow. Three double bedrooms and cot available. Children and pets welcome. Sittingroom, dining room; bathroom, toilet; kitchen with electric cooker. Available all year round. Electric heating metered. Everything supplied except linen. Terms from £75 to £250 weekly. Please apply to **Mrs M.E. Williams, Natsley Farm, Brayford, Barnstaple EX32 7QR (01598 710358).**

MIDSHIPS

Instow, Bideford

A comfortable old cottage, less than 50yds from the sandy, estuary beach. 'Midships' sleeps up to four, with gas central heating, colour TV, washing machine, dryer and fridge/freezer and a small walled courtyard with flower tubs at the back. The Tarka trail runs through Instow and there is cycling, sailing and walking, plus boat trips to Lundy Island, all nearby. The village has several good restaurants and pubs for meals out, as well as a small Post Office and village shop. The market towns of Bideford and Barnstaple are within easy reach for cinema and leisure centre etc. Contact: **Mrs M. Baxter, Panorama, Millards Hill, Instow, Bideford EX39 4JS.**

Tel: 01271 861146

BIDEFORD

No.5 Forest Gardens, Buck's Mills, Near Bideford. Sleeps 4 + cot. Cosy, traditional, comfortable, well equipped Devon cottage, three minutes' walk from the beach, in the quiet conservation village of Buck's Mills. Two bedrooms, bathroom, livingroom with old but very efficient coal burning range, plus storage heaters. Kitchen with electric cooker, fridge, toaster, microwave etc. Buck's Mills beach has sand, pebbles and rocks with lovely rock pools - catch your own prawn cocktail! - safe swimming. Coastal Path leaves the village in both directions: Peppercombe one way, Clovelly the other. Shop and Post Office, half a mile. Terms from £150 to £398. 10% discount for previous visitors. Approved under the North Devon Marketing Bureau Stepping Stones scheme. Details:- **Mrs J. Stevens, Court Barn Cottage, West Bradley, Near Glastonbury, Somerset BA6 8LR (01458 850349).**

BIDEFORD

Honeysuckle Cottage, Weare-Giffard, Bideford. Sleeps 4-6. Honeysuckle is a picturesque thatched property, comfortably and tastefully furnished, with many original features including inglenook fireplace, wall lighting, beams etc. Fully centrally heated; two bedrooms (family room and twin-bedded room); enclosed front garden with patio and garden furniture. Off-road parking. Weare-Giffard lies on the river, off the A386, twixt Bideford and Torrington. Village inn five minutes' walk, golf course one mile and Tarka Trail for cycling easily accessible from the village. Rosemoor (RHS) Gardens three and a half miles, equally not far from the coast and other attractions. Terms £140 to £385 per week excluding gas/electricity. Open all year. Contact: **Mrs Curtis, "Bracken Haven", Weare-Giffard, Bideford EX39 4QR (01237 472918).**

BIDEFORD

Yapham Cottages, Hartland, Bideford. Sleep 2-4. Three beautifully furnished and equipped, centrally heated, quality cottages in an Area of Outstanding Natural Beauty with marvellous views, breathtaking coastal scenery, wonderful clifftop walks and secluded beaches. Each has cooker, microwave, fridge, washing machine, colour TV, video, radio, duvets with linen, garden furniture, barbecue and own garden/sitting out area. Laundry room also available. Ample car parking space. Set down our own private drive, the location offers complete tranquillity yet is perfect for visiting nearby tourist attractions: Hartland Abbey and Clovelly; the Tarka Trail for cyclists; Lundy Island for naturalists and the South West Coastal Path for walkers. Pets most welcome. Cream teas on arrival. **ETC ★★★★**. Please

contact: **Jane and Jimmy Young, Yapham Farm, Hartland, Bideford, Devon EX39 6AN (01237 441916).** e-mail: **jane.yapham@virgin.net**   website: **www.yaphamcottages.com**

ENGLAND

ENGLAND

CREDITON

Stewart & Sandra Turner, Creedy Manor, Long Barn, Crediton EX17 4AB (01363 772684). Rural tranquillity situated in Devonshire heartland. An ideal location for visiting moorlands, coasts, historic/heritage sites or attractions, all corners of Devon accessible. Just one mile from Crediton, convenient for shops, amenities, leisure centre, golf and restaurants. Eight miles away lies the cathedral city of Exeter, offering extensive activities. Stroll around our on-site former estate lakes (carp and tench fishing), abundant with wildlife. Comfortable ground floor apartments within Manor farmhouse, good facilities, wheelchair accessible. Reasonably priced - opt for a hearty farmhouse breakfast for £3. Quaint local inns, restaurants and takeaways nearby.
e-mail: info@creedymanor.com
website: www.creedymanor.com

DARTMOOR NATIONAL PARK

Badger's Holt, Dartmeet, Dartmoor PL20 6SG (01364 631213; Fax: 01364 631475). Luxury self catering holiday accommodation nestling by the River Dart at the foot of Yar Tor adjacent to the famous Badger's Holt tea rooms – a traditional Devonshire cream tea not to be missed! Three purpose-built apartments all fully equipped and maintained to the highest standard. "Bench Tor" and "Fox Tor" have two bedrooms and sleep four, "Yar Tor" has three bedrooms and two bathrooms and sleeps from six to eight. Accommodation available all year. Pets welcome. Tea rooms open March to October.

DARTMOUTH

Torcross Apartments, Slapton Sands, Torcross, South Devon TQ7 2TQ (01548 580206; Fax: 01548 580996). Situated directly on the beach in the unspoilt countryside of the South Hams between the blue waters of Start Bay and the Slapton Ley Nature Reserve. Seven miles to Dartmouth. Winter breaks. Central heating. Ground floor apartments and lift to all floors. In-house bar and restaurant, take-away food service. Lovely walks. Brochure with pleasure or visit our website.
e-mail: enquiries@torcross.net
website: www.torcross.net

DAWLISH WARREN

Oakcliff Holiday Park, Mount Pleasant Road, Dawlish Warren, South Devon EX7 0ND (01626 863347). Award-winning self catering holidays on the glorious South Devon coast. Lodges, chalets, caravans & apartments. Heated outdoor pool with slide. Club with live family entertainment. Please contact us for a colour brochure and information. *ROSE AWARD, DAVID BELLAMY CONSERVATION GOLD AWARD.* ETC ★★★★
website: www.oakcliff.co.uk

EXMOUTH

Raleigh Holiday Homes. Comfortable family flats and house sleeping 2-11 people in quiet road near sea and shops. One home suitable for wheelchair. Dogs by arrangement. Terms reasonable £199 to £650 per week inclusive. Open mid-June to mid-September only. Please write or telephone: **Mrs C. E. Duncan (Dept FHG), 24 Raleigh Road, Exmouth, Devon EX8 2SB (01395 266967).**

HEMYOCK

Mrs Anthea Edwards, Chapel Farm, Culm Davy, Hemyock, Cullompton EX15 3UR (01823 680430). Sleeps 4. Chapel Cottage is a secluded detached period cottage with beautiful views in the unspoilt Blackdown Hills, an Area of Outstanding Natural Beauty. It has a pleasant garden. The large lounge has a feature inglenook fireplace, with the original bread oven and beams. The cottage is spacious with excellent facilities including a washer/dryer, an extra downstairs toilet and incoming calls telephone. Hemyock is central for the north and south coasts and Exmoor and Dartmoor National Parks. Shopping at Exeter, Taunton and Honiton, famous for lace, pottery and antiques. Take a steam journey with the West Somerset Railway, or a local walk to a conservation area. Sorry, no pets. Terms from £160 to £295 including linen and heating. **ETC ★★★**

See also Colour Display Advertisement

HIGHAMPTON

Valerie & Dave Langdown, Kingslake, Chilla, Highampton EX21 5JS (Tel & Fax: 01409 231401). Four well-stocked fishing lakes with a choice of self-catering accommodation in cottages or lodges set in 22 acres of beautiful Devon countryside. They have wonderful views of woodland, farmland, the fishing lakes or the tranquil water garden. We offer a choice of one, two, three or four bedroom cottages, or a two or three bedroom lodge; all are tastefully furnished and decorated, with central heating in the cottages and gas or electric fires for cooler evenings. All cottages have their own patio or garden area; barbecues available. Fishing is for residents only – carp, tench and mixed species. No pets.
e-mail: vlangdown@talk21.com
website: www.kingslakes.co.uk

HOLSWORTHY

David & Sue Tucker, Blagdon Farm Country Holidays, Ashwater EX21 5DF. Eight luxury 4/5 Star cottages set in 24 acres of Devon countryside, all south-facing and overlooking our fishing lake. Totally wheelchair accessible throughout. Other facilities include indoor heated pool complex with hoist and shallow steps, licensed bar with meals and takeaways, games room, pets corner. **For brochure phone 01409 211509. ETC ★★★★/★★★★★**
website: www.blagdon-farm.co.uk

See also Colour Display Advertisement

HOPE COVE

Mike and Judy Tromans, Hope Barton Barns, Hope Cove, Near Salcombe TQ7 3HT (01548 561393). Sleep 2/10. Nestling in its own valley, close to the sandy cove, Hope Barton Barns is an exclusive group of 17 stone barns in two courtyards and three luxury apartments in the converted farmhouse. Superbly furnished and fully equipped accommodation ranges from a studio to four bedrooms. Heated indoor pool, sauna, gym, lounge bar, tennis court, trout lake and a children's play barn. We have 35 acres of pastures and streams. Farmhouse meals from our menu. Ample parking. Golf, sailing and coastal walks nearby. Open all year. A perfect setting for family Summer holidays, a week's walking in Spring/Autumn or just a get away from it all break. Free range children and well behaved dogs welcome. Open all year. For a colour brochure please contact **Mike or Judy.** ★★★★
website: www.hopebarton.co.uk

Readers are requested to mention this guidebook when seeking accommodation (and please enclose a stamped addressed envelope).

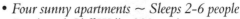

ILFRACOMBE

Waterside Holidays. Sleep 2/10. For North Devon's spectacular coastline with some of Europe's best and cleanest beaches and Exmoor National Park visit our 400 year-old four-bedroomed cottage on Ilfracombe's unspoilt harbour, only ten yards from the beach. Or one of our six Victorian hotel apartments sleeping between two and eight. All completely self contained with livingroom with TV and video; bathroom; kitchen fully equipped for the preparation of breakfasts and lunches for a flexible and relaxing holiday. There is a cafe/bar with a balcony onto the sea. Both on the coast path. Excellent dog walks from the doorsteps. Dogs most welcome here in all local pubs and beaches nearby. Open all year. Short breaks. For brochure, please phone **Ellie or Brian Greenwood, Marine Lodge, Capstone Crescent, Ilfracombe, Devon EX34 9BT (01271 865768).**
website: www.watersidehols.co.uk

INSTOW

Beach Haven Cottage. Sea front cottage overlooking the sandy beach. Instow is a quiet yachting village with soft yellow sands and a pretty promenade of shops, old cottages, pubs and cafes serving drinks and meals. Beach Haven has extensive beach and sea views from the house and garden (as photo opposite), sleeps five, has its own parking, gas-fired central heating, colour TV and washing machine. There is a lawned garden overlooking the sea, with a terrace and garden furniture. Locally are coastal walks and cycle trails, a boat to Lundy Island and most sporting activities. Dog welcome. Please send SAE for colour brochure of this and other sea edge cottages to **S.I. Barnes, 140 Bay View Road, Northam, Bideford EX39 1BJ (01237 473801).**

KINGSBRIDGE (Near)

Mill Cottage, Marsh Mills, Aveton Gifford, Kingsbridge TQ7 4JW (Tel & Fax: 01548 550549). In the beautiful Avon Valley, four miles from Kingsbridge, eight miles south of Dartmoor, Mill Cottage offers single-storey holiday accommodation for two to three people (children 12 years and over) and well-trained dogs. Bedroom with double and single beds, en suite bathroom with separate WC. Large, well-equipped kitchen with electric cooker, combination microwave, refrigerator and freezer. Lounge/dining room with sofa-bed, colour TV and video. This room, which overlooks the mill race and pond, opens on to a private, south-facing sun terrace. We have large gardens and orchard, which you are welcome to share. Electric storage radiators plus electric fire in lounge. Rates £250 per week all inclusive.
e-mail: Newsham@Marshmills.co.uk
website: www.Marshmills.co.uk

NEWTON ABBOT

John and Helen Griffiths, Lookweep Farm, Liverton, Newton Abbot TQ12 6HT (01626 833277; Fax: 01626 834412). Sleeps 4/5. Two attractive well-equipped stone cottages. Clean, characterful and comfortable accommodation. Tranquil setting surrounded by open farmland and woods. Perfectly placed to explore Dartmoor National Park and the charming villages and coastline of South Devon. Golf, riding, fishing and outstanding walking all nearby. Heated pool. Short breaks available. Pets welcome. Mastercard and Visa accepted. **ETC ★★★**
e-mail: holidays@lookweep.co.uk
website: www.lookweep.co.uk

NEWTON ABBOT

Mrs M. A. Gale, Twelve Oaks Holiday Cottages, Twelve Oaks Farm, Teigngrace, Newton Abbot TQ12 6QT (Tel & Fax: 01626 352769). Working farm, join in. Sleeps 4. Join us at one of the two carefully converted cottages on our 220 acre beef farm, bordered by the River Teign, on the edge of the village of Teigngrace. Each self-contained cottage has one double and one twin room with bathroom and shower room. Heating, TV, fridge, microwave and laundry facilties. Parking. Children welcome. Non-smoking accommodation available. Find us off the A38 Expressway. Rates from £250 to £450. **ETC ★★★** *HOLIDAY COTTAGES*. Also Twelve Oaks Caravan Park (**ETC ★★★★**) with electric hook-ups, TV hook-ups and awnings available. Hot water, shower, pets and swimming pool free of charge.

OKEHAMPTON

East Hook Cottages. An outstanding location in the heart of Devon, with a beautiful panoramic view of the Dartmoor National Park, on the Tarka Trail and Devon Coast to Coast Cycle Route. Three comfortably furnished country cottages with exposed beams, log fire and full of character. Sleep 2/6. Quiet and peaceful, set in own large grounds with garden furniture. Ample parking. Very accessible, one mile from Okehampton, less than two miles from Dartmoor, three miles from the A30. The most central point for leisure In the West Country. Children and pets welcome. Open all year. Flexible short breaks. Terms £145 to £395 per week. Guests return yearly! **Mrs M.E. Stevens, West Hook Farm, Okehampton EX20 1RL (01837 52305).**
E-mail: marystevens@westhookfarm.fsnet.co.uk

The FHG Directory of Website Addresses
on pages 243 – 272 is a useful quick reference guide for holiday accommodation with e-mail and/or website details

Galford Springs
Self-catering Farm Holidays

- Barn conversion with newly built interior ◆ On a working farm
- Designed for large families and groups – can accommodate up to 18
- Main area open-plan; two separate en suite bedrooms
- Kitchen with fridge, freezer, washing machine, microwave etc
- Adaptable interior – beds, bunks and furniture can be moved around
- Suitable for disabled visitors – interior all on one level
- Ideal for walking, riding, fishing and sightseeing

Tel: 01566 783264 • e-mail: galfordsprings@aol.com

Galford Springs Holiday Centre, Galford Farm, Lewdown, Okehampton, Devon EX20 4PL

See also Colour Advertisement

See also Colour Display Advertisement

PAIGNTON

Christine & Mike Grindrod, Serena Lodge 15 Cliff Road, Paignton TQ4 6DG (01803 550330). Sleep 2-7. Fully equipped, centrally heated, self-contained holiday apartments in superb level position adjacent Headland Gardens; 250 yards harbour and two beaches. Immaculate throughout; bed linen, hot water and central heating for those cooler months supplied free of charge. Sea views and balconies from some apartments. Microwave, colour TV and video; payphone. Parking on premises. Ground floor units available. Write or phone for terms and brochure.
website: www.serenalodge.com

See also Colour Display Advertisement

SIDMOUTH

Boswell Farm Cottage, Sidford, Sidmouth EX10 0PP (Tel & Fax: 01395 514162). Listed 17th century farmhouse with seven individual cottages lovingly converted from period farm buildings, each with its enclosed, delightful garden. Cradled in 45 acres of peaceful valley amid glorious Devon countryside. Abundant wildlife. Art studio facilities in restored Victorian kennels with stunning views. All weather-tennis court and trout pond. Idyllic walks in Area of Outstanding Natural Beauty, two miles from beaches and World Heritage Coastline. 14th century inn and amenities within walking distance. Open all year. **ETC ★★★★**
e-mail: dillon@boswell-farm.co.uk
website: www.boswell-farm.co.uk

SOUTH MOLTON

Rebecca Evans, North Lee Holiday Cottages, North Lee Farm, South Molton, EX36 3EH (01598 740248; Fax: 01598 740248). Situated on the southern edge of Exmoor with stunning views over the surrounding countryside. The old courtyard and stables have been converted into five holiday cottages. Sleep two to eight people. Pets welcome. **ETC ★★★★**
e-mail: beck@northleeholidaycottages.co.uk
website: www.northleeholidaycottages.co.uk

e-mail: wmbselfcatering@aol.com

SOUTH MOLTON

Mike and Rose Courtney, West Millbrook, Twitchen, South Molton EX36 3LP (01598 740382). Properties sleep 2/8. Adjoining Exmoor. Two fully-equipped bungalows and one farmhouse annexe in lovely surroundings bordering Exmoor National Park. Ideal for touring North Devon and West Somerset including moor and coast with beautiful walks, lovely scenery and many other attractions. North Molton village is only one mile away. All units have electric cooker, fridge/freezer, microwave and colour TV; two bungalows also have washing machines. Children's play area; cots and high chairs available free. Linen hire available. Games room. Car parking. Central heating if required. Electricity metered. Out of season short breaks. Weekly prices from £70 to £365. Colour brochure available. **ETC ★★/★★★ website: www.westcountrynow.com**

SOUTH MOLTON (Near)

Court Green, Bishop's Nympton, Near South Molton. Sleeps 5. A most attractive well equipped, south-facing cottage with large garden, on edge of the village of Bishop's Nympton, three miles from South Molton. Ideal holiday centre, easy reach of Exmoor, the coast, sporting activities and places of interest. Three bedrooms - one double, one twin-bedded with washbasin and one single. Two bathrooms with toilets. Sitting and dining rooms, large kitchen. Central heating, electric wood/coal effect fires, TV. One mile sea trout/trout fishing on River Mole. Well behaved pets welcome. Terms April to October £180 to £220. **Mrs J. Greenwell, Tregeiriog, Near Llangollen, North Wales LL20 7HU (01691 600672).**

TORQUAY

Atherton Holiday Flats, 41 Morgan Avenue, Torquay TQ2 5RR (01803 296884). A warm welcome is assured at Atherton. Run by an ex-Yorkshire couple who still give the famous Yorkshire hospitality. We aim for high standards particularly regarding cleanliness. Our self-contained flats are modern and comfortable with own showers and toilets. Very centrally located being 300 yards from town centre. Riviera Centre and beach within walking distance. Flats sleep 2-4 people, have bed linen provided, microwave and colour TV. Car parking. Open all year with out of season short breaks available. Reasonable rates with prices from £75 per week for two people. Full central heating included in price. Brochure from resident proprietors **Beatrice and Terry Kaye.**

TORQUAY

Atlantis Holiday Apartments, Solsbro Rd, Chelston, Torquay TQ2 6PF (01803 607929; Fax: 01803 391313). Set in a charming Victorian house which is totally non-smoking. There is a pleasant garden and ample car parking. Within easy walking distance along tree-lined streets are the main beaches, shops and railway station. Although sited close to all of Torquay's main facilities, the area is quiet and peaceful. The apartments have fully equipped kitchens including microwaves. Linen and towels, colour TV and video recorder are included in the tariff. All major credit and debit cards accepted. Open all year. **ETC ★★★ e-mail: enquiry@atlantistorquay.co.uk website: www.atlantistorquay.co.uk**

CHELSTON DENE
HOLIDAY APARTMENTS
CHELSTON ROAD, TORQUAY, DEVON TQ2 6PU

Set in its own spacious grounds, this house offers 9 well-equipped, self-contained holiday apartments, sleeping up to four people. It is close to beaches, shops, and the railway station and within walking distance of Torquay Harbour, The Riviera Centre and Cockington Village. All bed linen is provided and cleanliness is of a high priority. There is a laundry room and central heating in some apartments for winter bookings. Many guests return, especially for our short breaks between September and June, with prices starting at £60.

No smokers, but well-behaved pets and children welcome.   ETC ★★★

Tel/Fax: 01803 605180   e-mail: info@chelstondene.com   website: www.chelstondene.com

TORQUAY

South Sands Apartments. These well-appointed apartments have been under the same ownership since 1986, with many regular guests. They are conveniently situated on the seafront, with a good bus service. Apartments are on the ground floor and first floor only; linen, heating, electricity and hot water included in the price. Riviera 'Commitment to Quality' Award. Open all year. ETC ★★★. Full details from: **South Sands Apartments, Torbay Road, Torquay TQ2 6RG (01803 293521; Fax: 01803 293502).**
e-mail: southsands.torquay@virgin.net
website: www.southsands.co.uk

TORQUAY

See also Colour Display Advertisement

Sunningdale Apartments, 11 Babbacombe Downs Road, Torquay TQ1 3LF. Spacious one and two bedroom apartments. All self-contained with bathroom with shower. Separate fitted kitchens, many apartments with stunning sea views over Lyme Bay. All are fully equipped with everything necessary for guests to enjoy the highest levels of comfort and convenience. Large private car park. Laundry room. Fully double glazed with central heating. Level walk to shops and restaurant, bars and theatre, and most sporting activities. Close to beaches and moors. Excellent touring centre for south west. Terms from £195 to £595 per week. **ETC ★★★**. For brochure and further details please telephone: **Mrs H. Carr (01803 325786).**
website: www.sunningdaleapartments.co.uk

TOTNES

Mrs Anne Torr, Downe Lodge, Broadhempston, Totnes TQ9 6BY (01803 812828). Sleeps 2-6. Centrally situated for Dartmoor and the coast, our beautiful stone cottage is set in its own south-facing garden next to the owner's property. Peaceful location with woodland walks from the doorstep, a birdwatcher's paradise, quiet lanes for easy cycling. Three-quarters of a mile from excellent 15th century village pub with fabulous food. Four miles from the fascinating historic towns of Totnes and Ashburton. Two acres of land with Dartmoor ponies and rarebreed poultry. Three bedrooms – one double, one single and one with bunks. Sofa bed. Two bathrooms with bath/shower. TV and video. Central heating. Washing machine, microwave. Children welcome. Available with one double room, one bathroom and sofa bed. Terms from £200. B&B available.

ENGLAND

Flear Farm Cottages

Discover nine superb cottages set in 75 acres of a beautiful South Devon valley - just five miles from the sea. As well as peace and quiet, we offer a 40ft indoor heated swimming pool, sauna, all weather tennis court, large indoor and outdoor play areas.

Non-smokers only. Children and dogs welcome. Log fires and full central heating – perfect for off-season breaks.

ETC ★★★★/★★★★★
East Allington, Totnes, South Devon TQ9 7RF
Website: www.flearfarm.co.uk

Phone (01548) 521227 or Fax (01548) 521600 For our Colour Brochure

---

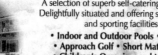

WOOLACOMBE BAY APARTMENTS
Woolacombe • Devon

ENGLAND FOR EXCELLENCE GOLD AWARD WINNER FOR BEST FAMILY RESORT

A selection of superb self-catering apartments and suites sleeping between 4-8. Delightfully situated and offering seclusion and privacy with the extensive leisure and sporting facilities offered in our luxury 3 star hotel.

- Indoor and Outdoor Pools • Sauna • Steam Room • Tennis • Squash
- Approach Golf • Short Mat Bowls • Gym • Beautician and Masseur
- Children's Organiser and teenage activities in high season • Crèche

Tel: **01271 870388** www.woolacombe-bay-hotel.co.uk

See also Colour Display Advertisement

WOOLACOMBE
Chichester House Holiday Apartments, The Esplanade, Woolacombe EX34 7DJ (Tel: 01271 870761). Quiet, relaxing, fully furnished apartments situated opposite Barricane Shell Beach – central seafront position with outstanding sea and coastal views. Equipment including colour TV, fridge, cooker etc. Watch the sun go down into the sea from your own balcony. Open all year. Free parking. Pets by arrangement. Off-peak reductions. Short Break details on request. SAE to resident proprietor, **Mrs Joyce Bagnall**.

WOOLACOMBE
Mrs B.A. Watts, Resthaven Holiday Flats, The Esplanade, Woolacombe EX34 7DJ (01271 870248). Situated on the sea front opposite the beautiful Combesgate Beach, with uninterrupted views of the coastline. Two self-contained flats – ground floor sleeps five, first floor sleeps nine. Family, double and single bedrooms, all with washbasins. Comfortable lounges with sea views, colour TV and videos. Fully equipped electric kitchens. Bathrooms have bath and shower. Electricity by £1 meter. Payphone. Free lighting, parking, hot water and laundry facility. Terms from £160 to £800 per week. Please write, or phone, for brochure.

FHG

FHG PUBLICATIONS publish a large range of well-known accommodation guides. We will be happy to send you details or you can use the order form at the back of this book.

DORSET

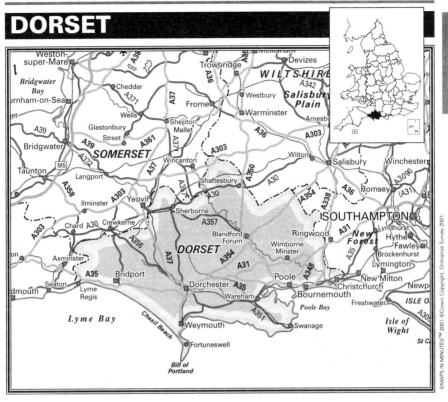

Visit the **FHG** website
www.holidayguides.com
for details of the wide choice of accommodation
featured in the full range of FHG titles

BEAMINSTER

33A St Mary Well Street. Sleeps 7. Delightful two-bedroomed bungalow, peacefully located in a small town, nestling in the rolling hills of west Dorset. Each bedroom has a washhand basin, one has a double bed and the second has two single divans. Z-bed and cot available, also settee converts into double bed in lounge. Bathroom and toilet are separate. Well-equipped kitchen/dining room. Spacious lounge overlooking patio and garden. Separate utility room. Car parking on private drive. Ideal for walking, fishing and fossil hunting, with the stunning Dorset coastline only seven miles away with picturesque harbours, beaches and coastal path. West Bay, Lyme Regis, Hardy's Cottage, Cricket St Thomas, Forde Abbey all nearby. No pets. Terms from £140 to £330. For brochure SAE to: **Mrs L. Watts, 53 Higshill Street, Beaminster, Dorset DT8 3AG (01308 863088).**

BEXINGTON

Mrs Josephine Pearse, Tamarisk Farm, West Bexington, Dorchester DT2 9DF (01308 897784). Sleep 4/6. On slope overlooking Chesil Beach between Abbotsbury and Burton Bradstock. Three large (one suitable for Disabled Category 1 - M3) and two small cottages and two secluded chalets (not ETC Graded). Each cottage stands in own fenced garden. Terms from £105 to £620. Glorious views along West Dorset and Devon coasts. Lovely walks by sea and inland. Mixed organic farm with arable, sheep, cattle, horses and market garden - vegetables available. Sea fishing, riding in Burton Bradstock, lots of tourist attractions and good markets in Bridport (six miles), Dorchester, Weymouth and Portland, all 13 miles. Good centre for touring Thomas Hardy's Wessex. Very quiet, safe for children, and pets can be quite free. ETC ★★★/★★★★

SEAWAY HOLIDAY FLATS

Seaway, 41 Grand Avenue, Southbourne, Bournemouth BH6 3SY
Tel: 01202 300351

- Self-contained holiday flats with garden and parking.
- Three minutes' level walk between shops and cliffs, with lift to fine sandy beach. Exercise area in garden for pets.
- Most reasonable terms early and late season.

BLANDFORD

Mrs M. J. Waldie, The Old Rectory, Lower Blandford St Mary, Near Blandford Forum DT11 9ND (01258 453220). Sleeps 6. Completely self-contained wing of Georgian Old Rectory, one mile from the market town of Blandford Forum, within easy reach of the south coast, Poole, Bournemouth, Salisbury and Thomas Hardy country around Dorchester. Local fishing and many places of historic interest. Accommodation for six in three rooms, one double bedded, one twin bedded and smaller room with bunk beds, cot. Large well equipped kitchen, spacious sitting/diningroom with colour TV; cloakroom downstairs; bathroom and separate toilet upstairs. Pets allowed by prior arrangement. Children welcome. Parking spaces. Use of secluded garden. Everything provided except bed linen and towels. Terms from £185 to £235 per week. May to September. SAE, please, for further details.

BLANDFORD FORUM

Murray & Amanda Kayll, Luccombe Country Holidays, Luccombe, Milton Abbas, Blandford Forum DT11 0BE (01258 880558; Fax: 01258 881384). Superior self-catering holiday cottages. Set in the heart of beautiful and unspoilt Dorset countryside with stunning views and a peaceful, traffic-free environment. Luccombe offers quality accommodation for two to seven people in a variety of converted and historic farm buildings, with original timbers and panelling. Well-equipped kitchens. Large shower or bath. Cosy lounge/dining room with colour TV. Bed linen, duvets, towels provided. Laundry room. Children and well behaved pets welcome. Ample parking. Disabled access. Riding, tennis, swimming pool and gymnasium/games room (new for 2003). Clay pigeon shooting and fishing nearby. Post Office and stores in local village. Open throughout the year. Group/family enquiries welcome. Short breaks available. **ETC ★★★★**
e-mail: mkayll@aol.com   website: www.luccombeholidays.co.uk

BRIDPORT (Near)

Court Farm Cottages, Askerswell, Dorchester DT2 9EJ (01308 485668). A Grade II Listed barn has been converted into delightful holiday cottages, fully equipped with all modern conveniences to make your holiday as relaxing as possible. Wheatsheaf and Haywain sleep four and feature king-sized four-poster beds. Threshers has three bedrooms and sleeps five. South Barn has four bedrooms and two bathrooms and sleeps seven. A games room and large garden are provided for guests. Askerswell is an idyllic village in an Area of Outstanding Natural Beauty just four miles from the coast. Perfect for walking and touring holidays. Open all year. Low season short breaks available. From £210 to £690 per week. **ETC ★★★★/★★★★★**
e-mail: courtfarmcottages@eclipse.co.uk
website: www.eclipse.co.uk/CourtFarmCottages/WEBPG2

BRIDPORT/NETTLECOMBE

The Studio, The Old Station, Nettlecombe, Bridport. Sleeps 2. Enjoy a peaceful stay in beautiful countryside. Off-road parking, two-and-a-half acres of garden. The 150-year-old stone building, originally the linesmen's hut at Powerstock Station, was later enlarged, forming a fashion designer's studio. Recently double glazed, it has a bedsit, kitchen, shower room, toilet, for one to two non-smoking adult guests (no children or pets). Two single beds; duvets, bed linen and towels provided. Electricity also included (small winter surcharge). Microwave, fridge, TV, heating. Garden furniture, putting, tennis. Available extras include , laundry facilities and badger-watching at the adjacent Old Station. Terms from £130 per week, B&B also available. Low season short stays by arrangement. SAE please: **Mrs D.P. Read, The Old Station, Powerstock, Bridport DT6 3ST (01308 485301).**

LYME REGIS

Mrs M.J. Tedbury, Little Paddocks, Yawl Hill Lane, Lyme Regis DT7 3RW (01297 443085). Sleeps 2. A chalet situated in the garden of a smallholding which overlooks Lyme Bay and surrounding countryside for perfect peace and quiet. Two-and-a-half miles Lyme Regis, three-and-a-half miles Charmouth. Easy driving distance Seaton, Beer, Sidmouth. The chalet is ideal for two people liking plenty of room; it has a double bedroom and is fully equipped except linen. Mains water, hot and cold, flush toilet and shower, electric light, fridge, fire, TV. Parking space for cars. Pets welcome. Terms from £90. Also six berth caravan from £100. SAE, please.

MEYRICK PARK

Mr & Mrs B. W. Lonnen, Langlea House, 18 St Anthony's Road, Meyrick Park, Bournemouth BH2 6PD (01202 558426). Langlea House Self Catering Apartments are open all year, delightfully situated, peaceful and central. Few minutes' walk to town, beaches and gardens. Attractive apartments with a high standard of cleanliness. Parking, Sky TV. Linen and hand towels at cost. Guest telephone. Central heating. Pets, children and disabled welcome. Member of Bournemouth Holiday Flats Association. Weekly terms from £80 to £150 per person.

MILTON ABBAS

Little Hewish Barn. A 150 year-old brick and flint barn, converted to provide comfortable accommodation of a very high standard, including oil-fired central heating. There are two double bedrooms (one converts to twin), both with en suite bath/shower facilities. Spacious open-plan living/dining area features a wood-burning stove, fully-equipped kitchen, dishwasher, washer/dryer, TV/video, stereo etc. Children and well-behaved pets are very welcome. Fully-enclosed private garden and secure on-site parking. Prices are all inclusive – no hidden extras. ETC ★★★★★. **Little Hewish Barn, Milton Abbas, Blandford Forum, Dorset DT11 0DP (01258 881235; Fax: 01258 881393).** e-mail: terry@littlehewish.co.uk

SHERBORNE

White Horse Farm, Middlemarsh, Sherborne DT9 5QN (01963 210222). Toad Hall sleeps 4; Badger's sleeps 2; Ratty's sleeps 2/4; Moley's sleeps 2. Set in beautiful Hardy countryside, we have four cottages furnished to high standards and surrounded by three acres of paddock and garden with a duck-pond. We lie between the historic towns of Sherborne, Dorchester and Cerne Abbas. Delightful coastal attractions are some 30-40 minutes' drive away. Situated next door to an inn serving good food, we welcome children, partially disabled guests and pets. All cottages have central heating, colour TV and video recorder with unlimited free video-film rental. Electricity, bed linen, towels inclusive. Ample parking. Good value at £150 to £370 per week. Discounted two weeks or more. B&B holidays available in our attractive farmhouse. Contact: **David, Hazel, Mary and Gerry Wilding on 01963 210222. ETC ★★★★** e-mail: enquiries@whitehorsefarm.co.uk website: www.whitehorsefarm.co.uk

STURMINSTER NEWTON

Mrs Sheila Martin, Moorcourt Farm, Moorside, Marnhull, Sturminster Newton DT10 1HH (01258 820271). Working farm. Ground floor flat with own entrance and front door key. It is part of the farmhouse, kept immaculately clean and furnished to the highest order. We are a 117-acre dairy farm in the middle of the Blackmore Vale. Guests are welcome to wander round, watch the farm activities and laze in the large garden – we have some garden loungers for your use. We are very central for touring with easy access to New Forest, Longleat Wildlife Park, Cheddar, Stonehenge and the lovely Dorset coast. Accommodation for four people in two double bedrooms, one with a double bed, the other with twin beds. Bathroom, separate toilet. Sittingroom with colour TV and door leading straight on to the back garden. Well-equipped kitchen/diner with fridge/freezer, microwave and washing machine; all utensils colour co-ordinated, matching crockery etc. Beds made up with fresh linen on arrival. Towels, tea towels, etc provided. Sheila creates a friendly atmosphere here "down on the farm" and does her best to make your holiday an enjoyable one. Open April to November. Car essential. Sorry, no pets. Weekly terms from £190 to £295. SAE please.

TARRANT GUNVILLE/BLANDFORD

Mrs M.E. Belbin, Home Farm, Tarrant Gunville, Blandford DT11 8JW (01258 830208). Sleeps 4. Beautifully situated in the Cranborne Chase, a secluded bungalow on a working farm. Furnished and equipped to a high standard, comprising one double and one twin bedded room; large lounge, dining area and kitchen. Large fenced garden with drive and parking area. Wonderful rural walks and an abundance of wildlife all round. Other amenities close by - golf, riding, leisure centres, etc. Half-an-hour from New Forest, Bournemouth, Purbecks. Open all year. Long weekends available out of season. Brochure on request. **ETC ★★★**

TOLLER PORCORUM

Barton Cottage. Toller Porcorum is situated in picturesque rural Dorset, mid-way between the market towns of Dorchester and Bridport (20 minutes), and only six miles to West Bay and Heritage Coast. Shop selling groceries and provisions, newsagent, post office, bakery and public house two miles away in Maiden Newton. The accommodation, a self-contained cottage with front and rear entrance, adjoins Barton Farmhouse at the end of the village High Street, and is adjacent to a working organic dairy farm. Own driveway with ample parking for two cars and garden to both front and rear. Upstairs accommodation comprises one double and one single bedroom, and a modern bathroom, all fully carpeted. The downstairs is open-plan, with a spacious well-equipped modern kitchen/diner, which includes fridge, electric cooker and washing machine. The lounge is comfortably furnished, fully carpeted, with colour TV. Cloakroom and second toilet on the ground floor. Heating and hot water by electric meter (£1 coins). All linen supplied. Pets by arrangement. Terms: £100 – £170 per week, deposit required. For bookings and enquiries contact: **T.G. Billen, Barton Farmhouse, Toller Porcorum, Dorchester DT2 0DN (01300 320648).**

ENGLAND

WAREHAM (near)

"Dormer Cottage", Woodlands, Hyde, Near Wareham. Sleeps 5. This secluded cottage, cosy and modern, is a converted old barn of Woodlands House. Standing in its own grounds, it is fronted by a small wood with a walled paddock at the back. Pleasant walks in wooded forests nearby. In the midst of "Hardy Country" and ideal for a family holiday and for those who value seclusion. All linen included, beds ready made on guests' arrival and basic shopping arranged on request. Amusements at Bournemouth, Poole and Dorchester within easy reach. Five people and a baby can be accommodated in two double and one single bedrooms; cot and high chair available. Bathroom, two toilets; lounge and diningroom, colour TV. Kitchen with cooker, fridge, washing machine, small deep freeze, etc. Pets welcome. Open all year. Golf course half-mile; pony trekking, riding nearby. **SAE, please, for terms. Mrs M.J.M. Constantinides, "Woodlands", Hyde, near Wareham BH20 7NT (01929 471239).**

WAREHAM (near)

Mrs M.J.M. Constantinides, "Woodlands", Hyde, Near Wareham BH20 7NT (01929 471239). Secluded house, formerly Dower House of Hyde Estate, stands alone on a meadow of the River Piddle in four-and-a-half acres in the midst of "Hardy Country". Accommodation comprises: upstairs lounge with colour TV; one bedroom (two single beds); downstairs large kitchen-diner, small entrance hall, bathroom; electric cooker (in addition to Aga cooker), refrigerator. Independent side entrance. Extra bedroom (two single beds) on request at £35 per week. Visitors are welcome to use house grounds; children can fish or play in the boundary stream. Pleasant walks in woods and heath nearby. Golf course half-a-mile; pony trekking/riding nearby. All linen included, beds ready made and basic shopping arranged on arrival day. Ideal for a quiet holiday far from the madding crowd. Cot and high chair available and children welcome to bring their pets. SAE, please, for terms and further particulars.

WEST BAY

Robins, Meadway, West Bay, Bridport. Sleeps 6. This comfortably furnished bungalow, with attractive garden in a quiet cul-de-sac at West Bay, overlooks open field, only three minutes' walk to the harbour and beach. Ideal for family holidays, walking, fishing, visiting many places of interest or just relaxing. Three bedrooms, two double and one twin bedded, sleeping six, cot available if required. Sitting room with colour TV. Well equipped kitchen/dining room. Bathroom and separate toilet. Garden and parking space. Open all year, out of season short breaks available. Personally supervised. **Mrs B. Loosmore, Barlands, Lower Street, West Chinnock, Crewkerne, Somerset TA18 7PT (01935 881790).**

The medieval bridge over the River Stour at Sturminster Newton

DURHAM

HARTLEPOOL

Joy and Tony Pinto, Ash Vale Holiday Homes Park, Easington Road, Hartlepool TS24 9RF (01429 862111). Quiet and pretty country park. Situated only one mile from Crimdon's long and sandy beach, three miles from centre of Hartlepool with its historic quay; Durham 15 miles, Newcastle 20 miles. A walker's paradise: The Cleveland Way, North Yorkshire Moors, the North Pennines, the Northumberland Coast, Hadrian's Wall and the Border Counties. Beautiful "Catherine Cookson" country. Holiday homes for sale and hire. Modern six-berth caravans and tourers with hook-ups. On site laundry, showers with hot water. Children and pets welcome. Terms from £10. Open Easter to end October, Short Breaks and last minute deals available. Golf, stables, fishing, bowling and recreation centre nearby. **ETC ★★**
e-mail: joy@ashvalepark.fsnet.co.uk

LANCHESTER

Mrs Ann Darlington, Hall Hill Farm, Lanchester, Durham DH7 0TA (01207 521476; Tel & Fax: 01388 730300). Two country cottages. Well-equipped and comfortable. Both cottages have one double and one twin room – sleep up to four people. Downstairs is a livingroom and large kitchen/dining room, upstairs two bedrooms and bathroom. Kitchen contains washing machine/tumble dryer, microwave and fridge/freezer. Linen and towels are provided. Both cottages are heated. The cottages are in an ideal location for Durham City and Beamish Museum. You will have a free pass for the week to visit our own open farm. Prices from £160 per week. Children welcome. Sorry no pets. Please write or telephone for brochure. **ETC ★★★**
e-mail: hhf@freenetname.co.uk
website: www.hallhillfarm.co.uk

PLEASE NOTE

All the information in this book is given in good faith in the belief that it is correct. However, the publishers cannot guarantee the facts given in these pages, neither are they responsible for changes in policy, ownership or terms that may take place after the date of going to press. Readers should always satisfy themselves that the facilities they require are available and that the terms, if quoted, still apply.

FHG
Visit the website
www.holidayguides.com
for details of the wide choice of accommodation
featured in the full range of FHG titles

GLOUCESTERSHIRE

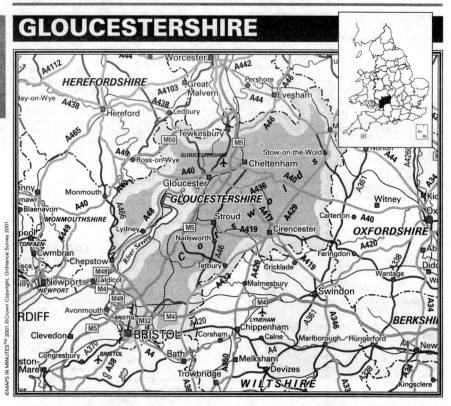

FHG PUBLICATIONS publish a large range of well-known accommodation guides. We will be happy to send you details or you can use the order form at the back of this book.

See also Colour Display Advertisement

UNIVERSITY ACCOMMODATION & FACILITIES

Budget accommodation or fully tailored packages (0870 712 5002; Fax: 020 7017 8273). En suite designer halls across the UK. Groups of any age or size. Sports facilities all year. Tell us your needs and we'll find a location and package to suit.
e-mail: enquiries@thesv.com

DURSLEY

Two Springbank, 37 Hopton Road, Upper Cam GL11 5PD. Sleeps 4 + cot. Fully restored mid-terraced cottage in pleasant village opposite 14th century church with open fields to rear and about one mile from Dursley where the amenities include a swimming pool and sports centre. Superb base for Cotswold Way, touring Severn Vale and Forest of Dean. Few miles from Slimbridge Wildfowl Trust, Berkeley Castle and Westonbirt Arboretum and within easy reach of Gloucester, Bristol, Bath and Cirencester. The ground floor accommodation comprises comfortable sitting room with TV/video and electric fire, dining area with multi-fuel stove, and fitted kitchen with fridge/freezer, electric cooker and microwave. A utility room with washing machine gives access to a rear lawn. On the first floor are two bedrooms (one double, one twin) and a bathroom. There are fitted staircates. Linen and towels included, also cot and high-chair if required. Sorry no pets or smoking. Electricity, including night storage heaters, charged extra by meter readings. Rates from £132 to £219 per week. Off-peak breaks (3 nights) from £85 to £125. **ETC ★★★. Mrs F.A. Jones, Everlands, Cam, Dursley, Gloucestershire GL11 5NL (01453 543047).**

DURSLEY (Near)

Mrs Coates, Hill House, Crawley Hill, Uley, Dursley GL11 5BH (01453 860267). Sleeps 2. The flat is a separate part of this Cotswold stone house which stands in four and a half acres and is situated on top of a hill with beautiful views of the surrounding countryside. The accommodation consists of double bedroom, kitchen with cooker, microwave, fridge, etc., lounge with TV and video, toilet and shower. Car port and garden area. We supply a comprehensive set of maps and tourist information as well as routes to the many places of interest in the area. Bed linen and towels not supplied. Electricity by meter. Open all year. Sorry, no pets. Non-smoking. Terms from £140 per week. Please telephone, or write, for brochure.

HAMPSHIRE

Netley Abbey, Netley, Hampshire

LOCKERLEY

No. 2 Thatched Cottage, Carter's Clay, Lockerley, Near Romsey. Sleeps 5. Delightful thatched self-catering cottage. Set in beautiful countryside, in rural hamlet four miles from Romsey. Ideally situated for exploring New Forest and within easy reach of many places of interest and tourist attractions. Cottage has modern conveniences - TV, fridge etc. - with linen provided. It is clean, homely and very comfortable with a large garden. A warm welcome awaits all visitors, including children and pets. Terms from £164 to £275 weekly. For further details SAE to: **Mrs R.J. Crane, 1 Thatched Cottage, Carter's Clay, Lockerley, Romsey SO51 0GN (01794 340460).**

LYNDHURST

The Penny Farthing Hotel, Romsey Road, Lyndhurst, Hampshire SO43 7AA (023 8028 4422; Fax: 023 8028 4488). We have some neighbouring cottages available as Hotel annexe rooms or on a self-catering basis. These have been totally refitted, much with "Laura Ashley", and offer quieter, more exclusive accommodation. The Penny Farthing is a cheerful small Hotel ideally situated in Lyndhurst village centre, the capital of "The New Forest". The Hotel offers en suite single, double, twin and family rooms with direct dial telephones, tea/coffee tray, colour TV and clock radios. The hotel has a licensed bar, private car park and bicycle store. Lyndhurst has a charming variety of shops, restaurants, pubs, and bistros and "The New Forest Information Centre and Museum". **ETC ★★★**
website: www.pennyfarthinghotel.co.uk

MILFORD-ON-SEA

Mrs Jean Halliday, Westover House, Westover Road, Milford-on-Sea, Lymington SO41 0PW (01590 642077). Sleeps 6. Westover House is a partly thatched period house 300 yards from the sea and half-a-mile from Milford's village green. Its East Wing, available for letting throughout the year, is self-contained and equipped for six, with modern services yet retaining an air of mature tranquillity reminiscent of a past age. There is a sheltered informal half-acre garden of unusual botanical interest, outstanding for its spring flowers. Milford is near the old-world market town of Lymington and the New Forest, yet is also convenient for Bournemouth and many popular holiday attractions of central Southern England. Terms from £140 per week, full tariff available on request.
e-mail: hallidaymos@tinyworld.co.uk

MILFORD-ON-SEA (New Forest)

Carolyn Plummer, Ha'Penny House, 16 Whitby Road, Milford-on-Sea, Lymington SO41 0ND (01590 641210). 'PENNYPOT' sleeping two, is a nicely furnished apartment adjoining Ha'penny House (a guest house offering luxury bed and breakfast accommodation). Set in a quiet area of the unspoilt village of Milford-on-Sea and just a few minutes' walk from both sea and village, it is ideally situated for touring the New Forest, Bournemouth, Salisbury and the Isle of Wight. The apartment has its own separate entrance, a double bedroom, lounge with TV and video, diningroom, fully equipped kitchen and bathroom, use of a large garden and summer house. Heating, power, linen and towels are included. Private parking. Non-smokers only; sorry no pets. Friday to Friday bookings from £140 to £240 per week. **ETC ★★★★**
website: www.SmoothHound.co.uk/hotels/hapenny.html

SWAY (Lymington)

Mrs H. J. Beale, Hackney Park, Mount Pleasant Lane, Sway, Lymington SO41 8LS (01590 682049). Sleep 2/6. Two very comfortable and modern self-catering apartments and Coach House Cottage sleep two/six people (further bedrooms available). Colour TV. Bed linen and electricity included. Hackney Park is situated in a commanding and tranquil setting, two miles from Lymington and the village of Sway. It is a delightful residence standing in its own extensive grounds adjoining New Forest Heath with superb walks, rides and drives from the property. We have first class stables for those wishing to bring their own horse and there are excellent riding facilities in the area. There are many famous places of interest nearby; close to the Isle of Wight ferry and within six miles of sandy beaches. Pets by prior arrangement. Open all year.

HEREFORDSHIRE

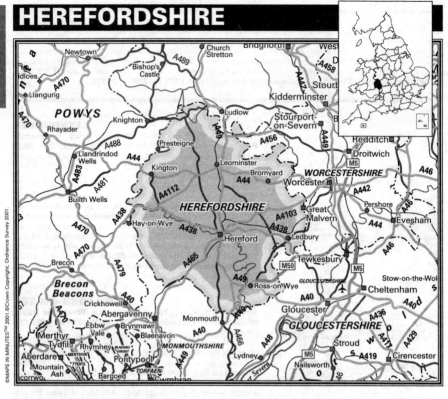

THE LODGE

The Lodge, being the former Verger's cottage, can be found in a tranquil setting just eight miles north of the historic cathedral town of Hereford. Peacefully located next to the Parish Church. Guests can enjoy the pleasure of the gardens of Felton House, the stone-built former Rectory, now a guest house. The Lodge has been completely renovated and restored to its Victorian character but with the convenience of central heating, a modern kitchen, two shower rooms, a dining room and a sitting room with TV. There are three bedrooms with accommodation for five people (One double room, one twin, one single), and in addition a cot is available. Linen may be hired. Children, and pets with responsible owners, are most welcome. Private parking, patio and garden. The Lodge is a cosy, restful cottage, spotlessly clean. Short Breaks catered for and weekly terms range from £150 to £250 per week, exclusive of electricity. Brochure available.

Marjorie and Brian Roby, Felton House, Felton, HR1 3PH Tel/Fax: (01432) 820366
Website: www.SmoothHound.co.uk/hotels/felton.html

See also Colour Advertisement

HEREFORD

**Carey Dene and Rock House, Hereford. Sleeps 4/8 + cot.
Working farm.** Two oak-beamed cottages on traditional farm overlooking River Wye. Beautiful area between Hereford and Ross-on-Wye, for a peaceful holiday or a short break. Access to the river, two minutes' walk to pub serving meals. Washing machine. microwave, colour TV, central heating. Electricity and linen included in charge. Open all year. Pets and children welcome. Non-smoking. Prices from £200 to £450. Please contact: **Mrs Milly Slater, Ruxton Farm, Kings Caple, Hereford HR1 4TX (Tel & Fax: 01432 840493).**
e-mail: milly@ruxton.co.uk
website: www.wyevalleycottages.com

HEREFORD

Rose Cottage, Craswall, Hereford. Sleeps 5. Rose Cottage is a modernised stone-built cottage, retaining its original character situated at the foot of Black Mountains, on a quiet country road. Hay-on-Wye, Hereford and Abergavenny are easily accessible and the cottage is the ideal base for walking and touring. Many churches and castles of historic interest; close to River Monnow where trout fishing is available. Pony trekking, hang-gliding nearby. A car is essential and there is ample parking. Rose Cottage is comfortably furnished with full central heating and wood fire (heating and hot water included). Linen provided free of charge, towels available if required. Electricity by meter reading. Two bedrooms, one with double bed, one with three single beds. Cot can be provided. Bathroom, toilet. Kitchen fully equipped with electric cooker, kettle, fridge, etc. Sittingroom; diningroom. TV. Dogs are allowed. Available all year round. Terms from £150 to £160. ETC ★★★. **Mrs M. Howard, The Three Horseshoes, Craswall, Hereford HR2 0PL (01981 510631).**

HEREFORD

Mrs S. Dixon, Swayns Diggins, Harewood End, Hereford HR2 8JU (01989 730358). This highly recommended first floor flat is completely self-contained at one end of the main house. The bedroom, sitting room and private balcony all face south with panoramic views over farmland towards Ross and Symonds Yat. The well-equipped kitchen overlooks the garden with grand views towards Orcop Hill and the Black Mountains. Open all year, rental from £130 to £140 per week includes electricity, linen, heating, colour TV. Ideal base for exploring the beautiful Wye Valley, Herefordshire, Gloucestershire and the historic Welsh Marches. There is much to see and do in the area. Write or phone for further particulars.

KINGTON

The Harbour, Upper Hergest, Kington. Properties sleep 5/9. This bungalow is on a good second-class road facing south with beautiful views from its elevated position, across the Hergest Ridge and Offa's Dyke. The Welsh border is a mile away. Shops are two-and-a-half miles away. Kington Golf Club nearby. Accommodation for five/nine in two double rooms (one with extra single bed) downstairs and two double dormer bedrooms; two cots; bathroom, toilet; sittingroom (TV); diningroom; sun porch for relaxing; kitchen with electric cooker, fridge, food store and usual equipment. No linen. Children and pets welcome. Car essential - parking. Available all year. SAE, please, to **Mrs B.F. Welson, New House Farm, Upper Hergest, Kington, Herefordshire HR5 3EW (01544 230533).**

LEOMINSTER

Nicholson Farm Holidays. Self-catering properties on a working dairy farm. Beautiful views. Wide choice of restaurants and bar meals in the area. Supermarket 10 minutes. Excellent walking, golf, riding, carp fishing available on the farm, swimming and tennis 10 minutes. Dogs are welcome but must not remain in during the owner's absence. Non-smoking. Contact: **Mrs J. Brooke, Brimstone Cottage, Docklow, Leominster HR6 0SL (01568 760346).**

LEOMINSTER

Mrs Audrey Pritchard, Eaton Farm Cottage, Eaton Court Farm, Stoke Prior Road, Leominster HR6 0NA (01568 612095). A self-contained cottage wing of Listed Georgian farmhouse with own entrance. Situated in the countryside but within easy reach of Leominster with interesting shops and antique markets. Many places to dine out, and plenty to see and do. Accommodation comprises one twin and one double bedroom; cot available. Lounge/dining room with TV/video. Downstairs bathroom with bath/shower, separate WC. Fully-equipped kitchen with Aga (oil), electric cooker, microwave, dishwasher, washing machine, larder with fridge. Linen supplied, including duvets, if required. Electricity, water, oil included. Terms from £215 to £295 per week, 10% deposit. Weekends £150. On short minor road linking A44 east of junction with A49. Non-smoking only. Sorry, no pets. ETC ★★★

ENGLAND

MALVERN

Kate and Dennis Kavanagh, Whitewells Farm Cottages, Ridgeway Cross, Near Malvern WR13 5JS (01886 880607; Fax: 01886 880360). Sleep 2-6. Charming converted cottages. Fully equipped with colour TV, microwave, barbecue, fridge, iron etc. Linen, towels also supplied. One cottage is equipped for the disabled with full wheelchair access. Children and pets welcome. Short breaks and long lets, suitable for relocation. Also see advert under Great Malvern, Worcestershire. **ETC ★★★★**
e-mail: whitewells.farm@btinternet.com

See also Colour Display Advertisement

ROSS-ON-WYE

Mainoaks Farm Cottages, Goodrich, Ross-on-Wye. Six units sleeping 2,4,6 & 7. Mainoaks is a 17th century Listed farm which has been converted to form six cottages of different size and individual character. It is set in 80 acres of pasture and woodland beside the River Wye in an Area of Outstanding Natural Beauty and an SSSI where there is an abundance of wildlife. All cottages have exposed beams, pine furniture, heating throughout, fully equipped kitchens with microwaves, washer/dryers, etc., colour TV. Private gardens, barbecue area and ample parking. Linen and towels provided. An ideal base for touring the local area with beautiful walks, fishing, canoeing, pony trekking, golf, bird watching or just relaxing in this beautiful tranquil spot. Open throughout the year. Short breaks available. Pets by arrangement.
Brochure on request. **ETC ★★★/★★★★.** Contact: **Mrs P. Unwin, Hill House, Chase End, Bromesberow, Ledbury, Herefordshire HR8 1SE (01531 650448).**
e-mail: mainoaks@lineone.net website: www.mainoaks.co.uk

ROSS-ON-WYE (Near)

A rendered stone cottage tucked away down a country lane in a tiny village on the edge of the Royal Forest of Dean in the Wye Valley, an Area of Outstanding Natural Beauty. Excellent acccommodation for up to 12 people. The cottage is typical of the Herefordshire countryside, but when entered, quality and high standards are very much in evidence. Five bedrooms, one with handmade oak four-poster, king-size bed; one of the bathrooms has a jacuzzi bath; two showers. Two beamed lounges with TV and video, open fires and storage heaters. Oak-fitted kitchen with dishwasher, fridge, freezer etc. Linen and towels for hire. Children and pets welcome. Ample parking. The River Wye is a haven for fishermen, with salmon, trout and coarse fishing. Also B&B (ETC Four Diamonds). Details from **Mrs H. Smith, The Old Kilns, Howle Hill, Ross-on-Wye HR9 5SP (Tel & Fax: 01989 562051).**

ROSS-ON-WYE (Near)

Kiln House, Yatton, Near Ross-on-Wye. Sleeps 6. The Kiln House is a converted hop kiln, situated just off the A449 in the peace and quiet of lovely Herefordshire countryside. The historic towns of Ledbury and Ross-on-Wye are nearby, as well as the Wye Valley, Forest of Dean, Malvern Hills and many more places of interest. The accommodation sleeps six in three bedrooms - two with double beds and one with single bed plus guest bed. Cot and high chair available. Large lounge with woodburner and TV; well-equipped kitchen; downstairs toilet, bathroom and toilet upstairs. Airing cupboard with immersion heater. Garden and ample parking, car essential. Children welcome. Sorry, no pets. Available all year. SAE for terms and further details to: **Mrs P.A. Ruck, Lower House, Yatton, Near Ross-on-Wye HR9 7RB (01531 660280).**

SYMONDS YAT

Mrs J. Rudge, Hilltop, Llangrove, Near Ross-on-Wye (01600 890279). Sleeps 4. Chalet bungalow with magnificent views over surrounding countryside. One mile off A40 dual carriageway and within easy reach of Forest of Dean, Monmouth and Black Mountains. The chalet stands in the gardens of a seven-acre smallholding, enjoying peace and quiet, yet close to local shops, public houses and the local attractions. Livingroom with TV. Kitchen and bathroom with all amenities. Two bedrooms, one with two single beds and one with double bed. Patio, sun lounge, garden. Children welcome. No pets. Accommodation particularly suitable for the elderly. No linen supplied. £1 meter. Terms from £175 to £225. SAE, please.

HERTFORDSHIRE

SOUTH MIMMS

Mr W.A.J. Marsterson, The Black Swan, 62/64 Blanche Lane, South Mimms, Potters Bar EN6 3PD (01707 644180; Fax: 01707 642344). Sleep 2/6. The Black Swan, a timber framed building dating from 1600, looks across the village green in South Mimms. Once a village inn, it is now our home. We have two flats and a cottage, convenient for M25 and A1(M), half-an-hour's drive, tube or train from central London. Near Junction 23 on M25. Follow signs to South Mimms village. Stay with us to see London and the South-East or use us as a staging post to or from the Channel Ports. Self-catering from £150 to £295 per week. Children and pets welcome. Non-smoking accommodation available. **ETC ★★/★★★**

ISLE OF WIGHT

Cowes, Isle of Wight PO31 8QE Ideally set in a countryside location, minutes' drive away from Cowes. Accommodation consists of pine lodges sleeping 2, 4 or 6 plus caravans and bungalows sleeping 4 or 6. Large range of leisure facilities for your enjoyment, including indoor and outdoor heated pools, all-weather floodlit tennis courts, hi-tech gymnasium, health suite with pine sauna, steam rooms and solarium, plus a health and beauty salon. Seasonal entertainment programme with visiting cabaret and Syril the Squirrel's children's club for 5 to 12 year olds, a play fort, crazy golf – and not forgetting the patio chess! Catering facilities within the centre include a top quality restaurant serving evening meals and Sunday lunches, and a coffee shop open during the day and early evening, serving hot and cold food, home-baked daily specials and takeaways. Open all year (please note that some facilities are seasonal only).

Tel: 01983 292395 • Fax: 01983 299415 • info@gurnardpines.co.uk • www.gurnardpines.co.uk

See also Colour Advertisement

Island Cottage Holidays. Charming individual cottages in lovely rural surroundings and close to the sea. Over 45 cottages situated throughout the Isle of Wight. Beautiful views, attractive gardens, delightful country walks. All are equipped to a high standard and graded for quality by the Tourist Board. Open all year. Terms from £132 to £1195 per week. Short Breaks available in low season (3 nights) £89 to £395. Sleep one to 14. For a brochure please contact: **Mrs Honor Vass, The Old Vicarage, Kingston, Wareham, Dorset BH20 5LH (01929 480080; Fax: 01929 481070). ETC ★★/ ★★★★★**
e-mail: enq@islandcottageholidays.com
website: www.islandcottageholidays.com

TOTLAND BAY

3 Seaview Cottages, Broadway, Totland Bay. Sleeps 5. This well-modernised cosy old coastguard cottage holds the Farm Holiday Guide Diploma for the highest standard of accommodation. It is warm and popular throughout the year. Four day winter break - £42; a week in summer £250. Located close to two beaches in beautiful walking country near mainland links. It comprises lounge/dinette/kitchenette; two bedrooms (sleeping five); bathroom/toilet. Well furnished, fully heated, TV, selection of books and other considerations. Another cottage is also available at Cowes, Isle of Wight. Non-smokers only. **Mrs C. Pitts, 11 York Avenue, New Milton, Hampshire BH25 6BT (01425 615215).**

ENGLAND

KENT

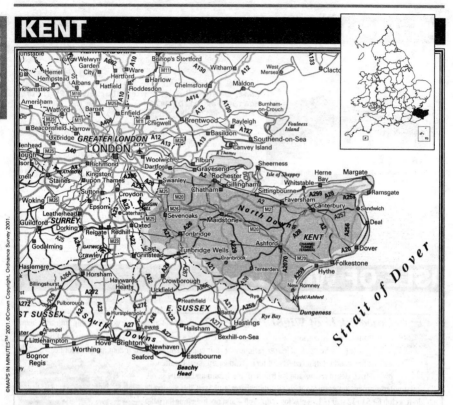

UNIVERSITY ACCOMMODATION & FACILITIES

Budget accommodation or fully tailored packages (0870 712 5002; Fax: 020 7017 8273). En suite designer halls across the UK. Groups of any age or size. Sports facilities all year. Tell us your needs and we'll find a location and package to suit.
e-mail: enquiries@thesv.com

Garden of England Cottages. Accommodation for all seasons in Kent and Sussex. Set in part of England's most beautiful countryside, our ETC quality graded cottages offer you a homely atmosphere and ideal locations for your perfect holiday. Visit pretty villages, explore historic castles and famous gardens and enjoy day trips to London and France. Available all year. Ideal for re-locating, visiting friends, ex-patriots and any short let that requires quality furnished accommodation. Prices include linen, towels, fuel and pets. Visit our website or contact us for a free brochure. Member of South East England Tourist Board. **Garden of England Cottages, The Mews Office, 189A High Street, Tonbridge, Kent TN9 1BX (01732 369168; Fax: 01732 358817).**

e-mail: holidays@gardenofenglandcottages.co.uk   **website: www.gardenofenglandcottages.co.uk**

LEYSDOWN

Isle of Sheppey. Privately owned three bedroomed bungalow on holiday park. Sleeps up to seven + cot. Shower, toilet, TV, fridge and cooker. Duvets supplied, bring your own linen. Quiet site with clubhouse, restaurant, bar, games room and heated swimming pool. Only five minutes' walk from beaches, shops and amusements. One dog welcome. Terms from £65 to £250 per week. Phone **Yvonne on 07771 644 529** for information and booking.
e-mail: leysdownchalet@aol.com

LYDD-ON-SEA

98 Coast Drive, Lydd-on-Sea, Romney Marsh. Sleeps 6.

Lydd-on-Sea is a small hamlet on the south coast near New Romney/Dungeness. We offer a three bedroomed bungalow situated opposite the sea front with uninterrupted sea views from the sun lounge/diner. There is an inner lounge. Colour TV, linen and duvets provided. Central Heating. A separate bathroom and toilet. Utility area in garage, tiled with worktops, washing machine, drawer unit and freezer. Lawns to front and rear plus expanse of natural garden. Small patio to rear with garden furniture. Easy access to Dover and Folkestone for cross-Channel trips. The ancient towns of Rye and Hastings are a short distance away. Good sea fishing off Dungeness Point. Romney, Hythe and Dymchurch small gauge railway passes rear of the house and buses stop a few yards away. Children welcome. Weekly terms from £175 to £375 plus £20 winter fuel supplement - October to April. No pets. Contact: **Mrs Frances I. Smith, Holts Farm House, Coopers Lane, Fordcombe, Near Tunbridge Wells TN3 0RN (01892 740338).**

• • *Some Useful Guidance for Guests and Hosts* • •

Every year literally thousands of holidays, short breaks and overnight stops are arranged through our guides, the vast majority without any problems at all. In a handful of cases, however, difficulties do arise about bookings, which often could have been prevented from the outset.

It is important to remember that when accommodation has been booked, both parties – guests and hosts – have entered into a form of contract. We hope that the following points will provide helpful guidance.

GUESTS:

• When enquiring about accommodation, be as precise as possible. Give exact dates, numbers in your party and the ages of any children.

• State the number and type of rooms wanted and also what catering you require – bed and breakfast, full board etc. Make sure that the position about evening meals is clear – and about pets, reductions for children or any other special points.

• Read our reviews carefully to ensure that the proprietors you are going to contact can supply what you want. Ask for a letter confirming all arrangements, if possible.

• If you have to cancel, do so as soon as possible. Proprietors do have the right to retain deposits and under certain circumstances to charge for cancelled holidays if adequate notice is not given and they cannot re-let the accommodation.

HOSTS:

• Give details about your facilities and about any special conditions. Explain your deposit system clearly and arrangements for cancellations, charges etc. and whether or not your terms include VAT.

• If for any reason you are unable to fulfil an agreed booking without adequate notice, you may be under an obligation to arrange suitable alternative accommodation or to make some form of compensation.

While every effort is made to ensure accuracy, we regret that FHG Publications cannot accept responsibility for errors, omissions or misrepresentations in our entries or any consequences thereof. Prices in particular should be checked because we go to press early. We will follow up complaints but cannot act as arbiters or agents for either party.

LANCASHIRE

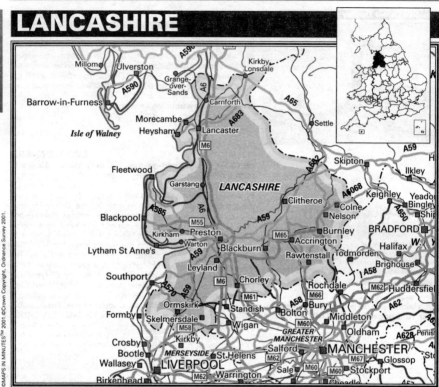

BLACKPOOL (Norbreck)

Mrs C. Moore, 'Cotswold', 2a Haddon Road, Norbreck, Blackpool FY2 9AH (01253 352227). The flats are situated in a quiet, select area on the edge of town adjoining the promenade with acres of grass and level walking. Our famous trams pass by frequently for the town centre, Cleveleys and Fleetwood. The Fylde is well known by golf and bowls enthusiasts. Our ground floor flat is spacious, fully self-contained and centrally heated. Sleeps up to six persons. We also have a flatlet with private bathroom and central heating sleeping up to two persons. Travel cot and high chair available. Pets welcome by arrangement. Midweek/Weekend Short Breaks can be arranged early season and during the illuminations. Rates from £110 per week. Phone or send SAE for brochure.

See also Colour Display Advertisement

CLITHEROE

Mrs P. M. Gifford, Rakefoot Farm, Chaigley, near Clitheroe BB7 3LY (Chipping 01995 61332; mobile: 07889 279063; Fax: 01995 61296). Family farm peacefully situated in the beautiful countryside of the Ribble Valley in the Forest of Bowland, with panoramic views. Ideally placed for touring coast, Dales and Lakes. Superb walks, golf and horse riding nearby or visit pretty villages and mill shops. Warm welcome whether on holiday or business, with refreshments on arrival. Bed and Breakfast or Self Catering available in 17th century farmhouse and traditional stone barn conversion. Four properties, three internally interlink. Wood-burning stoves, central heating, exposed beams and stonework. Most bedrooms en suite, some ground floor. Excellent home-cooked meals, laundry; pubs/restaurants nearby. Indoor/outdoor play areas, garden and patios. Dogs by arrangement. **ETC ★★★/★★★★★ (SC) / ETC ◆◆◆◆ (B&B).**
e-mail: info@rakefootfarm.co.uk   **website: www.rakefootfarm.co.uk**

ENGLAND

LUNE VALLEY

Barbara Mason, Oxenforth Green, Tatham, Lancaster LA2 8P (015242 61784). Working farm, join in. Sleeps 4 plus cot. Cottage and static caravan on working farm with panoramic views of Ingleborough and surrounding hills. Central for Lakes, dales and coast. Good walking, fishing and horse-riding nearby. Guests are welcome to watch the day-to-day workings of the farm. Our cottage sleeps four in one double and one twin room with lounge, fitted kitchen, ground and first floor shower rooms. The caravan sleeps four in one double and two single beds, with washbasin, shower, flushing toilet, colour TV. Garden and garden chairs available. Children welcome. One dog welcome. Three-quarters-of-a-mile to nearest pub. Prices from £200 to £270 per week. Caravan from £150 per week.

MORECAMBE

St Ives and Rydal Mount Holiday Flats, 360-361 Marine Road, East Promenade, Morecambe LA4 5AQ (01524 411858). Situated on the sea front overlooking the bay and Lakeland hills. Ideal base for touring the Lake District and Yorkshire Dales. Large one or two bedroom flats occupying one floor, each with their own TV, electric cooker, fridge and microwave. Stair lift. Car park. SAE please for brochure to **Mrs S M Holmes.**

MORECAMBE

Mrs G.A. Tamassy, Gizella Holiday Flats, 8 Marine Road, West End, Morecambe LA3 1BS (01524 418249). Sleep 5. Luxury holiday flats overlooking the gardens with a beautiful view of Morecambe Bay and Lakeland Hills. All modern facilities including en suite and colour TV. Easy access to Lake District, Lune Valley and Lancaster, and ideal for golf and birdwatching. Open all year. Overnight guests welcome. (Sorry, no children and no pets). Reasonable rates, with reductions for Senior Citizens. SAE please for confirmation. Member Morecambe Bay Warmth of Welcome. **websites: www.morecambeholidayflats.co.uk**
www.gizellaholidayflats.co.uk

FHG

FHG PUBLICATIONS

publish a large range of well-known accommodation guides. We will be happy to send you details or you can use the order form at the back of this book.

ENGLAND

LINCOLNSHIRE

See also Colour Display Advertisement

ALFORD

Mrs Stubbs, Woodthorpe Hall Country Cottages, Near Alford LN13 0DD (01507 450294; Fax: 01507 450885). Very well appointed luxury one and three bedroomed cottages, overlooking the golf course, all with central heating, colour TV, microwave, washer, dryer, dishwasher and fridge freezer. Woodthorpe is situated approximately six miles from the coastal resort of Mablethorpe and offers easy access to the picturesque Lincolnshire Wolds. Adjacent facilities include golf, fishing, garden centre, aquatic centre, snooker, pool and restaurant with bar and family room. **ETC** ★★★★
e-mail: enquiries@woodthorpehall.com
website: www.woodthorpehall.com

HORNCASTLE

Little London Cottages, Tetford, Horncastle. Three very well-equipped properties standing in their own gardens on our small estate six miles from Horncastle. Superb views over the pastures and parkland grazed by our pedigree Longhorn cattle and rare breed sheep. Lovely walks, fishing and pony trekking are available nearby. Golf courses and swimming pools less than 10 miles away. The Garth is a single storey conversion of farm buildings with open-plan sitting and dining room and three bedrooms. Cornerways is a mid-19th century cottage with a log fire in the sitting room, dining room and two bedrooms. Mansion Cottage is the latest addition, originally a thatched timber framed building from the late 17th or early 18th century with a cosy sitting room and two bedrooms. Short Breaks and special offers. Pets welcome free. **ETC** ★★★★/★★★★★. Further information from **Mrs S D Sutcliffe, The Mansion House, Little London, Tetford, Horncastle LN9 6QL (01507 533697; mobile: 07767 321213).**
e-mail: debbie@sutcliffell.freeserve.co.uk   **website: www.littlelondoncottages.co.uk**

SAXILBY

The Conifers Guest Annexe, Occupation Lane, Broadholme, Near Saxilby, Lincoln LNI 2NB (01522 703196). One bedroom self-catering cottage refurbished to a very high standard and set in a rural location. The historic city of Lincoln is seven miles away; local shops, etc one and a half miles. A No Smoking establishment. Well-equipped, with washer/dryer, dishwasher, electric cooker with separate grill, fridge/freezer, TV, video, CD player, electric shower, etc. Bed linen, towels, electricity and heating included. Single guest bed, cot and highchair available. Private courtyard garden, a real suntrap, weather permitting! Off-road parking. Sorry, no pets. Weekly prices from £170 to £270. Short Breaks all year. For further information contact **Mr M.J. Gray** at above.
e-mail: mjgtheconifers@supanet.com

WADDINGWORTH

Andrew and Alison Pritchard, Redhouse Farm, Waddingworth LN10 5EE (Tel & Fax: 01507 578285; mobile: 07702 678241). Working farm. Sleeps 4. This delightful, well-equipped cottage offers self-catering and Bed & Breakfast and is integral to the main farmhouse. Redhouse Farm stands within beautiful Lincolnshire countryside, overlooking St Margaret's Church, central point of Old Lincolnshire. The cottage makes the perfect base for the holidaymaker and the business person. Pets and children welcome. Weekly terms from £250 to £350, includes fuel and linen. Open all year, short breaks available. **ETC** ★★★★, *MEMBER FARMSTAY UK.*
e-mail: redhousefarm@waddingworth
website: www.redhousecottage.co.uk

NORFOLK

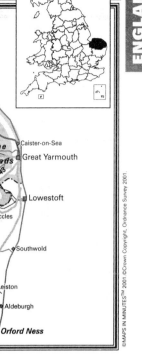

ENGLAND

FHG

Visit the FHG website
www.holidayguides.com
for details of the wide choice of accommodation
featured in the full range of FHG titles

*When making enquiries or bookings,
a stamped addressed envelope is always appreciated*

CROMER

Hobby Cottage, Driftway Farm, Felbrigg, Cromer. Sleeps 4/6 plus cot. Completely modernised, comfortable cottage at the end of a quiet farm lane. Two miles from sandy coast and within easy access of North Norfolk bird sanctuaries, stately homes and Norfolk Broads. The cottage sleeps four/six, having a sitting room with TV and bed settee; two double bedrooms (one with double bed, one with twin beds); diningroom, well-equipped kitchen and bathroom. Garden and parking for two cars. Own transport essential. Available March-October. From £130 - £270 per week, including electricity. No linen. Enquiries, with SAE please, to **Mrs E. Raggatt, The Ferns, Berkeley Street, Eynesbury, St Neots, Cambs PE19 2NE (01480 213884).**
website: http://web.onetel.net.uk/~raggatt/

DEREHAM

Moor Farm Stable Cottages, Foxley NR20 4QN (Tel & Fax: 01362 688523). Located on a working farm, a courtyard of two and three bedroomed self-catering chalets and two cottages. All fully equipped, and all with central heating which is included in the letting fee. Situated 20 miles from the coast and 15 miles from Norwich and the Broads. 365 acres of mature woodland adjoining owners' farm – ideal for walking. Fishing close by. Pets welcome at charge of £10. **ETC ★★/★★★**

FAKENHAM

Saddlery Cottage and Hillside Cottage, Colkirk, Fakenham. Sleep 2/7. Both cottages are situated near the farm on the outskirts of Colkirk village, overlooking farmland. Saddlery Cottage (shown in picture) has large sittingroom with beams and woodburner and colour TV, fully fitted kitchen/dining room with fridge and electric cooker, microwave, dishwasher; utility room with automatic washing machine. Garage, parking and fenced garden. Hillside Cottage has sittingroom with colour TV, large airy kitchen/dining room with fitted units, dish washer and washing machine. Fenced garden, parking. Saddlery Cottage has two ground-floor bedrooms. Both have central heating/Calor gas heating. Children and pets welcome. Cots available; linen supplied. **ETC ★★★**. Apply **Mrs C. Joice, Dept SC, Colkirk Hall, Fakenham NR21 7ND (01328 862261)**

HORNING (Norfolk Broads)

Wake Robin Village Chalet. Sleeps 4. Set in the picturesque village of Horning on the River Bure at the heart of the Norfolk Broads. The Chalet has one double and two single bedrooms. A comfortable lounge with river-view balcony and well-equipped kitchen make a relaxing holiday home in Summer or Winter. Large garage for a car and safe storage of fishing tackle, bicycles, etc. Wake Robin guests have private access to the River Bure a few yards from the door for mooring boats and renowned coarse fishing. Electricity and linen supplied. Pets are welcome. **Contact: Bob Oldershaw, Heroncote, Lower Street, Horning, Norfolk NRI2 8PF (O1692 631255).**
e-mail: bob.oldershaw@virgin.net

See also Colour Display Advertisement

MATTISHALL

The Old Mill, Mattishall. The Old Mill in the heart of Norfolk has been tastefully converted to provide peaceful holidays, away from the rush of modern living. Standing in the owners' delightful grounds, it has one round Victorian style double bedroom with French doors overlooking the paddock, lounge/diner with TV, kitchen, bathroom, scullery with fridge and microwave. Linen and towels provided. Electricity by £1 coin meter. Village has surgery, chemist, bakery, butcher, Post Office, etc. The market town of Dereham is four miles away, Norwich 12 miles. Convenient for Sandringham, Broads, etc. Your privacy respected. Warm welcome. Sorry, no smoking or pets. Open all year. Terms on request. **ETC** ★★★. Contact: **Margaret and Don Fisher, Ivydene, Mill Road, Mattishall, Dereham NR20 3RL (01362 850312).**

MUNDESLEY-ON-SEA

47 Seaward Crest, Mundesley-on-Sea. Sleeps 4. Mundesley-on-Sea is an attractive seaside village situated centrally on the Norfolk coast, within 10 miles of the Norfolk Broads, seven miles from Cromer and 20 miles from Norwich. The clean sandy beaches stretch for miles with safe bathing and natural paddling pools. This attractive west-facing brick-built chalet is in a delightful setting with lawns, flower beds, trees and parking. Beach 500 yards away and shops 800 yards. There is an excellent golf course nearby and bowls and riding are within easy reach. Large lounge/diningroom tastefully furnished including easy chairs, settee and colour TV. Kitchenette with electric cooker, fridge, sink unit, etc. One double, one twin-bedded rooms. Fully carpeted. Bathroom and toilet. Lighting, hot water, heating and cooking by electricity (£1 slot meter). Fully equipped except for linen. Weekly terms from £100. Details, SAE, please, **Mrs J. Doar, 4 Denbury Road, Ravenshead, Nottinghamshire NG15 9FQ (01623 798032).**

NORWICH

Sunnybank, Blofield. Sleeps 4/5 plus baby. Comfortable, well equipped, detached bungalow in quiet location close to village centre. Excellent road access providing ideal base for exploring Broadland, historic Norwich and Great Yarmouth Coast. Boating and fishing nearby. Comprises sun porch, fitted kitchen with automatic washing machine and microwave, sittingroom with colour TV, video, radio, toys, games. Double-bedded room, twin-bedded room with Z-bed (for child); bathroom. Ample parking. Attractive enclosed lawned garden. One well-behaved dog accepted. Railway one-and-a-half miles, bus stop 400 yards. Terms £160 to £320 per week, including holiday cancellation insurance. Inclusive central heating, electricity and linen. **Mrs C. Pritchard, 18 Danesbower Lane, Blofield, Norwich NR13 4LP (01603 713986).**
e-mail: gpritchard@farmersweekly.net   website: www.cottageguide.co.uk/sunnybank

SHERINGHAM

Beeston Hills Lodge, Sheringham. Sleeps up to 8. Edwardian lodge. Non-smoking, seaside holiday accommodation in Sheringham. Our house which is marvellously located next to the Norfolk Coastal Path, cliffs and ocean, obtains good views of the sea and green. Beeston Hills Lodge is one of the highest dwellings here, located opposite the putting green and the sea. Set back from the road so there is no passing traffic, the house is equipped with a four-poster, king-size bed, an old piano, satellite system, video player and several colour TVs with boosted feeds to the bedrooms, DVD player, washing machine, microwave, tumble dryer, dishwasher. Garden with garden furniture. Car parking for two cars. Ten to twenty minutes drive from the golf course and cinema. The Lodge can accommodate up to eight people in four bedrooms (cot available if required), all with sea views, including one bedroom with a shower and washbasins. There is also a bathroom with WC and two further WCs. Fitted carpets, central heating and storage heaters. Well behaved children and pets welcome. Pillows and duvets provided. Terms from £325 per week, early booking discounts available; Bargain Short Breaks £125. Creative writing courses available, as the owner, a writer and poet, has recently reached the finals of an International Writing competition. Please contact for further details. **(01603 766716 or 07974 381926; Fax: 001 775 542 2519).**

e-mail: enquiries@bhlodge.co.uk   **website: www.bhlodge.co.uk/lodge.htm**

STANFIELD

Mr & Mrs Moore, Mangreen Farm, Stanfield, Near Dereham NR20 4HZ (01328 700272). Come and enjoy the relaxing, friendly atmosphere of one of our converted barns, set in 35 acres of unspoilt countryside in the heart of Norfolk. Ideal for exploring the surrounding historic towns, coastal villages and bird sanctuary. Three cottages sleeping up to eight. TV, microwave, washing machine, tumble dryer. Terms from £150 to £600; power and linen included. Open all year, short breaks available. Children and pets welcome.

website: www.mangreen.co.uk

Blickling Hall, near Aylsham, Norfolk

NORTHUMBERLAND

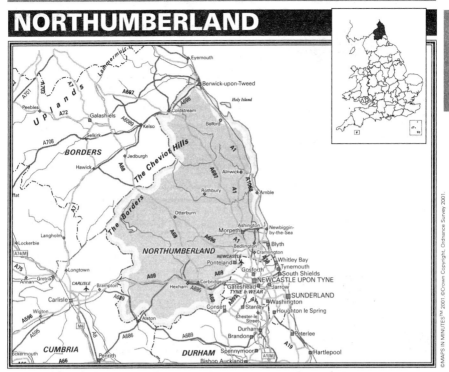

**Town Foot Farm, Shilbottle, Alnwick, Northumberland NE66 2HG Tel/Fax: 01665 575591
E-mail: crissy@villagefarmcottages.co.uk Website: www.villagefarmcottages.co.uk**

Choice of cosy cottages, airy chalets or 17th century farmhouse. Sleep between two and twelve. Perfectly situated; three miles from beaches and historic Alnwick. Fantastic facilities include an indoor forty-foot heated swimming pool, health club, sauna/steam room, sunshower, tennis court and a games room. Visit our beauty therapist. Also try fishing and riding.

Terms from £125 – £975.

VILLAGE FARM *SELF-CATERING*

Free colour brochure.   ETC ★★★★ to ★★★★★

ALNMOUTH

Mrs A. Stanton, Mount Pleasant Farm, Alnmouth, Alnwick NE66 3BY (01665 830215). Mount Pleasant is situated on top of a hill on the outskirts of the seaside village of Alnmouth with spectacular views of surrounding countryside. We offer fresh air, sea breezes, green fields, beautiful beaches, country roads and peace and quiet. There are two golf courses and a river meanders around the farm with all its bird life. Convenient for Holy Island, the Farnes and the Cheviots. The farmhouse has an annexe which is self-contained, and sleeps two adults. Pets welcome. Chalet available sleeping four plus six berth caravan available - prices on application.

BAMBURGH

Point Cottages, Bamburgh. POINT COTTAGES consist of a cluster of cottages in a superb location at the end of the Wynding, next to a beautiful golf course on the edge of Bamburgh, only a short drive away from many other attractive Links courses. Bamburgh is an unspoilt coastal village dominated by a magnificent castle and is an ideal base for visiting other parts of historic Northumbria. The cottages overlook the sea with fine views of the Farne Islands and Lindisfarne. Sandy beaches nearby. They share a large garden with lawns and a total of ten car parking spaces are provided (two per cottage). The cottages are in excellent order, have open fire or woodburning stove and are comfortably furnished. Each cottage has its own special atmosphere but all are warm, cosy and well-equipped. **ETC** ★★★. For further information, availability, prices and booking please contact: **John and Elizabeth Sanderson, 30 The Oval, Benton, Newcastle-upon-Tyne NE12 9PP (0191-266 2800 or 01665 720246 (weekends); Fax: 0191-215 1630).**
e-mail: info@bamburgh-cottages.co.uk   **website: www.bamburgh-cottages.co.uk**

BERWICK-UPON-TWEED

Janet Dunn, Lickar Lea, Bowsden, Berwick-Upon-Tweed TD15 2TP (01289 388500; Fax: 01289 388507). Situated in the former farm steading of Lickar Lea our one bedroom cottage offers the highest standard of accommodation and comfort. Full oil central heating combined with high insulation values ensure a warm and cosy stay. Accommodation comprises light, airy living room with French doors to patio, fully equipped kitchen, large bathroom with bath, washbasin and separate shower, and large double bedroom. The cottage is only four miles inland from Holy Island and has lovely views over the coast and local Kyloe hills. (ETC award pending) Rates: April - October £260, November - March £210, Christmas and New Year weeks £300.
e-mail: janet@lickarlea.co.uk
website: www.lickarlea.co.uk

BERWICK-UPON-TWEED

The Boathouse, Norham, Berwick-Upon-Tweed. Sleeps 10. A delightful south-facing, 18th century house offering spacious accommodation with frontage to the River Tweed and spectacular views over the surrounding countryside. The ground floor consists of a sitting room with TV, lounge with open fire and TV, dining room, kitchen with electric cooker, fridge/freezer, microwave, automatic washing machine, tumble dryer and dishwasher; bathroom with bath, shower, basin and WC; en suite bedroom with king-size bed. First floor has three bedrooms, all with washbasins and bathroom with bath/shower, WC and washbasin. Oil central heating, duvets and linen are provided (not towels).Sports centre, golf course, beaches, places of historic interest, salmon fishing and abundant wildlife. Tariffs from £350 to £750 per week. Open all year. **ETC** ★★★. For further information contact **Mrs M Chantler, Great Humphries Farm, Grafty Green, Maidstone, Kent ME17 2AX (Tel & Fax: 01622 859672).**
e-mail: chantler@humphreys46.fsnet.co.uk

HEXHAM

The Old Church, Chollerton, Hexham NE46 4TF. (01434 681930). Carefully converted church, with original features set in spacious gardens and beautiful countryside, just north of Chollerton and Hadrian's Wall, convenient for Newcastle, Gateshead Metro Centre, Carlisle, Edinburgh and the Scottish Borders. Kirkend (wheelchair access) sleeps four/five, Lonnenend sleeps four. Each has a double and a twin room, full oil-fired central heating, bed linen, towels, colour TV, microwave, patio, seating, pond and barbecue. Cot and high chair available. Village shop and pub one mile, superb restaurants within five miles. One well-behaved dog by arrangement. No smoking indoors. Car necessary (ample safe parking). Washing machine and dryer available.Terms from £250 to £450 a week, Short Breaks available (min. three nights), 20% off second week. Phone or e-mail for a brochure. **ETC** ★★★★
e-mail: oldchurch@supanet.com   **website: http://chollerton.urscene.net**

HEXHAM (Near)

R.A & A.G. Dodsworth, Station House, Catton, Allendale, Near Hexham NE47 9QF (01434 683362) Sleeps 4 plus full-size double bunk. Station House was the terminal station of the Hexham to Allendale Railway, closed in 1950. The Flat is the ground floor front of Station House and is made up of the former Station Master's Office, Staff Room, Booking Office and Waiting Room. Facing south-west, the rooms are in a line, with the second bedroom opening out of the first. Bedroom 1: two singles, Bedroom 2: two singles plus full-size double bunk. Living room with open fire, colour TV; kitchen with electric cooker, microwave, washing machine; bathroom with shower. Central heating by storage heaters included in weekly charge. Electricity for cooking, lighting etc by meter reading. Weekly terms from £140 to £190. Brochure available.

ROTHBURY

The Granary, Charity Hall Farm, Sharperton NE65 7AG (01669 650219). Sleeps up to 8 plus cot. This exceptional conversion of a former granary building provides the perfect setting for a carefree, country holiday. Spacious, fully equipped and tastefully furnished accommodation, with delightful features such as exposed roof beams, traditional stone flagged and timber floors. Cosy inglenook fireplace with cast iron stove. The views over the Coquet Valley are stunning. There's a large garden for enjoying barbecues and relaxing and a playing field for the more energetic. An excellent location for walking, mountain-biking and exploring Northumberland. Rates from £325 to £720 per week; Short Breaks from £200. **ETC ★★★★★**
website: www.charityhallfarm.com

WOOLER

Coach House Cottages, Ilderton Glebe, near Wooler. Sleeps 4/5. Two cottages converted from a Grade II Listed barn, offering comfortable accommodation. Electricity, fuel and linen included in rent. Ilderton is a hamlet on the edge of the Northumbrian National Park and close to the Cheviot Hills. It is an ideal spot for walking, bird watching, visiting historic houses and castles. There are beautiful beaches 15 miles away and trips to the Farne Islands and Holy Island. Both cottages have garages, ample parking, one has an open fire, night storage heating and fitted carpets throughout. There is a walled garden with garden chairs. Children and dogs welcome. Also Bed and Breakfast available at Ildderton Glebe. **ETC ★★★.** Contact: **Mrs Sale, Ilderton Glebe, Ilderton, near Wooler NE66 4YD. (01668 217293).**

OXFORDSHIRE

THAME

The Hollies, Thame. Sleeps 6/7. A beautifully situated luxury bungalow with a pretty, secluded garden only five minutes from the centre of the historic market town of Thame and conveniently situated for Oxford, M40 and trains to London and Birmingham. Three double bedrooms (one en suite shower), and one single bedroom. Bathroom and additional toilet. Modern fully fitted French kitchen and utility room with microwave, dishwasher, self-cleaning cooker, split level gas and electric hob, fridge and deep freeze, washing machine and tumble dryer. Off street parking for two cars. **ETC★★★★.** Contact: **Ms Julia Tanner, Little Acre, Tetsworth, Near Thame, Oxon OX9 7AT (01844 281423; mobile: 077986 25252).**
e-mail: info@theholliesthame.co.uk
website: www.theholliesthame.co.uk

SHROPSHIRE

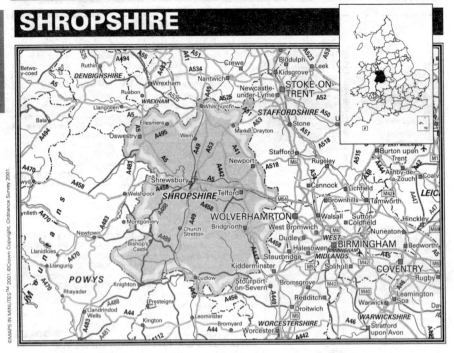

©MAPS IN MINUTES™ 2001 ©Crown Copyright, Ordnance Survey 2001.

CRAVEN ARMS

Mrs B. Freeman, Upper House, Clunbury, Craven Arms SY7 0HG (01588 660629). Sleeps 4. Welcome to Horseshoe Cottage which is situated in the beautiful gardens of Upper House (17th century Listed) in Clunbury, a village of archaeological interest in a designated Area of Outstanding Natural Beauty – A.E. Housman countryside. This private self-catering cottage is completely furnished and equipped; being on one level the accommodation is suitable for elderly and disabled persons. Colour TV. Children and pets welcome; cot available. Ample parking. This Welsh Border countryside is rich in medieval history, unspoilt villages and natural beauty. Enjoy walking on the Long Mynd and Offa's Dyke, or explore Ludlow and Ironbridge. £135 to £170 per week. Please write or phone for further details.

LUDLOW

Hazel Cottage, Duxmoor, Onibury, Craven Arms. Sleeps 4. Beautifully restored, semi-detached, yet private, period cottage, set in its own extensive cottage-style garden with its own drive and ample parking space. Amidst peaceful surroundings and panoramic views of the countryside, it is situated five miles north of historic Ludlow and one-and-a-half miles from the A49. The cottage retains all its original features and fittings with traditional decoration and is fully furnished, with antiques throughout. It comprises a comfortable living room with a Victorian range for coal and log fire; TV, wireless and telephone; diningroom with bread oven; fully equipped kitchen, hall, Victorian bathroom; two bedrooms (one double and one twin-bedded) with period washbasins. Electric central heating throughout. All linen included. Tourist information. Open all year. Short Breaks available. No pets. Terms from £90 to £395 per week. **ETC ★★★★. Mrs Rachel Sanders, Duxmoor Farm, Onibury, Craven Arms SY7 9BQ (01584 856342).**

ENGLAND

Ryton Farm
Holiday Cottages
Ryton, Dorrington, Shrewsbury SY5 7LY

Choose from a traditional country cottage sleeping six or a recently converted barn for either 2 or 4 persons. Some suitable for visitors with mobility difficulties. Ample parking, well-equipped kitchens, colour TV, fitted carpets. Coarse fishing available. Quietly situated 6 miles south of Shrewsbury overlooking Shropshire Hills, convenient for Ironbridge, Ludlow and Shrewsbury.

Open all year.   Weekly bookings or Short Breaks.

ETC ★★/★★★

Telephone:
01743 718449
www.rytonfarm.co.uk

LUDLOW

Sally and Tim Loft, Goosefoot Barn, Pinstones, Diddlebury, Craven Arms SY7 9LB (01584 861326). Converted in 2000 from stone and timbered barns, the three cottages are individually decorated and equipped to the highest standards. Fresh linen and towels are also provided for your comfort. Each cottage has en suite facilities and private garden or seating area. Situated in a secluded valley with walks from the doorstep through beautiful Corvedale. Ideally located for exploring South Shropshire, only eight miles from Ludlow. Cottages sleep up to six people and pets are welcome. There is a games rooms with a full sized snooker table. Short breaks available. **ETC ★★★★**
website: www.goosefootbarn.co.uk

OSWESTRY (Near)

Mr and Mrs Breeze, Lloran Isaf, Llansilin, Near Oswestry SY10 7QX (01691 791376 or 01691 780318). Working farm. Detached bungalow set on a working farm in its own valley which has wonderful scenery and walks. Kitchen with microwave, washer/dryer, fridge, cooker; lounge/dining area with colour TV and woodburning stove, small charge for logs; three bedrooms – two double and one single (duvets supplied but no linen); separate toilet and bathroom. Fitted carpets and electric heating in bedrooms and lounge; garden furniture in enclosed garden. One-and-a-half miles from village, wonderful touring area with lots of attractions. Open all year. Pets welcome. Sorry no children. Prices from £80. Electricity by meter reading. **WTB ★★★** *SELF-CATERING..*

SOMERSET

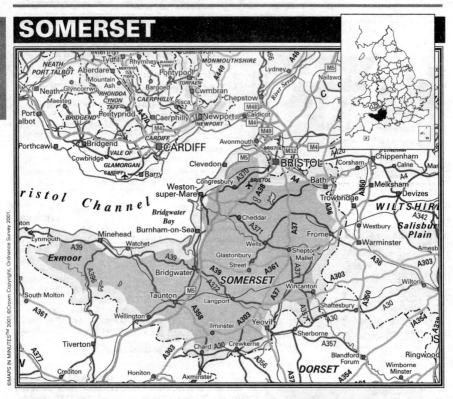

Dating from the late fourteenth century, the Grade II manor house and Listed farm buildings at Butcombe Farm have been sympathetically refurbished to provide every comfort while retaining original architectural features. The cottages are fully equipped and completely self-contained.

Set in eight acres amid Somerset's tranquil countryside, the farm is surrounded by fields and woodland, with many footpaths crossing the valley – including one starting at the farm itself.

On-site facilities include outdoor heated pool, gym and games room. Clay pigeon shooting, tank driving and aromatherapy massage can be arranged locally. Close by, Blagdon Lake offers world-renowned fly-fishing. Bristol, Bath, Cheddar, Wells, Glastonbury and the Mendip Hills are within easy reach.

Butcombe Farm, Aldwick Lane, Butcombe, North Somerset BS40 7UW
Tel: 01761 462380 • Fax: 01761 462300
e-mail: info@butcombe-farm.demon.co.uk   website: www.butcombe-farm.demon.co.uk

See also Colour Advertisement

See also Colour Display Advertisement

BRISTOL

Leigh Farm, Pensford, Near Bristol BS39 4BA (Tel & Fax: 01761 490281) Leigh Farm is situated in the old mining village of Pensford, seven miles to Bristol and eight miles to Bath. Overlooking the floodlit pool; a three-bedroomed cottage sleeping six plus baby. Terraced bungalow conversion built tastefully in natural stone with original oak beams. One or two bedroomed, with shower room, WC and basin. TV. Night storage heating. Bed linen is not supplied but can be hired. Cot and high chair available. Wander round the ponds where duck and moorhen nest. Park and ride for both cities near, and plenty of tourist information for your use. Safe floodlit car park. Open all year. No pets. Terms from £170 to £400 weekly. B&B available. For brochure contact: **Josephine Smart**.

See also Colour Display Advertisement

BURNHAM-ON-SEA (Near)

Mrs W. Baker, Withy Grove Farm, East Huntspill, near Burnham-on-Sea TA9 3NP (01278 784471). Sleep 4/5. Come and enjoy a relaxing and friendly holiday "Down on the Farm" set in beautiful Somerset countryside. Peaceful rural setting adjoining River Huntspill, famed for its coarse fishing. The farm is ideally situated for visiting the many local attractions including Cheddar Gorge, Glastonbury, Weston-super-Mare and the lovely sandy beach of Burnham-on-Sea. Self-catering cottages are tastefully converted and fully equipped including colour TV. Facilities also include heated swimming pool, licensed bar and entertainment in high season, games room, skittle alley. Reasonable rates. Please write or telephone for further details. ETC ★★

CATCOTT

'Upalong', 5 Weares Lane, Catcott. M5 six miles, midway Wells/Quantocks, edge of Levels; waterfowl, bird-watching (particularly winter/spring), coast 11 miles, coarse fishing two miles; quiet picturesque village. Shop; hairdresser; play area; two pubs serving good food. Homely, comfortable three-bedroomed bungalow sleeps five plus, all beds have king size duvets, electric blankets, matching curtains. Lounge with open fire (logs free), colour TV and video. Night storage central heating and immersion heater. All electricity by slot meter. Payphone. Bathroom with shower over bath, washbasin and toilet. Kitchen with dishwasher, washing machine, tumble dryer, full cooker, microwave, fridge, etc. All linen, towels, etc. supplied. Children welcome, cot available. Pets by arrangement. Large garden, patio set and barbecue. Off road parking. Terms from £150 to £235. Further details from: **Mrs Eileen Chilcott, 5 Langland Lane, Catcott, Bridgwater TA7 9HR (01278 722085).**

WOOLCHAMBER COTTAGES

Overlooking the River Barle in the heart of Exmoor, the cottages are converted to a very high standard from a 300 year-old Woolchamber. Sleeping between 2 and 6 people, all the cottages are centrally heated and come fully equipped with cooker, microwave, washing machine/ tumble dryer, fridge freezer, Colour TV and telephone. The perfect setting to explore the magnificent Exmoor countryside and coastline. Dogs welcome. Guided walks by arrangement.

Contact for more details:

(01643) 831259

e-mail: cottages@simonsbathhouse.co.uk
website: www.simonsbathhouse.co.uk

See also Colour Display Advertisement

CHEDDAR

Sungate Holiday Apartments. Sleep 2/4. In Cheddar village, close to Cheddar Gorge and the Mendip Hills, this Listed Georgian building has been thoughtfully converted into four holiday apartments. Each apartment has lounge with sofa bed, TV, bedroom, bathroom, fully-equipped kitchen plus microwave. Linen supplied. Laundry facilities. Pets welcome with prior approval. Private parking. Swimming and leisure facilities nearby. Competitively priced for a short break, longer holiday or a short-term let. Bookings: **Mrs Fieldhouse, "Pyrenmount", Parsons Way, Winscombe BS25 1BU (01934 742264; Fax: 01934 741411). ETC ★★★**

EXMOOR

Jane Styles, Wintershead Farm, Simonsbath, Exmoor TA24 7LF (01643 831222). Occupying a unique location with breathtaking views within the National Park, five quality stone cottages converted from original farm buildings, offering peace, tranquillity, privacy and all the comforts of home. A special place to recharge your batteries away from the stresses of everyday life. Stabling, grazing and DIY livery available. Please telephone, fax or write for a colour brochure. **ETC ★★★★**
website: www.wintershead.co.uk

GLASTONBURY

Mrs S. Kavanagh, Middlewick Holiday Cottages, Wick Lane, Glastonbury BA6 8JW. (Tel & Fax: 01458 832351). Eight delightful cottages set in eight acres of gardens and orchards. With far-reaching views over the Somerset Levels to the Mendip hills beyond. Centrally located for many places of interest. The cottages were converted from a 17th century Listed farmhouse and its barns. Retaining a wealth of beamed ceilings and inglenooks, each cottage is different; sleep from two to six. Set in a courtyard and complemented by a heated indoor swimming pool for guests' use only. Cots and highchairs available. Terms from £200 to £650 per cottage per week, depending on size and time of year.
e-mail: info@middlewickholidaycottages.co.uk
website: www.middlewickholidaycottages.co.uk

£1 per person OFF full admission price (max 5 persons) at
Wookey Hole Caves & Papermill
See our READERS' OFFER VOUCHER for details.

ENGLAND

MINEHEAD

St Audries Bay Holiday Club, West Quantoxhead, near Minehead TA4 4DY (01984 632515 Fax: 01984 632785). The family holiday centre on the Somerset coast. Facilities include indoor heated pool, family entertainment programme, wide range of sports and leisure facilities, licensed bar and restaurant and an all day snack bar. Situated only 15 miles from the M5, near Exmoor at the foot of the Quantock Hills. Well-maintained level site with sea views. On site shop. Family owned and managed. Half board holidays available in comfortable chalets, self-catering in luxury caravans. Touring caravans and tents welcome. Luxury holiday homes for sale.
e-mail: mrandle@staudriesbay.demon.co.uk
website: www.staudriesbay.co.uk

PORLOCK

Lucott Farm, Porlock, Minehead. Sleeps 2/10. Isolated farmhouse on Exmoor, with wood burning fireplaces and all modern conveniences. It lies at the head of Horner Valley and guests will delight in the wonderful scenery. Plenty of pony trekking in the area. Ten people accommodated in four double and two single bedrooms, cot; bathroom, two toilets; sittingroom; diningroom. Kitchen has oil-fired Aga and water heater. No linen supplied. Shops three miles; sea four miles. Car essential - parking. Open all year, Terms (including fuel) on application with SAE please to **Mrs E.A. Tucker, West Luccombe Farm Cottage, Porlock, Minehead TA24 8MT (01643 862810).**

SHEPTON MALLET

Knowle Farm, West Compton, Shepton Mallet BA4 4PD (01749 890482; Fax: 01749 890405). Working farm. Cottages sleep 2/5/8. Knowle Farm Cottages are converted from the old cowstall and stables, set around the old farmyard now laid out as a pleasant garden. Quiet location at the end of a private drive. Excellent views and plenty of wildlife. All cottages furnished to a high standard - bathroom (bath, shower, toilet, washbasin); fully fitted kitchen (automatic washing machine, fridge/freezer, microwave, full size cooker). Two cottages have kitchen/diner, separate lounge with colour TV, the other two have kitchen, lounge/diner, colour TV. Cot, high chair by prior arrangement. Bed linen supplied, towels by request. Surrounding area full of interesting places to visit. Five miles from Wells and Mendip Golf Clubs; the area also has a wide selection of family attractions, fishing, selection of pubs and restaurants. Around the farm plenty of walks, play area for children. Sorry no pets. Terms from £180 to £450. Car essential, ample parking. Payphone for guests. Open all year. **ETC ★★★**

WELLINGTON

Mrs A. Toogood, Dunns Farm, Langford Budville, Wellington TA21 0QP (01823 667808) Sleeps 4/6. Dunns is a working family farm situated in a beautiful and peaceful area near the Devon/Somerset border. Ideal for exploring the Quantock Hills and the North and South coasts. The West Somerset Steam Railway and Hestercombe Gardens are nearby. Accommodation is in the spacious self-contained wing of our 16th century farmhouse, which has inglenook fireplaces and beamed ceilings. The wing is well equipped with central heating, TV, dishwasher, washing machine and microwave. Electricity is included. Visitors are welcome to join in with the farming activities. Open from April to October.
e-mail: toogood@tinyonline.co.uk

WESTON-SUPER-MARE

Gwen Wilson, Seaford Lodge Holiday Flats, 28 Clifton Road, Weston-Super-Mare BS23 1BL (01934 429866/628105). Modernised and refurbished to a high standard, all flats are self-contained with their own toilet and shower room. Fully equipped with fridge/freezer, full electric cooker, electric kettle, ironing facilities, toaster, microwave and electric radiators. All flats have fitted carpets, 20'' colour television; own keys and meters. Cotton sheets, pillow cases and continental quilts provided, all freshly laundered. Heating with night storage heaters inclusive in early and late season. Towels and tea cloths not supplied. Regret, no pets. Parking. Fully fire protected.

ENGLAND

STAFFORDSHIRE

LEEK

Edith and Alwyn Mycock, 'Rosewood Cottage and Rosewood Flat', Lower Berkhamsytch Farm, Bottom House, Near Leek ST13 7QP (Tel & Fax: 01538 308213). Each sleeps 6. Situated in Staffordshire Moorlands, one cottage and one flat overlooking picturesque countryside. Fully equipped, comfortably furnished and carpeted throughout. Cottage, all on ground floor and with three bedrooms (one with four-poster) is suitable for the less able. An ideal base for visits to Alton Towers, the Potteries and Peak District. Patio, play area. Cot and high chair available. Laundry room with auto washer and dryer. Electricity and fresh linen inclusive. Terms from £150 to £305. **ETC ★★★**

See also Colour Display Advertisement

PEAK DISTRICT

Field Head Farmhouse Holidays, Calton. Situated midway between Leek and Ashbourne within the Southern Peak District and the Staffordshire Moorlands Grade II Listed farmhouse with stables, set within its own grounds with open views. Well equipped, with SKY TV. Sleeps 11 plus campbed and cot. Ample space for family caravan. Set in beautiful secluded surroundings close to Dovedale and the Manifold Valley. Ideal country for the walker, horse rider or cyclist. Alton Towers 15-minute drive. All pets and horses welcome. Open all year. Short winter breaks. Late booking discount. Contact **Janet Hudson (01538 308352). ETC ★★★★**
website: www.field-head.co.uk

Looking towards Steep Low, near Alstonefield, Staffs.

SUFFOLK

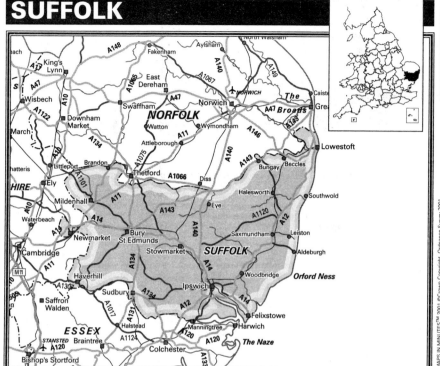

HITCHAM

Old Wetherden Hall Cottage. Sleeps 6 plus cot. 15th century Listed oak-beamed house, with large open inglenook fireplace (logs supplied). Full central heating. Surrounded by large moat stocked with carp and various other fish. Private fishing available. Abundance of wildlife with picturesque secluded setting. Large spacious garden. Close to Lavenham and Bury St Edmunds, well positioned to explore Suffolk. Terms from £175 to £350 per week. Open all year. **Mrs J. C. Elsden, Old Wetherden Hall, Hitcham, Ipswich IP7 7PZ (Tel & Fax: 01449 740574) e-mail: farm@wetherdenhall.force9.co.uk**

KESSINGLAND

Kessingland Cottages, Rider Haggard Lane, Kessingland. Sleeps 6. An exciting three-bedroomed recently built semi-detached cottage situated on the beach, three miles south of sandy beach at Lowestoft. Fully and attractively furnished with colour TV. Delightful sea and lawn views from floor-to-ceiling windows of lounge. Accommodation for up to six people. Well-equipped kitchen with electric cooker, fridge, hot and cold water; immersion heater. Electricity by £1 coin meter. Luxurious bathroom with coloured suite. No linen or towels provided. Only 30 yards to beach and sea fishing. One mile to wildlife country park with mini-train. Buses quarter-of-a-mile and shopping centre half-a-mile. Parking, but car not essential. Children and disabled persons welcome. Available 1st March to 7th January. Weekly terms from £50 in early March and late December to £225 in peak season. SAE to **Mr S. Mahmood, 156 Bromley Road, Beckenham, Kent BR3 6PG (020 8650 0539).**
e-mail: jeeptrek@kjti.freeserve.co.uk   website: www.k-cottage.co.uk

SAXMUNDHAM (Near)

Snape Maltings, Snape IP17 1SR (01728 688303). Sleep 2-6. Snape Maltings, a unique collection of granaries and malthouses nestling beside the River Alde, offers three superb self-catering units. The accommodation surrounds the main arch through which the historic railway link used to run. The Clock Flat and No.3 Maltings Cottages sleep six, No.4 Maltings Cottages sleeps two. All have been tastefully converted and finished to a high standard, with colour TV, electric heating and a fully equipped kitchen. Linen and towels are provided. Children permitted, but no pets except in No.3 cottage. Snape Village has a well-stocked village shop, Post Office, and three pubs. Saxmundham five miles.
e-mail: info@snapemaltings.co.uk
website: www.snapemaltings.co.uk

SOUTHWOLD/WALBERSWICK

H.A. Adnams, Estate Agents, 98 High Street, Southwold IP18 6DP (01502 723292; Fax: 01502 724794). Furnished Holiday Cottages, Houses and Flats, available in this charming unspoilt seaside town. Convenient for sandy beaches, with safe bathing, sailing, fishing, golf and tennis. Near to 300 acres of open Common. Attractive country walks and historic churches are to be found in this area, also the fine City of Norwich, the Festival Town of Aldeburgh and the Bird Sanctuary at Minsmere, all within easy driving distance. SAE, please, for brochure with full particulars.
website: www.haadnams.com

STANSFIELD

Plough Hill Bungalow, Stansfield, Sudbury. Sleeps 4. Plough Hill Bungalow, with attractive garden to front, is situated in a small village with pub, within 15 miles of Sudbury, Gainsborough's birthplace, Newmarket Racecourse and historic Bury St Edmunds, Long Melford and Lavenham. At picturesque Clare, five miles distant, there are good shopping facilities. The Bungalow is well equipped to acccommodate four people in twin-bedded rooms, sittingroom, kitchen/diner with electric cooker, microwave, fridge, cutlery and crockery. Colour TV. Bathroom, toilet. Car essential, parking. Children and pets welcome; cot available. Solid fuel heating or electric fires. Linen supplied on request. Open all year round at very reasonable rates. Terms from £59 to £120 per week. For further details send SAE to **Mrs M. Winch, Plough House, Stansfield, Sudbury CO10 8LT (01284 789253).**

WENHASTON

Holmview. Sleeps 4/5. Delightful detached cottage in pretty Suffolk village, near Southwold, Minsmere and Heritage Coast. Three bedrooms, one twin, one double and one with bunk beds. Well equipped kitchen with electric cooker, microwave, fridge/freezer, washing machine. Electric heating in all rooms. Parking. Very pleasant garden with table and chairs. Good location for walking, bird watching, fishing, golf and horse riding. Terms from £195 per week. Brochure available from **Mr. J. Saunders, Foxdale, 159 The Street, Rockland St Mary, Norwich NR14 7HL (01508 538340).**

SURREY

ENGLAND

KINGSTON-UPON-THAMES (Near)

Sunny House. An attractive alternative to staying in hotels. Designed to suit the discerning business executive or independent traveller away from home, Sunny House has the appeal of a modern upmarket establishment whilst still retaining the charm and characteristics of a well-cared for home. Easy availability of transport to almost anywhere in London, overlooking the quaint surroundings of Royal Bushy Park. All accommodation equipped with en suite facilities, colour TV with satellite, fridge, tea/coffee facilities, direct-dial telephone; use of spacious well-fitted kitchen and dishwasher, washing machine, microwave etc. Also use of beautiful lounge; six-day maid service; full parking facilities. For full details contact: **Chase Lodge Hotel, 10 Park Road, Hampton Wick, Kingston-upon-Thames KT1 4AS (020 8943 1862; Fax: 020 8943 9363).**
e-mail: info@sunnyhouse.com
website: www.sunnyhouse.co.uk

┌ THE FHG DIPLOMA ┐

HELP IMPROVE BRITISH TOURIST STANDARDS

You are choosing holiday accommodation from our very popular FHG Publications.
Whether it be a hotel, guest house, farmhouse or self-catering accommodation, we think you will find it hospitable, comfortable and clean, and your host and hostess friendly and helpful.

Why not write and tell us about it?

As a recognition of the generally well-run and excellent holiday accommodation reviewed in our publications, we at FHG Publications Ltd. present a diploma to proprietors who receive the highest recommendation from their guests who are also readers of our Guides. If you care to write to us praising the holiday you have booked through FHG Publications Ltd. – whether this be board, self-catering accommodation, a sporting or a caravan holiday, what you say will be evaluated and the proprietors who reach our final list will be contacted.

The winning proprietor will receive an attractive framed diploma to display on his premises as recognition of a high standard of comfort, amenity and hospitality. FHG Publications Ltd. offer this diploma as a contribution towards the improvement of standards in tourist accommodation in Britain. Help your excellent host or hostess to win it!

FHG DIPLOMA

We nominate ....

....

Because

Name ....

Address..

....

Telephone No...

SUSSEX

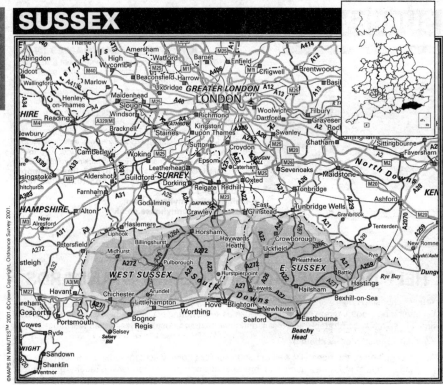

EAST SUSSEX

CROWHURST PARK

Telham Lane, Battle, East Sussex TN33 0SL
Telephone 01424 773344

Award winning holiday park featuring luxury log cabin accommodation.
Magnificent heated pool complex with children's paddling area,
Jacuzzi, steam room, sauna, gym with cardiovascular and resistance
training equipment, solarium, beauty therapies, aquafit classes, tennis
court, children's adventure play area, a 90 acre "Country Pursuits"
activity centre, restaurant, bars and clubhouse.
All this plus beautiful, historic 1066 Country on your doorstep and the
Sussex coast just five miles away. Call for a brochure today.

virtual tour: www.crowhurstpark.co.uk

See also Colour Advertisement

TWO for the price of ONE
Wilderness Wood
See our READERS' OFFER VOUCHER for details.

Cadborough Farm

Udimore Road, Rye, East Sussex TN31 6AA
Tel: 01797 225426; Fax: 01797 224097

Five newly converted individual cottages. Each sleeps two, some with own courtyards. Direct access to '1066' country walks and cliff track with sea views to Rye (1 mile). Full GCH & CTV and CD player. Rates from £150 - £395 per week. Double and Twin available. Minimum two day lets from £50/night. Linen, towels, gas and electricity inclusive. Full G.C.H. Sorry no children and no smoking. One small well-behaved pet welcome.

Website: www.cadborough.co.uk   E-mail: info@cadborough.co.uk

See also Colour Display Advertisement

FAIRLIGHT

Little Oaks, Farley Way, Fairlight. Luxury bungalow on one level, situated in quiet coastal village with clifftop parklands, close to ancient towns of Rye, Battle and Hastings. Furnished to a very high standard, the spacious accommodation comprises double bedroom with en suite shower and sauna, twin bedroom, lounge with TV, dining room, fully equipped kitchen/diner, bathroom, conservatory and balcony overlooking beautiful secluded garden, garage. No smoking in bungalow. Pets welcome. Rates on application, which include central heating, electricity, bed linen and towels. **ETC ★★★★**. Contact: **Ray and Janet Adams, Fairlight Cottage, Warren Road, Fairlight, East Sussex TN35 4AG (Tel & Fax: 01424 812545).**

WEST SUSSEX

HENFIELD

The Holiday Flat and Cottage, New Hall, Small Dole, Henfield. New Hall, the manor house of Henfield, stands in three-and-a-half acres of mature gardens, surrounded by farmland with abundant footpaths. The holiday cottage is the orginal 1600 farmhouse. It has one en suite bedroom, a large livingroom, dining room with two folding beds, and kitchen; a door opens into the walled garden. The holiday flat is the upper part of the dairy wing. Its front door opens from a Georgian courtyard and it has three bedrooms sleeping five, lounge/diner, kitchen and bathroom. Both units are fully equipped and comfortably furnished. Children welcome. Open all year. Terms from £160 to £325 per week. **ETC ★★★**. Send SAE for details to **Mrs M.W. Carreck, New Hall, Small Dole, Henfield BN5 9YJ** or phone **(01273 492546).**

ENGLAND

WARWICKSHIRE

WARWICK

Copes Flat, Brook Street, Warwick. Sleeps 3. Warwick town centre, secluded first floor flat dating from the mid 17th century has its own entrance and high level garden, ideal for al fresco meals. The timber framed sitting/dining room is comfortably furnished for eating and relaxing and has a colour TV and telephone. A bathroom, bedroom with twin or double bed and fully fitted kitchen with washing machine and tumble dryer complete this charming accommodation in the interesting, historic town of Warwick. Sorry, no pets. No smoking. We are ideally situated for visiting Stratford-upon-Avon, Oxford, the Cotswolds and the main towns and attractions in the Heart of England. Terms from £190 to £310. **ETC ★★★**. **Mrs Elizabeth Draisey, Forth House, 44 High Street, Warwick CV34 4AX (01926401512; Fax: 01926 490809).**
e-mail: info@forthhouseuk.co.uk   website: www.forthhouseuk.co.uk

WILTSHIRE

CHIPPENHAM

Kate and David Humphrey, Roward Farm, Draycot Cerne, Chippenham SN15 4SG (01249 758147). Sleep 2/4. Roward Farm offers three holiday cottages, converted from traditional farm buildings, full of character and charm. Overlooking open fields, they provide the perfect base for visiting the Cotswolds and Bath, with Castle Combe, Lacock Abbey and Bowood House all close by. All cottages are fully-equipped and furnished to a high standard. Welcome pack on arrival. Non-smoking throughout. Pets welcome. Open all year. Short breaks and long lets suitable for relocation. Tariffs from £190 per week. Linen, electricity and heating included in the price. **ETC ★★★**
e-mail: d.humphrey@roward.demon.co.uk
website: www.roward.demon.co.uk

See also Colour Display Advertisement

DEVIZES

Colin and Cynthia Fletcher, Lower Foxhangers Farm, Rowde, Devizes SN10 1SS (Tel & Fax: 01380 828795; Fax: 01380 828254). Sleep 4/6. Enjoy your holiday with us on our small farm/marina with its many diverse attractions. Hear the near musical clatter of the windlass heralding the lock gate opening and the arrival of yet another narrowboat. Relax on the patios of our rural retreats - four holiday mobile homes sleeping four/six in a setting close to the canal locks. Bed and Breakfast accommodation in 18th century spacious farmhouse from £22 per person. Self-catering rates from £210 per week. Also available weekly hire with our narrowboat holidays or small camp site with electricity and facilities.

DEVIZES

The Gate House Annexe, Wick Lane, Devizes. Large ground floor annexe accommodation – 'home from home'. Very well equipped to a high standard. Well kept large, quiet garden. Only 15 minutes' walk into the market townof Devizes. **Mrs Stratton, The Gate House, Wick Lane, Devizes SN10 5DW (01380 725283; Fax: 01380 722382).**
e-mail: info@visitdevizes.co.uk
website: www.visitdevizes.co.uk

LACOCK (Near Bath)

The Cheese House & The Cyder House. The Cheese House, with exposed elm and oak timbers, sleeps up to five and consists of an open living/dining room with an arch leading to a fitted kitchen. The first floor has one double and one single bedroom and a shower room/toilet. The second floor has one twin-bedded room and a gallery with casual seating area. The Cyder House, with stepped fireplace and wood-burning stove, sleeps up to four persons. The first floor has two single bedrooms and a shower room/toilet. On the second floor there is a gabled double bedroom. The Cyder House also has the attraction of having the original cyder press on the ground floor, separating the fitted kitchen from the sitting room. Each has a garden with seating and barbecue and a separate drive. Both properties are non-smoking.

Short breaks and business stays are welcome. **ETC ★★★★.** *WELCOME HOST, FARM STAY UK MEMBER.* **Sue and Philip King, Wick Farm, Lacock, Chippenham SN15 2LU (01249 730244; Fax: 01249 730072). e-mail: kingsilverlands2@btinternet.com website: www.cheeseandcyderhouses.co.uk**

TROWBRIDGE

John and Elizabeth Moody, Gaston Farm, Holt, Trowbridge BA14 6QA (01225 782203). The self-contained accommodation is part of a farmhouse, which dates from the 16th century, on the edge of the village of Holt with views across open farmland. Within 10 miles of Bath, Bradford-on-Avon two miles, Lacock eight miles. Private fishing on River Avon available. The apartment consists of a large lounge/dining room with open fire and sofa which converts into a double bed; two generously proportioned bedrooms upstairs, one twin-bedded, one with a double bed, both with washbasins; a separate toilet (downstairs); a large kitchen in the single storey wing, fitted with light oak finish units, electric cooker, microwave, refrigerator and automatic washing machine; shower room which opens off the kitchen. Off road parking. Choice of pubs in village. Terms £170 to £195. Brochure and further details available.

WORCESTERSHIRE

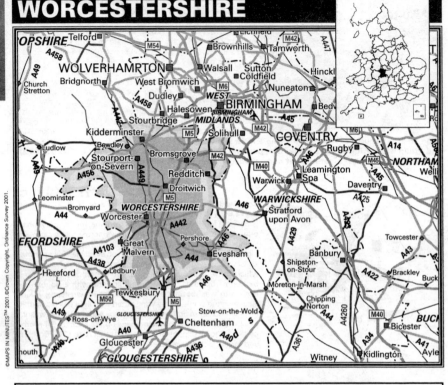

WHITEWELLS FARM COTTAGES

Ridgeway Cross, Near Malvern, Worcestershire WR13 5JS   ETC ★★★★
Tel: 01886 880607   Fax: 01886 880360   E-mail: Whitewells.Farm@btinternet.com

Seven well-established cottages converted from old farm buildings and a hop kiln, full of charm and character with original exposed timbering. These award-winning cottages are exceptionally clean and comfortable and equipped to the highest standards. One cottage is equipped for the disabled with full wheelchair access. Idyllically set around a duckpond in 10 acres, with 2 ½ acres of the property being a fully-fenced woodland plantation, ideal for exercising dogs, on or off the lead. Set in unspoilt countryside on the Herefordshire/Worcestershire border, with outstanding views of the Malvern Hills . Children and pets welcome. Short breaks and long lets; suitable for relocation.

Colour brochure available from: Kate and Denis Kavanagh.

MALVERN

Greenbank Garden Flat, Malvern. Greenbank Garden Flat is situated in the Malvern Hills overlooking Herefordshire. It is self-contained and fully equipped with gas cooker, microwave, central heating, fridge, TV, bath and shower, immersion heater. Large conservatory. Sleeping two/four (double bed and studio couch which converts for two); Z-bed also available. Inclusive charge covers bedlinen for the double bed, towels and all fuel etc. Village shop and public house within five minutes' walk of Greenbank. Terms £130 to £200 weekly. Guests have the use of our garden. An excellent base. Dogs welcome by arrangement, £10 charged per pet. **ETC ★★★**. Apply: **Mr D.G. Matthews, Greenbank, 236 West Malvern Road, Malvern WR14 4BG (01684 567328).**

YORKSHIRE

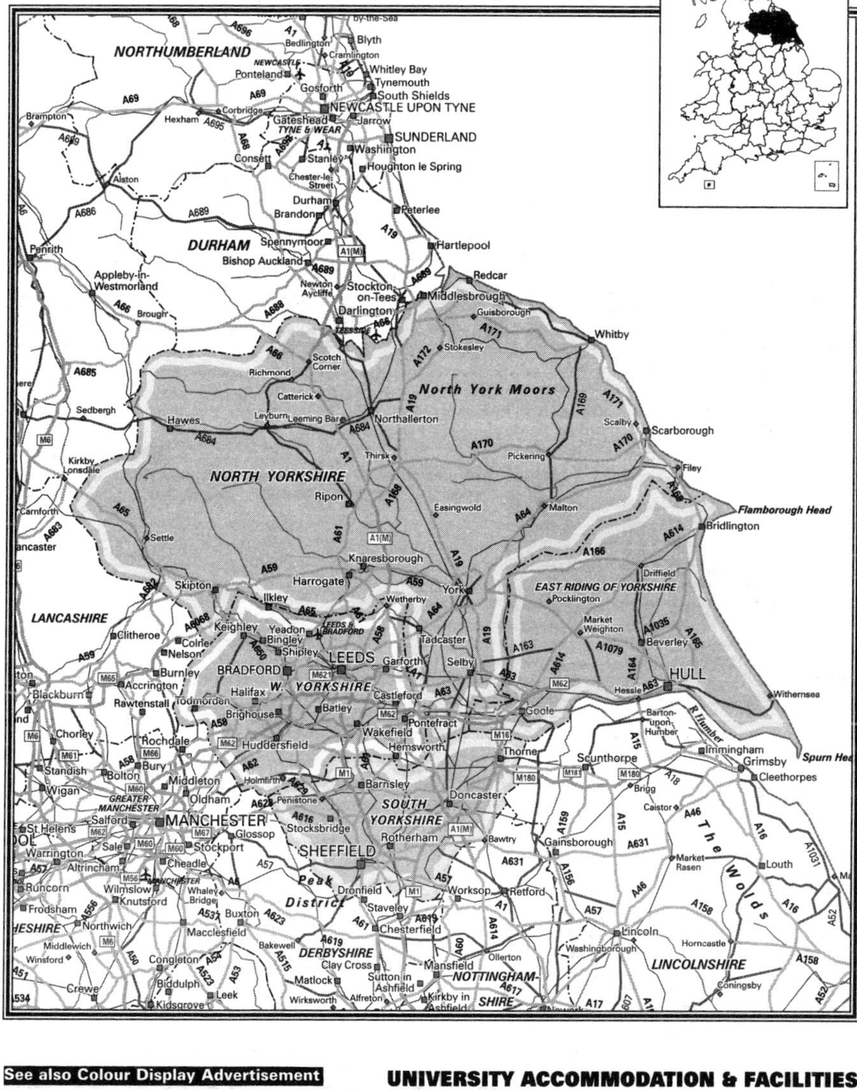

UNIVERSITY ACCOMMODATION & FACILITIES

Budget accommodation or fully tailored packages (0870 712 5002; Fax: 020 7017 8273). En suite designer halls across the UK. Groups of any age or size. Sports facilities all year. Tell us your needs and we'll find a location and package to suit.
e-mail: enquiries@thesv.com

The FHG Directory of Website Addresses
on pages 243 – 272 is a useful quick reference guide for holiday accommodation with e-mail and/or website details

ENGLAND

EAST YORKSHIRE

BRIDLINGTON

Ash-Lee Holiday Apartments, 4 Vernon Road, Bridlington YO15 2HQ (01262 400485). Sleeps 2-6. Situated close to shops and beach, only five minutes from Leisure World. Well established and highly recommended, the apartments are furnished to a high standard, with bed linen included. All have colour TV, fridge and micowave; own shower and toilet. Large apartments have two bedrooms. Chalet also available, sleeps six. Open all year, reduction for late and early season. Winner of Bridlington in Bloom 2000-2001.Send S.A.E with dates and number in party to resident proprietor **Mrs Janet Greatorex.**
website: www.bridlington-flats.co.uk

BRIDLINGTON

Mrs Audrey Marshall, Rialto Holiday Flats, 63/ 65 Trinity Road, Bridlington YO15 2HF (01262 677653). Sleep 2-8. Well established and highly recommended fully equipped flats situated close to the North Beach. All flats have their own private facilities and include a colour TV. Car park and public telephone available. Bed linen and cots may be hired. Close to shops, Leisure World and North Beach. Phone for a brochure. Prices from £90 to £230. Fully Fire Certificated. **ETC ★★**
e-mail: enquiries@rialto-bridlington.co.uk
website: www.rialto-bridlington.co.uk

Why Yorkshire?

With ruined abbeys and castles, great houses and gardens framed by high moors and wooded hills, Yorkshire is a place of great natural beauty. This beauty is conserved in three national parks: the Yorkshire Dales, the Peak District and the North York Moors. In contrast to nature, Yorkshire is also home to The West Yorkshire Playhouse, The Yorkshire Sculpture Park and The National Museum of Photography, Film & Television. The Millennium Galleries, the new multi-million MAGNA and The Deep all make it a worthwhile place to visit.
For further information contact the Yorkshire Tourist Board,
Tel: **01904 707070** or visit **www.yorkshirevisitor.com**

BRIDLINGTON

Lunbelle Holiday Flats, 49 Trinity Road, Bridlington YO15 2HF. Sleep 2-6. Spotless, sound-proof, well-equipped flats situated two minutes from the beach and five minutes from the town centre. Flats have their own facilities, including controlled central heating, TV, microwave and ironing facilities. Chairlift to first floor. Small dogs accepted. Parking for three/five cars on a first come, first served basis. NEW four–six berth 35' x 12' caravan situated on the superb Thornwick Seafarm Holiday Centre at Flamborough, only four miles from Bridlington, with a choice of four bays within a half to two miles. Accommodation comprises: double bedroom, twin bedroom and bed settee in lounge – bed linen provided. Site facilities include three bars (with entertainment), indoor pool, kids' club, cafeteria, food takeaway and supermarket. Contact address only: **Mrs L.E. Ward, 19 Birch Close, Priory Grange, Hull HU5 5YR (01482 572641; mobile: 07771 754656) e-mail: brid-accom@talk21.com**   **website: www.bridlington.net/business/lunbelle**

DRIFFIELD

The Wold Cottage, Driffield. Brand new barn conversion comprising two self-catering cottages and one apartment. "The Granary" has spacious ground floor accommodation, entrance with cloakroom, kitchen, dining area and lounge with sofa bed if needed. First floor has one double and one twin bedroom both with en suite facilities. "The Hayloft" has ground floor double room with shower en suite, first floor twin room with bath en suite. Kitchen, dining area, sitting area with arched window, south-facing with open views of the Wolds. " Bar End" is a four-poster suite with kitchen and sitting area, en suite corner bath with walk-in shower. Prices from £160 - £380 per week, includes VAT, heating, bed linen, towels, electricity and laundry facilities. Non-smoking. No pets. Contact: **Mrs K Gray, The Wold Cottage, Wold Newton, Driffield YO25 3HL (Tel & Fax: 01262 470696).**

KILHAM

Mrs P.M. Savile, Raven Hill Farm, Kilham, Driffield YO25 4EG (01377 267217). Working farm. Sleeps 8+2 plus cots. With delightful views overlooking the Yorkshire Wolds, ideally situated for touring the East Coast, Bridlington, Scarborough, Moors and York, this secluded and private four-bedroomed farmhouse is set in its own acre of woodland lawns and orchard, with garden furniture, summerhouse and children's play area. Games room in converted Granary in the main farm area 200 yards away. Clean and comfortable and very well equipped including dishwasher, microwave, automatic washing machine and dryer; two bathrooms, payphone, TV and video. Fully centrally heated. Beds are made up for your arrival; cots and high chair available. Three miles to the nearest village of Kilham with Post Office, general stores, garage and public houses. Available all year. Terms from £270 to £380 (low season), £380 to £505 (high season) per week. Brochure on request. **ETC ★★★**

PUBLISHER'S NOTE

FHG

While every effort is made to ensure accuracy, we regret that FHG Publications cannot accept responsibility for errors, misrepresentations or omissions in our entries or any consequences thereof. Prices in particular should be checked because we go to press early. We will follow up complaints but cannot act as arbiters or agents for either party.

ENGLAND

GRASSINGTON

Mrs Judith M. Joy, Jerry and Ben's, Hebden, Skipton BD23 5DL (01756 752369; Fax: 01756 753370). Properties sleep 3/6/8/9. Jerry and Ben's stands in two acres of grounds in one of the most attractive parts of the Yorkshire Dales National Park. Seven properties; Ghyll Cottage (sleeps eight) with dishwasher; Mamie's Cottage (sleeps eight) with dishwasher; Paradise End (sleeps six); Robin Middle (sleeps six); High Close (sleeps nine); Cruck Rise (sleeps six); Raikes Side (sleeps two/three). All have parking, electric cooker, microwave, toaster, fridge, colour TV, electric heating and immersion heater; lounge, dining area, bathroom and shower; cots if required. Fully equipped, including linen if requested. Washing machine and telephone available. Well behaved pets accepted. Open all year. Fishing and bathing close by. Terms from £90 to £375. SAE, please, for detailed brochure. Suitable for some disabled guests.
e-mail: dawjoy@aol.com

HARROGATE

Mrs Hardcastle, Southfield Farm, Darley, Harrogate HG3 2PR (01423 780258). Two well equipped holiday cottages on a farm in an attractive area between Harrogate and Pateley Bridge. An ideal place to explore the whole of the dale with York and Herriot country within easy driving distance. Riverside walks, village shop and post office within quarter-of-a-mile, and local pub one mile away. Each cottage has two bedrooms, one double and one with bunk beds. Games room. Large lawn for ball games, with garden chairs and barbecue. Pets welcome. Ample car parking. Prices from £170 to £200 low season, £200 to £270 high season.

See also Colour Display Advertisement

RUDDING
HOLIDAY PARK

HARROGATE

Rudding Holiday Park, Follifoot, Harrogate HG3 1JH (01423 870439; Fax: 01423 870859). These superior holiday cottages and lodges are set in picturesque surroundings just south of Harrogate. The luxury cottages have been completely restored retaining many of their original features (sleep 2-10 persons). The Timber Lodges are situated in beautiful parkland, many overlooking a small lake (sleep 2-6 persons). All are centrally heated and fully equipped. Facilities within the private country estate include; heated swimming pool and paddling pool, children's adventure playground, Deer House, games room, 18 hole Pay and Play golf course plus floodlit driving range. Please send for free illustrated brochure. **ETC ★★★★★ Lodges, ★★★ Cottages.**
e-mail: holiday-park@ruddingpark.com   **website: www.ruddingpark.com**

HARROGATE

Mrs Janet Hollings, Dougill Hall, Summerbridge, Harrogate HG3 4JR (01423 780277). Working farm. Sleeps 4. Dougill Hall is of Georgian design, built in 1722 by the Dougill family who lived on this farm from 1496 to 1803. It is in Nidderdale, half-a-mile from the village of Summerbridge, just by the River Nidd, where there is fishing available for visitors. There are good facilities for horse riding, tennis, swimming, squash, etc. Well situated for the walking enthusiast and within easy reach of the Dales, the beautiful and ancient city of York, Fountains Abbey, How Stean Gorge and many other places of interest. The Old Cooling House flat sleeps up to four people. Well equipped, with electric cooker and fridge, iron, vacuum cleaner. Linen by arrangement. Pets permitted. Car essential, parking. Terms from £135 to £220. SAE please for details.

HAWES

Jane Allison, Gaudy House Farm, Gayle, Near Hawes DL8 3NA (01969 667231). Sleeps 2/5. Traditional stone barns converted into three spacious self-contained dwellings with log fires. Sleeping two/five people. Set in 25 acres of farmland. Peaceful, comfortable, unique setting on the Pennine Way with magnificent views over Wensleydale, ideal for exploring the Dales. One mile from the market town of Hawes. Reasonable rentals all year round from £150 to £320 per week. **ETC ★★**

HELMSLEY (Near)

Mrs Rickatson, Summerfield Farm, Harome, York YO62 5JJ (01439 748238). Working farm. Sleeps 6. Enjoy walking or touring in North Yorkshire Moors National Park. Lovely area 20 miles north of York. Comfortable and well-equipped farmhouse wing with electric cooker, fridge, microwave and automatic washing machine. Sit beside a log fire in the evenings. Linen supplied. Trout stream on farm. Children and dogs welcome. Weekly terms £95 to £230. Mid-week and weekend bookings are possible. For further information phone or write for leaflet.

HORTON-IN-RIBBLESDALE

The Byres Sleeps 6 plus cot and **Selside Farm Cottage Sleeps 4 plus cot.** Both situated in the hamlet of Selside in the heart of the Three Peaks, Ingleborough, Whernside and Pen-y-ghent. Ideal for walking, touring, caving, the Dales, west coast, Settle to Carlisle railway. Sorry no pets. THE BYRES: one double and two twin bedrooms; bathroom, lounge with coal fire, dining room, kitchen, patio, garden. Washer, electric cooker, fridge, freezer, microwave, colour TV, video. Electricity, coal, heating, linen, towels included in rent. From £230 to £370 per week. SELSIDE FARM COTTAGE: one double and one twin bedroom, bathroom, lounge with dining area, kitchen, garden. Electric cooker, fridge, spin dryer, microwave, colour TV. Heating, linen and towels included in rent. Electricity included. From £140 to

£245 per week. **ETC ★★★/★★★★**. SAE please to: **Mrs S.E. Lambert, Selside Farm, Selside, Horton-in-Ribblesdale, Settle BD24 0HZ (Tel & Fax: 01729 860367).**

A useful index of towns and counties appears at the back of this book on pages 273-276. Refer also to Contents Pages 44/45.

ENGLAND

ENGLAND

LEYBURN

Park Grange Farm Cottage. A working farm situated just a mile from the picturesque market town of Leyburn, Wensleydale. Comfortable self-catering cottage. Superb views of beautiful countryside. Ideal for walking, cycling, fishing, horse-riding, playing golf and touring the Dales. The cottage comprises two double rooms, one bunk-bed room and a double bed-settee if required. The kitchen is equipped with cooker, fridge, dishwasher and washer. Children, dogs and horses welcome. Grazing/stabling for your equine friends, and kennels available if you wish to bring working dogs on holiday. We cater for special occasions, and include a Yorkshire welcome pack with each booking. Short breaks available. For brochure and rates, contact: **Pam Sheppard, Low Gill Farm, Agglethorpe, Leyburn DL8 4TN (01969 640258).**

LEYBURN (Wensleydale)

Thorney Holiday Cottages, Spennithorne, Leyburn. Sleep 2-6. Two cottages and one flat in delightful village of Spennithorne. Modernised to high standard, with one, two or three bedrooms; fully equipped with microwave ovens, colour TV and video recorder; bed linen and towels provided. Children welcome, pets by arrangement only. Cottages are available all year, short break bookings taken; wood-burning stoves and night storage heaters for chilly evenings. FREE electricity. Set in their own grounds, these cottages provide comfortable accommodation for a stay in "Herriot" country, with its castles, waterfalls, museums, fishing, walks and magnificent views. Terms from £75 to £380. Details from **Michael and Ann Gaines, No.1 Thorney Cottage, Spennithorne, Leyburn DL8 5PR (01969 622496).**

LOW BENTHAM

Mrs L.J. Story, Holmes Farm, Low Bentham, Lancaster LA2 7DE (015242 61198). Sleeps 4. Attractively converted and well equipped stone cottage adjoining 17th century farm house. In a secluded position surrounded by 127 acres of beautiful pastureland. Ideal base for visiting Dales, Lake District and coast. ETC ★★★★

MARTON

Mr & Mrs A.W. Turnbull, Oak Lodge, White Thorn Farm, Rook Barugh, Kirkbymoorside YO62 6PF (01751 431298). Charming, detached former stable with open beams and log burners, tastefully furnished and well equipped throughout. On a family-run farm (beef, cows, sheep) surrounded by open countryside with easy access to bridleways and footpaths. Centrally situated for the North York Moors with its famous steam railway (four miles); York 27 miles, coast 22 miles, Castle Howard just 20 minutes. Available all year. Terms from £200 to £350 per week.
e-mail: turnbull@whitethornfarm.fsnet.co.uk
website: www.cottageguide.co.uk/oak-lodge

Terms quoted in this publication may be subject to increase if rises in costs necessitate

NORTHALLERTON

Julie & Jim Griffith, Hill House Farm, Little Langton, Northallerton DL7 0PZ (01609 770643; Fax: 01609 760438). Sleep 2-6. These former farm buildings have been converted into four well-equipped cottages, retaining original beams. Cosily heated for year round appeal. Peaceful setting with magnificent views. Centrally located between Dales and Moors with York, Whitby and Scarborough all within easy driving distance. Pets welcome. Weekly rates from £150 inclusive of all linen, towels, heating and electricity. Short breaks available. Pub food one mile. Golf two miles, shops three miles. Please telephone for a free brochure.
e-mail: info@Hillhousefarmcottages.com

ROBIN HOOD'S BAY

Mrs F. Harland, Lingers Hill Farm, Thorpe Lane, Robin Hood's Bay, Whitby YO22 4TQ (01947 880608). This semi-detached cosy character cottage, situated on the edge of the village at Robin Hood's Bay and overlooking the coastline and countryside, makes an excellent home from which to walk, cycle or tour the magnificent surroundings of the North York Moors National Park. Accommodating two to four guests, the cottage has a lounge with beamed ceiling, colour TV, fully-equipped kitchen/dining area, two bedrooms, bathroom and toilet. There is a gas fire and central heating and guests have use of a garden with picnic tables and benches. There are shops, a post office and pubs within 250 yards. Electricity is by £1 coin meter, with gas and bed linen included in rent. Private parking. Open all year. Terms from £165 to £295, with short breaks available from November to March. Please telephone or send SAE for our brochure. **ETC ★★★**

ROBIN HOOD'S BAY (Near)

Ken and Nealia Pattinson, South House Farm, Fylingthorpe, Whitby YO22 4UQ (01947 880243). Glorious countryside in North York Moors National Park. Five minutes' walk to beach at Boggle Hole. Super large farmhouse sleeps 10/12 people. Two spacious detached cottages sleep four and six. All inclusive and fully-equipped. Gardens. Parking. Terms from £120 to £1000.

SCARBOROUGH

Mr & Mrs J Donnelly, Gowland Farm, Gowland Lane, Cloughton, Scarborough YO13 0DU (01723 870924). Sleeps 2/7. Four charming converted stone barns situated within the beautiful North Yorkshire Moors National Park enjoying wonderful views of Harwood Dale and only two miles from the coast. The cottages have been sympathetically converted from traditional farm buildings, furnished and fitted to a very high standard, retaining the old features as well as having modern comforts. They are fully carpeted, warm and cosy with central heating and double glazing. Electric fires and colour TVs in all lounges. Well equipped kitchens. All linen and bedding provided (duvets). Large garden with plenty of car parking space. Garden furniture and laundry facilities. Sorry, no pets. Open all year. From £120 to £450 per week. *WHITE ROSE AWARD SELF-CATERING HOLIDAY OF THE YEAR RUNNER-UP 1993.*
website: www.gowlandfarm.co.uk

ENGLAND

SKIPTON

Mrs Brenda Jones, New Close Farm, Kirkby Malham, Skipton BD23 4DP (01729 830240; Fax: 01729 830179). Sleeps 5. A supa dupa cottage on New Close Farm in the heart of Craven Dales with panoramic views over the Aire Valley. Excellent area for walking, cycling, fishing, golf and touring. Two double and one single bedrooms; bathroom. Colour TV and video. Full central heating and double glazing. Bed linen, towels and all amenities included in the price. Low Season £250, High Season £300; deposit required. Sorry, no young children and no pets. Non-smokers preferred. The weather can't be guaranteed but your comfort can. *FHG DIPLOMA AWARD PAST WINNER*.
e-mail: brendajones@newclosefarmyorkshire.co.uk
website: www.newclosefarmyorkshire.co.uk

SKIPTON

Anthea and John Cowan, Ellershaw Farm, Halton Gill, Skipton BD23 5QN (01756 770241). In the heart of the beautiful Yorkshire Dales National Park, Halton Gill, the last village in Littondale, is quiet and unspoilt. The two traditional stone barns have been converted to provide high quality, low cost accommodation for groups of 10-40. Both are warm, welcoming and spacious, with oil-fired central heating and every facility. HALTON GILL BUNKBARN sleeps 40 in eight bedrooms and ELLERGILL sleeps 12 in three bedrooms. Please ring or e-mail for availability, further information, prices and special out of season offers.
e-mail: info@halton-gill-bunkbarn.fsnet.co.uk   website: www.haltongillbunkbarns.co.uk

STOCKTON-ON-FOREST

Orillia Cottages, Stockton-on-Forest, York. Four converted farm workers' cottages in a courtyard setting at the rear of the 300-year-old farmhouse in Stockton-on-Forest three miles from York. Golf course nearby, pub 200 yards away serving good food; post office, newsagents and general stores within easy reach. Convenient half-hourly bus service to York and the coast. Fully furnished and equipped for two to eight, the cottages comprise lounge with colour TV, etc; kitchen area with microwave, oven, grill and hob; bedrooms have double and twin beds. Gas central heating. Non-smokers preferred. Children and pets welcome. Available Easter to October - Short Breaks may be available. Terms from £195 to £495 weekly includes heating, linen, etc. Please contact **Mr & Mrs G. Hudson, Orillia House, 89 The Village, Stockton-on-Forest, York (01904 400600).**
website: www.orilliacottages.co.uk

SUTTON-ON-FOREST (Near York)

Stable and Wren Cottages. Working farm. Sleeping 2 and 4 plus cot. Converted from old working stables these single storey cottages while retaining the old roof beams are spacious, comfortable and fully equipped. Storage heating plus electric fire and bed linen are all included in the price - no extras! Cot available. Set on a mainly arable farm one mile from Sutton the cottages are in a very peaceful rural location yet are very handy for trips into the old city of York, with many stores and shops on the outskirts of town. This is a good central touring base for visits to the North Yorkshire Moors, East Coast and Dales. Well insulated and cosy these cottages are also ideal for winter holidays/short breaks too. Plenty of excellent reasonable eating places all round the area. Prices from £140 to £310 per week. **ETC ★★★.** Brochures from **Mrs H. Knowlson, Thrush House, Sutton-on-Forest, York YO61 1ED (Tel & Fax: 01347 810225).**
e-mail: kmkholcottyksuk@aol.com

THIRSK

Foxhills Hideaways, Felixkirk, Thirsk YO7 2DS (01845 537575). Quiet and secluded, but easily accessible, these four Scandinavian log cabins are situated between the North York Moors and the Dales National Parks. Convenient for the coast and the city of York, with wonderful walks from the top of Sutton Bank. Pretty garden setting, centrally heated and fully equipped. Pets are welcome. There is a village pub just around the corner and we are open all year. Fully inclusive prices (£180 to £340 per week). Out of season short breaks from £90 inc. Please write or phone for brochure.

THIRSK

Mrs M. Backhouse, Mowbray Stable Cottages, Stockton Road, South Kilvington YO7 2LY (01845 522605). Situated within a mile of Thirsk and the village of South Kilvington, these recently converted cottages provide an ideal base for exploring the North Yorkshire Moors, Yorkshire Dales, and within easy reach of York, Durham, and the east coast. COTTAGE NO. 1 sleeps four. One double bedroom, one twin, a large shower room, combined living/kitchen/dining room. Ramped access for wheelchairs, wider doors throughout, handrails etc. in shower room. COTTAGE NO. 2 sleeps two/four. One double bedroom, en suite shower room, living room with bed settee, separate kitchen/dining room. Not suitable for wheelchair users. Both cottages are equipped with an electric oven/hob, fridge, microwave, colour TV, shaver point and gas central heating. Linen, but not towels, are included in price. Pets welcome by arrangement. Car essential. Terms from £180 to £290 for Cottage No.1, £150 to £240 for Cottage No. 2. Short breaks available.

See also Colour Display Advertisement

THORNTON LE DALE

Easthill Farm House and Gardens, Thornton le Dale, Near Pickering YO18 7QP (01751 474561). Three luxury apartments and one cottage sleeping two to ten. All beautifully equipped and furnished to a very high standard. Set in two-and-a-half acres of landscaped gardens/woodland on the edge of the picturesque village of Thornton-le-Dale. Also three Scandinavian 'A' Frame chalets nestling in the pine wood with magnificent views over open countryside (sleep two/six). Ideally situated for visiting North York Moors, forestry, coast or York. Feed the hens and pigs enclosed in some of the woodland. Children very welcome. Friendly family-run business to high standards. Tennis court, games room, putting green, barbecue, jacuzzi and play area. Open all year. Sorry, no pets. Terms from £170 to £798 per week fully inclusive. Special terms for off-season breaks. **ETC ★★★★.** Contact: **Diane Stenton** for brochure.
e-mail: info@easthill-farm-holidays.co.uk   **website: www.easthill-farm-holidays.co.uk**

See also Colour Display Advertisement

WEST SCRAFTON

Westclose House (Allaker), West Scrafton, Coverdale, Leyburn DL8 4RM. Stone farmhouse with panoramic views, high in the Yorkshire Dales National Park (Herriot family's house in 'All Creatures Great and Small' on TV). Three bedrooms (sleeps six/eight), sitting and dining rooms with wood-burning stoves, kitchen, bathroom, WC. House has electric storage heating, cooker, microwave, fridge, washing machine, colour TV, telephone. Garden, large barn, stables. Access from lane, private parking, no through traffic. Excellent walking from front door, near Wensleydale. Pets welcome. Self-catering from £400 per week. For bookings telephone: **020 8567 4862**
e-mail: ac@adriancave.com
website: www.adriancave.com/allaker

WHITBY

Swallow Holiday Cottages, The Farm, Stainsacre, Whitby YO22 4NT (01947 603790). Stainsacre is an excellent base for many popular tourist areas. Discover historic Whitby, two miles away, pretty fishing villages, countryside with waymarked walks, etc. Four cottages with panoramic view of the Esk valley each with one or two bedrooms, plus a three bedroom detached house. All are fully furnished, including linen. Private parking. Children and dogs welcome. Non-smoking accommodation available. Resident owners Jill and Brian McNeil look forward to welcoming you. Please phone or write for a brochure. Weekly rates from £110 to £410.

YORK

Homefinders Holidays, 11 Walmgate, York YO1 9TX (01904 632660). Quality flats and town houses. Central location, all facilities. Garages/parking. Brochure.

YORK

Baile Hill Cottage, Bishophill, York. Sleeps 4 to 5. This Victorian town cottage is in a peaceful area within the historic city centre and overlooks the ancient city walls with roadside parking outside the front door. It is furnished and equipped to a very high standard including a fully fitted modern kitchen with a microwave. The master bedroom has a four-poster bed, the second has twin single pine beds. The lounge has a cosy coal-effect gas fire and a colour teletext TV. The Victorian style bathroom has gold plated and dark mahogany fittings with an over bath shower. There is a private patio garden area, barbecue and utlilty room with an automatic washing machine and tumble dryer. **ETC ★★★.** For further information contact: **Mrs Hodgson, Avalon, North Lane, Wheldrake, York YO19 6AY (01904 448670; Fax: 01904 448908).**

e-mail: enquires@holiday-cottage.org.uk   website: www.holiday-cottage.org.uk

YORK

Mr Chris Tinkler, Kirby Mills, Kirkbymoorside, York YO62 6NP (01751 432000; Fax: 01751 432300). Sympathetically restored stable mews cottages in converted two-acre 18th century watermill complex on the River Dove. Tranquil, luxury accommodation with linen and towels, TV, video and central heating included as standard. Bed and bath downstairs, living upstairs with "indoor balcony". Garden and barbecue by millrace. Breakfasts and dinners can be provided in the Mill by arrangement. On-site parking. Open all year round.
e-mail: cornmill@kirbymills.demon.co.uk
website: www.kirbymills.demon.co.uk

YORK

Merricote Cottages, Malton Road, York. Sleep 2-8. Eight cottages set in a beautiful rural location. The well-equipped, single storey accommodation includes living room with TV/VCR, kitchen area with microwave, fridge, oven and hob, and either double or twin bedrooms. Merricote Farm is set in eight acres adjacent to a plant nursery, three miles east of the city of York. An ideal location for exploring York, the North York Moors and the east coast towns of Bridlington, Filey and Scarborough. Bed linen, towels, heating and electricity, laundry facilities and a large garden are included.Terms from £150 to £585 per week. **ETC ★★★.** **Andrew Williamson, Merricote Farm, Malton Road, York YO32 9TL (01904 400256).**
e-mail: merricote@hotmail.com
website: www.merricote-holiday-cottages.co.uk

YORK

Wolds View Holiday Cottages, Yapham, Pocklington. Attractive, well-equipped accommodation situated in unspoilt countryside at the foot of the Yorkshire Wolds. Four units, sleeping from three to six, three of which are suitable for wheelchairs. Themed holidays, with transport provided, exploring the villages and countryside nearby; York only 12 miles. Terms from £145 to £540 per week. Short Breaks available. Pets welcome. Category 1,2 and 3 National Accessible Scheme. For further details contact: **E. and M.S.A. Woodliffe, Mill Farm, Yapham, Pocklington, York YO42 1PH (01759 302172).**

The FHG Directory of Website Addresses

on pages 243 – 272 is a useful quick reference guide for holiday accommodation with e-mail and/or website details

Richmond Castle, North Yorkshire

𝔉𝔥𝔊 Diploma Winners 2002

Each year we award a small number of diplomas to holiday proprietors whose services have been specially commended by our readers. The following were our FHG Diploma Winners for 2002.

England

DEVON
Woolacombe Bay Holiday Park,
Woolacombe, North Devon
EX34 7HW (01271 870343).

LANCASHIRE
Mrs Holdsworth,
Broadwater Hotel,
356 Marine Road, East Promenade
Morecambe, Lancashire LA4 5AQ
(01524 411333).

Peter & Susan Bicker,
Kelvin Private Hotel,
Reads Avenue, Blackpool,
Lancashire FY1 4JJ
(01253 620293).

LINCOLNSHIRE
Sue Phillips & John Lister,
Cawthorpe Farm, Cawthorpe
Bourne, Lincolnshire PE10 0AB
(01778 426697).

OXFORDSHIRE
Liz Roach, The Old Bakery,
Skirmett, Nr Henley on Thames
Oxfordshire RG9 6TD
(01491 638309).

SOMERSET
Pat & Sue Weir, Slipper Cottage,
41 Bishopston, Montacute,
Somerset TA15 6UX
(01935 823073)

Scotland

ARGYLL & BUTE
David Quibell,
Rosneath Castle Caravan Park
Near Helensburgh,
Argyll & Bute G84 0QS
(01436 831208)

DUNDEE & ANGUS
Carlogie House Hotel,
Carlogie Road, Carnoustie,
Dundee DD7 6LD
(01241 853185)

EDINBURGH & LOTHIANS
Geraldine Hamilton,
Crosswoodhill Farm, West Calder
Edinburgh & Lothians EH55 8LP
(01501 785205)

FIFE
Mr Alastair Clark,
Old Manor Country House Hotel,
Lundin Links, Nr St Andrews
Fife KY8 6AJ
(01333 320368)

HIGHLANDS
N & J McCallum, The Neuk
Corpach, Fort William PH33 7LE
(01397 772244)

HELP IMPROVE BRITISH TOURISM STANDARDS

Why not write and tell us about the holiday accommodation you have chosen from one of our popular publications? Complete a nomination form giving details of why you think YOUR host or hostess should win one of our attractive framed diplomas and send it to:
FHG Publications, Abbey Mill Business Centre, Seedhill, Paisley PA1 1TJ

THE FHG DIPLOMA

HELP IMPROVE BRITISH TOURIST STANDARDS

You are choosing holiday accommodation from our very popular FHG Publications.
Whether it be a hotel, guest house, farmhouse or self-catering accommodation, we think you will find it hospitable, comfortable and clean, and your host and hostess friendly and helpful.

Why not write and tell us about it?

As a recognition of the generally well-run and excellent holiday accommodation reviewed in our publications, we at FHG Publications Ltd. present a diploma to proprietors who receive the highest recommendation from their guests who are also readers of our Guides. If you care to write to us praising the holiday you have booked through FHG Publications Ltd. – whether this be board, self-catering accommodation, a sporting or a caravan holiday, what you say will be evaluated and the proprietors who reach our final list will be contacted.

The winning proprietor will receive an attractive framed diploma to display on his premises as recognition of a high standard of comfort, amenity and hospitality. FHG Publications Ltd. offer this diploma as a contribution towards the improvement of standards in tourist accommodation in Britain. Help your excellent host or hostess to win it!

FHG DIPLOMA

We nominate ....

....

Because

Name ....

Address ....

....

Telephone No...

Ratings You Can Trust

ENGLAND

The English Tourism Council (formerly the English Tourist Board) has joined with the **AA** and **RAC** to create a new, easily understood quality rating for serviced accommodation, giving a clear guide of what to expect.

HOTELS are given a rating from One to Five **Stars** – the more Stars, the higher the quality and the greater the range of facilities and level of services provided.

GUEST ACCOMMODATION, which includes guest houses, bed and breakfasts, inns and farmhouses, is rated from One to Five **Diamonds**. Progressively higher levels of quality and customer care must be provided for each one of the One to Five Diamond ratings.

HOLIDAY PARKS, TOURING PARKS and CAMPING PARKS are now also assessed using **Stars**. Standards of quality range from a One Star (acceptable) to a Five Star (exceptional) park.

Look out also for the new **SELF-CATERING** Star ratings. The more **Stars** (from One to Five) awarded to an establishment, the higher the levels of quality you can expect. Establishments at higher rating levels also have to meet some additional requirements for facilities.

SCOTLAND

Star Quality Grades will reflect the most important aspects of a visit, such as the warmth of welcome, efficiency and friendliness of service, the quality of the food and the cleanliness and condition of the furnishings, fittings and decor.

THE MORE STARS, THE HIGHER THE STANDARDS.

The description, such as Hotel, Guest House, Bed and Breakfast, Lodge, Holiday Park, Self-catering etc tells you the type of property and style of operation.

WALES

Places which score highly will have an especially welcoming atmosphere and pleasing ambience, high levels of comfort and guest care, and attractive surroundings enhanced by thoughtful design and attention to detail

STAR QUALITY GUIDE FOR

HOTELS, GUEST HOUSES AND FARMHOUSES

SELF-CATERING ACCOMMODATION
(Cottages, Apartments, Houses)

CARAVAN HOLIDAY HOME PARKS
(Holiday Parks, Touring Parks, Camping Parks)

★★★★★ Exceptional quality
★★★★ Excellent quality
★★★ Very good quality
★★ Good quality
★ Fair to good quality

In England, Scotland and Wales, all graded properties are inspected annually by Tourist Authority trained Assessors.

SCOTLAND
Self-catering Holidays

See also Colour Display Advertisement **UNIVERSITY ACCOMMODATION & FACILITIES**
Budget accommodation or fully tailored packages (0870 712 5002; Fax: 020 7017 8273). En suite designer halls across the UK. Groups of any age or size. Sports facilities all year. Tell us your needs and we'll find a location and package to suit. **e-mail: enquiries@thesv.com**

U.K. AND EMERALD
Cottage Holidays

www.selfcottages.co.uk
BEST EVER BROCHURE OUT NOW
IN SCOTLAND

✓ **DISCOUNTS FOR COUPLES**   ✓ **PETS GO FREE**

Most cottages provide linen and include fuel and power in the price.
**MANY LESS THAN £199 PER WEEK FROM OCTOBER TO APRIL.
LOTS AT LESS THAN £380 PER WEEK IN JULY AND AUGUST.**

**CALL FOR YOUR FREE
2003 COLOUR BROCHURE** **01756 697346**

SCOTLAND

ABERDEEN, BANFF & MORAY

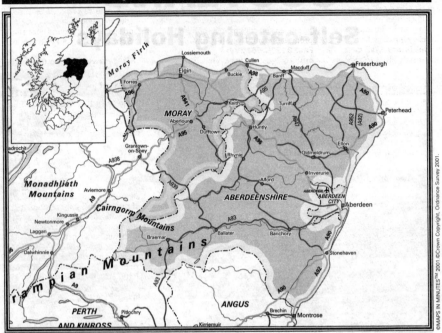

ABERDEEN

University of Aberdeen, Sales Office, Residential and Catering Services, Kings College, Aberdeen AB24 3FY. (01224 273444; Fax: 01224 276246) Sleep 4/7. Situated on the edge of Seaton Park and Old Aberdeen, the Hillhead Halls Complex of self-catering accommodation is available during Easter and Summer vacations. Sleeping four to seven guests, the flats are centrally heated, fully furnished and suitable for children. Bed linen, telephone and cooking utensils are provided along with a 'Welcome Pack` on arrival to get you started. Other facilities on site include a laundry, shop, TV lounge, bar, leisure facilities and a car park. **STB ★★** *SELF-CATERING.*
e-mail: accommodation@abdn.ac.uk
website: www.abdn.ac.uk/catering

See also Colour Display Advertisement

ABERDEEN

The Robert Gordon University, Business & Vacation Accommodation, Schoolhill, Aberdeen AB10 1FR (01224 262134; Fax: 01224 262144). The Robert Gordon University in the heart of Aberdeen offers a variety of accommodation in the city centre to visitors from June through to August. Aberdeen is ideal for visiting Royal Deeside, castles and historic buildings, playing golf or touring the Malt Whisky Trail. The city itself is a place to discover and Aberdonians are friendly and welcoming people. We offer 2-Star self-catering accommodation for individuals or groups at superb rates in either en suite or shared facility flats. Each party has exclusive use of their own flat during their stay. The flats are self-contained, centrally heated, fully furnished and suitable for children and disabled guests. All flats have colour TV, microwave, bedlinen, towels, all cooking utensils and a complimentary "welcome pack" of basic groceries. There are laundry and telephone facilities on site as well as ample car parking spaces. *ASSC MEMBER.*
e-mail: p.macinnes@rgu.ac.uk   **website: www.scotland2000.com/rgu**

ABERDEEN

Holiday Flat. To suit couple or small family. Clean, comfortable and conveniently located for Aberdeen city centre and attractions. Lounge, double bedroom, bathroom with shower, fully equipped galley kitchen. heating, lighting and all bedding included. Regular bus service to city centre. No smoking and no pets. STB ★★★ *SELF-CATERING.* ALSO PROPERTY IN WICK. Sleeps up to 6. Close to airport, bus and rail stations. Lounge with DVD, SKY TV, Playstation; dining kitchen, bathroom, en suite double bedroom, twin/double and single/twin; ground floor single. Fully equipped. Details of both properties from: **Donald Campbell, The Old Schoolhouse, Ulbster, Lybster, Caithness KW2 6AA (Tel & Fax: 01955 651297)**
e-mail: ulbster@ntlworld.com   **www.visit.ourflat.co.uk**   **www.assc.co.uk**

`See also Colour Display Advertisement`   ## ELGIN

Mrs J.M. Shaw, Sheriffston Farm Chalet, Sheriffston, Elgin IV30 8LA (01343 842695). An "A" frame chalet situated on a working farm. "Habitat" furnished, fully equipped for two to six people, colour TV, bed linen, duvets. Beautiful rural location in Moray – famous for flowers – district of lowlands, highlands, rivers, forests, lovely beaches, historic towns, welcoming people. Excellent local facilities. Moray golf tickets available. From £180 to £300. January to December. **STB ★★** *SELF-CATERING. ASSC MEMBER.*
e-mail: jennifer_m_shaw@hotmail.com

`See also Colour Display Advertisement`   ## FORRES

Tulloch Lodges. Peace, Relaxation and Comfort in beautiful Natural Surroundings. One of the loveliest self-catering sites in Scotland. Modern, spacious, attractive and beautifully equipped Scandinavian lodges for up to six in glorious woodland/water setting. Perfect for the Highlands and Historic Grampian, especially the Golden Moray Coast and the Golf, Castle and Malt Whisky Trails. £235 to £675 per week. **STB ★★★★** *SELF-CATERING..* For a brochure contact: **Tulloch Lodges, Rafford, Forres, Moray IV36 2RU (01309 673311; Fax: 01309 671515).** *ASSC MEMBER.*
website: www.tullochlodges.co.uk

GRANTOWN-ON-SPEY

Mr & Mrs J.R. Taylor, Milton of Cromdale, Grantown-on-Spey PH26 3PH (01479 872415). Sleeps 4. Fully modernised cottage available Easter to October. Excellent centre for touring with golf, tennis and trekking within easy reach. Large garden with views of River Spey and Cromdale Hills. Fully equipped except linen. Refrigerator, electric cooker. Two double bedrooms sleeping four. Bathroom with shower. Colour TV. Children and pets welcome. Car desirable. Terms £100 per week.

`See also Colour Display Advertisement`   ## INVERURIE

Mr and Mrs P. A. Lumsden, Kingsfield House, Kingsfield Road, Kintore, Inverurie AB51 0UD (01467 632366; Fax: 01467 632399). 'The Greenknowe' is a comfortable detached and renovated cottage in a quiet location at the southern edge of the village of Kintore. It is in an ideal situation for touring castles, historic sites and distilleries, or for walking, fishing and even golf. The cottage is all on one level with a large south-facing sittingroom overlooking the garden. It sleeps four people in one double and one twin room. A cot is available. Parking adjacent. Open from March to November. Prices from £275 to £475 per week, inclusive of electricity (the cottage is all-electric) and linen. Walkers Welcome Scheme. **STB ★★★★** *SELF-CATERING. ASSC MEMBER.*
e-mail: kfield@clara.net

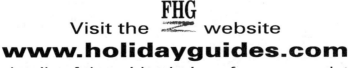

Visit the **FHG** website
www.holidayguides.com
for details of the wide choice of accommodation
featured in the full range of FHG titles

ARGYLL & BUTE

SCOTLAND

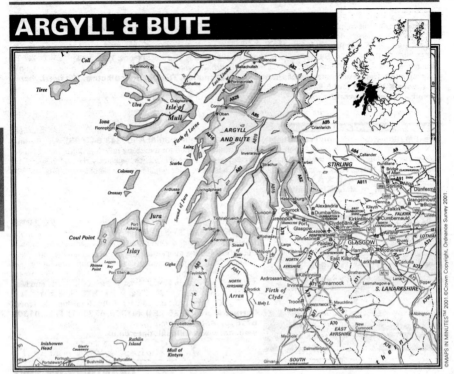

APPIN

Ardtur Cottages, Appin. Two adjacent cottages in secluded surroundings on promontory between Port Appin and Castle Stalker, opposite north end of Isle of Lismore. Ideal centre for hill walking, climbing, etc. (Glen Coe and Ben Nevis half-hour drive). Direct access across the field to sea (Loch Linnhe). Tennis court available by arrangement. Boat hire, pony trekking, fly fishing all available locally. Accommodation in first cottage for eight people in four double bedrooms, large dining/sittingroom/ kitchenette and two bathrooms. Second cottage accommodates six people in three twin-bedded rooms, dining/sittingroom, kitchenette and bathroom. Everything is provided except linen. Shops one mile; sea 200 yards. Pets allowed. Car essential, parking. Open March/October. Terms from £165 to £375 weekly. SAE, please, for full details to **Mrs J. Pery, Ardtur, Appin PA38 4DD (01631 730223 or 01626 834172).**

See also Colour Display Advertisement

CONNEL

West Coast Character Cottages. Sleep 2 to 7. Six interesting and individual privately-owned holiday homes, beautifully located in rural areas within easy driving distance of Oban. Each has a large garden and pleasant outlook, some have stunning views. All are equipped and presented to a high standard and are personally supervised by the local owners. Walking, fishing and many other pursuits to be enjoyed amidst wonderful scenery. Electricity included. Linen available. Call for a brochure. **Tigh Beag, Connel, By Oban PA37 1PJ (01631 710504).** e-mail: **johnandjanet@wccc.sol.co.uk**

Mr & Mrs E. Crawford, Blarghour Farm, Lochaweside, By Dalmally, Argyll PA33 1BW
Tel: (01866) 833246; Fax: (01866) 833338

E-mail: blarghour@aol.com Website: www.self-catering-argyll.co.uk

At Blarghour, a working hill farm on the shores of lovely Loch Awe, the holiday guest has a choice of high quality, well appointed, centrally heated, double glazed accommodation of individual character, each enjoying its own splendid view over loch and mountains in this highly scenic area.

Barn House sleeps two in one ground floor bedroom with twin or zip-linked beds, has a bathroom adjacent to bedroom and open lounge/dining/kitchen on the first floor which is well lit and has a pleasing view.

Stable House accommodates four in two first floor bedrooms with twin or zip-linked bed arrangements, has one bathroom and large lounge/dining room with an elegant spiral staircase and full length windows with an oustanding view.

Barr-beithe Lower sleeps five in three bedrooms, one twin or zip-linked, one double and one single. There is a bathroom and shower room. The lounge/dining/sun lounge enjoys an outstanding loch view.

Barr-beithe Upper sleeps six in three bedrooms, one king-sized double, one twin or zip-linked double, and one twin. There is a bathroom and shower room, and a large kitchen/diner. The lounge and conservatory enjoy lovely views of hill and loch. Set in a mature garden.

All have modern kitchens with fridge/freezer, washer/dryer, microwave and electric cooker and the two larger houses have dishwashers. Cots and high chairs are available in the two larger houses. All have telephones and televisions. Linen and towels are supplied.

Cars may be parked beside each house. Barn and Stable Houses are unsuitable for children under five years. No pets are allowed. Open all year. The area, centrally situated for touring, offers opportunities for walking, bird-watching, boating and fishing. Golf is available at Dalmally and Inveraray.

Colour brochure sent on request.   *See also colour advertisement*

See also Colour Display Advertisement

DALMALLY

Ardbrecknish House, South Lochaweside, by Dalmally PA33 1BH (01866 833223 or 833242). Set in 20 acres of garden woodland on the south shore of spectacular Loch Awe in the heart of Argyll, Ardbrecknish House dates back to the early seventeenth century when it was a fortified tower house. The house has been carefully converted to provide ten delightful self-catering apartments accommodating parties from two to twelve with facilities for larger groups. In the grounds are seven custom-designed holiday cottages, carefully spaced for optimum privacy and outlook, yet easily accessible to the central facilities. The house and grounds command breathtaking panoramic views over loch, mountain and glen. Two night breaks from £80 for two persons low season, to £960 weekly rental for 12-person apartment. STB ★★★ *SELF-CATERING.*
e-mail: ardbreck01@aol.com   website: www.ardbrecknish.com

See also Colour Display Advertisement

DALMALLY

Mr and Mrs Whalley, Rockhill Waterside Cottages, Ardbrecknish, Dalmally PA33 1BH (01866 833218). Secluded, clean, comfortable, well equipped, peaceful waterside bungalow and cottage on Loch Awe side-1200 metres free trout fishing. Both sleep seven and have outstanding views over loch to Cruachan Mountains and towards Glencoe. Small private Highland estate breeding Hanoverian competition horses. Wonderful central area for walking, climbing, bird and rare animal watching. Boat trips, gardens, castles and all kinds of attractions to visit. Just one-and-a-half hours travelling time north of Glasgow. Ample parking by door. Good restaurants, pony trekking, golf nearby. Take a ferry trip from Oban (30 miles) to Muli, Iona and other islands. Early booking discount scheme. Colour brochure on request. Pets welcome.

SCOTLAND

INVERARAY

Minard Castle, Minard PA32 8YB (Tel & Fax: 01546 886272). 19th century Minard Castle beside Loch Fyne is a peaceful location for a quiet break. Stroll in the grounds, walk by the loch, explore the woods, or tour this scenic area with lochs, hills, gardens, castles and historic sites. THE LODGE, a comfortable bungalow with small garden and view through trees to the loch, sleeps four to six. THE MEWS APARTMENTS both sleep four to five. Well equipped; central heating, hot water, linen and towels included. Terms £120 to £370 per week. Open all year. STB ★★★ *SELF-CATERING*. Also Four Star B&B in Minard Castle; £40-£45pppn, open April to October.
e-mail: reinoldgayre@minardcastle.com
website: www.minardcastle.com

See also Colour Display Advertisement

INVERARAY

Bralecken House, Brenchoille Farm, Inveraray PA32 8XN (Tel & Fax: 01499 500662). A mid 19th century stone building carefully restored to provide two comfortable houses situated on private upland farm. Each comprises sitting room, fully-fitted kitchen, two bedrooms, bathroom and shower room. Both are completely private or suitable for two families wishing to holiday together. Large parking area and garden. Children most welcome, but regretfully no pets. STB ★★★ *SELF-CATERING*. Contact **Mr and Mrs Crawford**. *ASSC MEMBER.*

See also Colour Display Advertisement

ISLE OF GIGHA

Gigha Hotel, Isle of Gigha PA41 7AA (01583 505254, Fax: 01583 505244). Situated in the Inner Hebrides, the community owned Isle of Gigha (God's Island) is surely one of Scotland's most beautiful and tranquil islands. Explore the white sandy bays and lochs. Easy walking, bike hire, birds, wildlife and wild flowers. Home to the famous Achamore Gardens with rhododendrons, azaleas and semi-exotic plants. Grass Airstrip, 9-hole golf course and regular ferry service (only 20 minutes from the mainland). We are dog-friendly. Holiday cottages also available. STB ★★★ *SMALL HOTEL.*
website: www.isle-of-gigha.co.uk

See also Colour Display Advertisement

OBAN

Cologin Country Chalets. Set in a tranquil glen less than three miles from Oban, our cosy chalets and atmospheric country pub/ restaurant are a winning combination. Enjoy the waymarked forest trails in the hills above our farm, or relax in front of the fire and sample home-cooked local produce in the pub. The attractions of Oban – "Gateway to the Islands" – are minutes away. Pets and children are welcome – we have a playpark, games byre, and 17,000 acres to walk the dog. Disabled access chalets are available. Free fishing on our hill loch; boats and rods provided. Short breaks from £30, weekly lets from £160 to £495. STB ★★★ to ★★★★ *SELF CATERING*. **Mrs Linda Battison, Cologin House, Lerags Glen, By Oban PA34 4SE (01631 564501; Fax: 01631 566925).** *ASSC MEMBER.*
e-mail: cologin@west-highland-holidays.co.uk   **website: www.west-highland-holidays.co.uk**

ELLARY ESTATE

While you are at ELLARY you are free to go wherever you please. There are hill walks, numerous lochs and burns where you can fish, a wealth of ancient ruins for archaeologists, numerous wild animals and flowers for naturalists and plenty of scope for the nautical people.

Chalets and cottages are available on the Estate. All are fully modernised with all-electric kitchens and modern bathrooms. Most accommodate parties of six, but one will take eight and full details are available on request.

The Estate staff are very helpful and can often point out an attractive place for a picnic or an interesting walk. Cars may be driven on the Estate roads and once you know Ellary you will want to return.

All correspondence to:
ELLARY ESTATE OFFICE,
LOCHGILPHEAD, ARGYLL PA31 8PA

(01880) 770209/770232
or 01546 850223 • Fax: 01880 770386
website: www.ellary.com

ELERAIG HIGHLAND LODGES

Near OBAN, ARGYLL
Gateway to the Highlands and Islands
STB ★★★ and ★★ Self-Catering

Well equipped
Norwegian chalets on
secluded Eleraig estate
12 miles from Oban.

Seven well equipped chalets are set in breathtaking scenery in a private glen 12 miles south of Oban. The chalets are widely spaced, and close to Loch Tralaig where there is free brown trout fishing and boating - or bring your own boat. Chalets sleep 4-7. Peace and tranquillity are features of the site, located within an 1,800 acre working sheep farm. Children and pets are especially welcome. Cots and high chairs are available. Walkers' and bird watchers' paradise. Pony-trekking, sailing, golf, diving, water skiing and other sports, pastimes and evening entertainment are available locally. Car parking by each chalet. Open March - November.

From £205 weekly per chalet, including electricity & bedlinen.
Colour brochure from resident owners:
Anne and Robin Grey,
Eleraig Highland Chalets, Kilninver,
By Oban, Argyll PA34 4UX
Tel/Fax: 01852 200225
Website: www.scotland2000.com/eleraig

SCOTLAND

PORT APPIN

The Cottage, Port Appin. Sleeps 7. Situated on small bay 50 yards from beach. Sheltered position, completely on its own, five minutes from the village. Area offers hill-walking, pony trekking, boating, windsurfing, sea fishing. Ideal for children. Oban and Fort William are within easy reach. Accommodation: four bedrooms (one en suite); dining-room; sittingroom, kitchen and bathroom. Sleeps seven. Fully equipped. Electric cooker, fridge/freezer, microwave, washing machine, colour TV. No linen. Heating by electricity and coal fires. Available March-September £285 to £350 weekly. For details send SAE to **Mrs A. V. Livingstone, Bachuil, Isle of Lismore, By Oban PA34 5UL (01631 760256).**
e-mail: bachuil@talk21.com

ROTHESAY

"Morningside" and "Prospect House" Sleep 3/5. Luxury holiday flats, Isle of Bute. "MORNINGSIDE" is a charming Victorian villa with magnificent views. Tastefully converted one and two bed-roomed self-contained apartments with spacious sittingroom, fitted kitchen, bath/shower room and central heating. Minutes from the Pier, golf course, indoor pool and town centre. "PROSPECT HOUSE" is on the sea front with private parking, toddlers' play area and all the above facilities. Also cottage with conservatory within own garden. Communal laundry. Terms from £189 to £389 weekly including heating, hot water and linen. STB ★★★ *SELF-CATERING.* For a colour brochure contact: **Mr & Mrs Shaw, 21 Battery Place, Rothesay, Isle of Bute PA20 9DU (Tel & Fax: 01700 503526).**
e-mail: islebute@aol.com
website: www.prospecthousebute.co.uk

•• *Some Useful Guidance for Guests and Hosts* ••

Every year literally thousands of holidays, short breaks and overnight stops are arranged through our guides, the vast majority without any problems at all. In a handful of cases, however, difficulties do arise about bookings, which often could have been prevented from the outset.

It is important to remember that when accommodation has been booked, both parties – guests and hosts – have entered into a form of contract. We hope that the following points will provide helpful guidance.

GUESTS:

• When enquiring about accommodation, be as precise as possible. Give exact dates, numbers in your party and the ages of any children.

• State the number and type of rooms wanted and also what catering you require – bed and breakfast, full board etc. Make sure that the position about evening meals is clear – and about pets, reductions for children or any other special points.

• Read our reviews carefully to ensure that the proprietors you are going to contact can supply what you want. Ask for a letter confirming all arrangements, if possible.

• If you have to cancel, do so as soon as possible. Proprietors do have the right to retain deposits and under certain circumstances to charge for cancelled holidays if adequate notice is not given and they cannot re-let the accommodation.

HOSTS:

• Give details about your facilities and about any special conditions. Explain your deposit system clearly and arrangements for cancellations, charges etc. and whether or not your terms include VAT.

• If for any reason you are unable to fulfil an agreed booking without adequate notice, you may be under an obligation to arrange suitable alternative accommodation or to make some form of compensation.

While every effort is made to ensure accuracy, we regret that FHG Publications cannot accept responsibility for errors, omissions or misrepresentations in our entries or any consequences thereof. Prices in particular should be checked because we go to press early. We will follow up complaints but cannot act as arbiters or agents for either party.

The FHG Directory of Website Addresses
on pages 243 – 272 is a useful quick reference guide for
holiday accommodation with e-mail and/or website details

SCOTLAND

SCOTLAND

AYRSHIRE & ARRAN

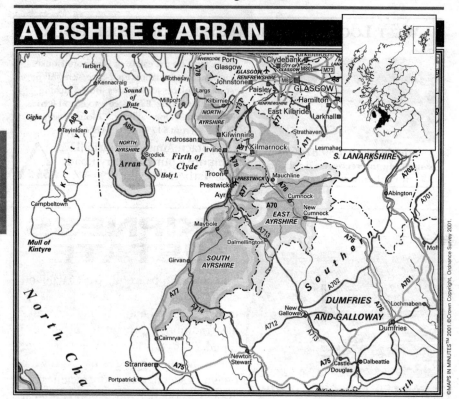

THE ISLE OF ARRAN

See also Colour Display Advertisement

ARRAN

Arran Hideaways, Invercloy House, Brodick, Isle of Arran KA27 8AJ. Choice of properties on the island, available throughout the year. All villages, all dates. Self-catering and bunk house accommodation available. STB Quality Assured. Short breaks available. Major credit cards accepted. Please ask for our brochure. On-line booking and availability. Our staff are here to help you seven days a week. **Call 01770 302303/302310.** *ASSC MEMBER.*
e-mail: holidays@arran-hideaways.co.uk
website: www.arran-hideaways.co.uk

FHG PUBLICATIONS

publish a large range of well-known accommodation guides. We will be happy to send you details or you can use the order form at the back of this book.

BORDERS

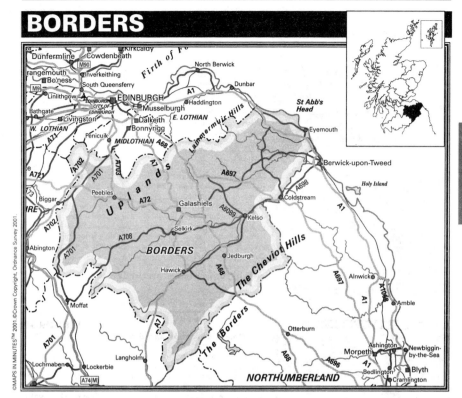

SCOTLAND

COLDSTREAM

'Meg's' and 'Nellie's' Cottages. Sleep 6/7. These comfortable and homely semi-detached cottages have lovely views across the River Tweed and rolling Border country to the Cheviot Hills. They are heated throughout, and in winter the sittingrooms have a welcoming open fire. Both have a sittingroom, kitchen, bathroom and double bedroom on the ground floor. 'Meg's' has one twin and one family room on the first floor; 'Nellie's' has two twin rooms. Full linen included. Both have colour TV, fridge, washing machine and garden furniture. Electricity by meter reading. Cot and high chair can be provided. Ample parking. Dogs by prior arrangement. Details from: **Mrs Sheila Letham, Fireburn Mill, Coldstream TD12 4LN (01890 882124; Fax: 01890 883838).** **e-mail: letham@tinyworld.co.uk**

DUNS

Cockburn Mill Cottage, Duns. A stone-built, traditional cottage nestling in the Whiteadder River valley and enjoying all the comforts with dishwasher, microwave, TV/video etc. Cockburn Mill is a place of peace and tranquillity where children can play and adults can relax in comfort. Well situated for exploring the scenic Berwickshire coastline and beaches and the historic Scottish Borderland with its Abbeys, castles and stately homes. Ideal for artists, golfers and walkers. Trout fishing included. Weekly from £145 to £320, Short break enquiries welcomed. Prices include night storage heating and bed linen. Dining/kitchen, sitting room with single sofa-bed, bathroom and two twin bedrooms. Cot and high chair available. Contact: **Mrs A M Prentice, Cockburn Mill, Duns, Berwickshire TD11 3TL (01361 882811).** **e-mail: amp@co-mill.freeserve.co.uk**

SCOTLAND

DUNS

Ellem Old Cottage, Ellemford, By Duns TD11 3SG (01361 890329). Sleeps 3/5. In a picturesque spot one hour south of Edinburgh and six miles north of Duns in the Scottish Borders. Ideal for walking the Southern Upland Way, fishing or getting away from it all. The cottage has one bedroom (sleeps three), bathroom and open-plan kitchen/living room with double sofa bed. It is self-contained and private, with central heating, washing machine, microwave, oven, TV, and shower over bath. French windows open onto cobbled yard with views of the Lammermuirs. Terms from £200 per week; short breaks available.
e-mail: enquiries@ellemfordcentre.co.uk
website: www.ellemfordcentre.co.uk

HAWICK

Mrs Anne Scott, Overhall Farm Cottage, Hawick TD9 7LJ (01450 375045; Fax: 01450 375446). Situated on the edge of Hawick in the beautiful Border country, this is an excellent base from which to explore the surrounding area, rich in history, with the remains of the Border abbeys testament to our turbulent past, and many stately homes to visit. Close by is the award-winning Wilton Lodge Park, with its walled garden, museum and art gallery, and children's play area. Hawick's Teviotdale Leisure Centre offers an excellent pool with flume attraction, and the town is famous for its quality knitwear and rugby.
website: www.overhall-scotland.co.uk

JEDBURGH

See also Colour Display Advertisement

Mill House, Letterbox and Stockman's Cottages. Three recently renovated, quality Cottages, each sleeping four, on a working farm three miles from Jedburgh. Ideal centres for exploring, sporting holidays or getting away from it all. Each cottage has two public rooms (ground floor available). Minimum let two days. Terms £190–£330. Open all year. Bus three miles, airport 54 miles.
STB ★★★★ SELF-CATERING. **Mrs A. Fraser, Overwells, Jedburgh TD8 6LT (01835 863020; Fax: 01835 864334).** ASSC MEMBER.
e-mail: abfraser@btinternet.com
website: www.overwells.co.uk

KELSO

See also Colour Display Advertisement

Edenmouth Holiday Cottages, near Kelso. Unique, quality cottages, recently converted from a traditional farm steading. Magnificent views across the Tweed Valley. Ideal base for fishermen, golfers, walkers, families and couples wanting a relaxing break. Comfortable, well-equipped cottages on ground level. All bedrooms have en suite facilities. Central heating, linen, towels and electricity included in rates. Large grass garden, games room, laundry/drying room, bicycle lock-up. Pets by arrangement. Open all year. Cottages sleep 1 – 8. Parties of up to 18 catered for. Weekly lets from £160. Short Breaks – 3 nights for 2 people £100. Bed and Breakfast £20pppn. **Mrs Geraldine O'Driscoll, Edenmouth Farm, Near Kelso, Scottish Borders TD5 7QB (01890 830391). STB ★★★** SELF-CATERING/B&B.
e-mail: edenmouth.odris@virgin.net
website: www.edenmouth.co.uk

SCOTLAND (side tab)

NEWCASTLETON

Pamela Copeland, Bailey Mill Courtyard Apartments and Trekking Centre, Bailey Mill, Newcastleton TD9 0TR (016977 48617; Fax: 016977 48074). A warm welcome awaits you from Pam and Ian on this small farm holiday complex, nestling on the Roxburghshire/Cumbrian border. The rural self-contained apartments create a courtyard setting or enjoy Bed and Breakfast or Full Board riding holidays in the farmhouse. Forest trekking and lessons in outdoor school. Colour TV, heating (oil), electricity and linen included in the rent. On site sauna, jacuzzi, toning table, games room, laundry, babysitting, fully licensed bar and meals. Enjoy walking or trekking through surrounding forests. Central touring area for Lake District, Hadrian's Wall and Scotland. Colour brochure available.

Self-catering £88-£498; Bed and Breakfast from £20 per person. **ETC ★★/★★★**
e-mail: pam@baileymill.fsnet.co.uk   **website: www.holidaycottagescumbria.co.uk**

PAXTON

Rose and Lodge Cottages, Spital House, Paxton, Berwickshire TD15 1TD (01289 386139) Each sleeps 4. Situated in the grounds of a private country house estate in a beautiful location in the Tweed Valley only a few miles from the ancient walled town of Berwick-Upon-Tweed, these charming cottages are located in private gardens amidst peaceful surroundings. Tastefully furnished to a very high standard and containing all the conveniences required for a relaxing holiday, these properties provide exclusive accommodation and a superb base for touring the whole of the Border region as well as the magnificent Northumbrian coastline. **ETC ★★★★**

`See also Colour Display Advertisement`

WEST LINTON

Slipperfield House, West Linton, Peeblesshire EH46 7AA (Tel & Fax: 01968 660401). Two well-equipped cottages a mile from West Linton at the foot of the Pentland Hills, set in 100 acres of lochs and woodlands. Only 19 miles from Edinburgh City Centre. Both cottages have sitting room with dining area and colour TV; modern bathroom and kitchen with washing and drying machine, microwave oven and telephone. Within easy driving distance of golf courses in Borders; private fishing. Car essential. Ample parking. Available all year. **STB ★★★ SELF-CATERING.** Details from **Mrs C.M. Kilpatrick.**
e-mail: cottages@slipperfield.com
website: www.slipperfield.com

SCOTLAND

DUMFRIES & GALLOWAY

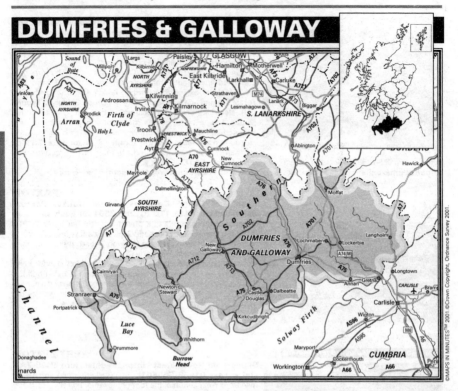

©MAPS IN MINUTES™ 2001. ©Crown Copyright, Ordnance Survey 2001.

The ROSSAN

Stable Cottage, The Rossan, Auchencairn, Castle Douglas DG7 1QR

Self-catering cottage, sleeps 5, close to two sandy beaches. Ideal for bird watching, golf, hill walking. Bicycles for hire. B&B also available.

Brochure from Mrs Bardsley, or apply on website.

- • Tel: 01556 640269
- • e-mail: bardsley@rossan.freeserve.co.uk
- • website: www.the-rossan.co.uk

CASTLE DOUGLAS

Kerr and Sheila Steele, Rose Cottage, Gelston, Castle Douglas DG7 1SH (Tel & Fax: 01556 502513). Detached country cottage in village two-and-a-half miles from Castle Douglas, one-and-a-half miles from Threave Gardens and centrally situated for exploring Galloway. The cottage contains four double bedrooms (one en suite), bathroom with bath and shower. Bedrooms have washbasin, TV, bedlinen and towels supplied. Lounge with television and video, dining room/ conservatory and large modern kitchen. Facilities include central heating, gas hob, electric oven, fridge, freezer, microwave and washing machine. Large garden with stream and waterfall. Rural views surround property. Private parking for six cars. Weekly terms from £350 to £550. Three night breaks from £200 to £314. Heating included. Electricity £25 extra November–March.

Let the Key Unwind!

Relax by the sea in a row of three cottages and two houses (sleep 2 to 6) overlooking Luce Bay. Patio at rear benefits from southerly aspect. Open fires give evening relaxation. Yards from the sea and sand/shingle beach. Highest quality furnishings and equipment. All linen/towels included. Garden/children's play area. Open all year.

Short Breaks available. Pets welcome. Terms from £195 per week. Electricity extra

Details from Mrs S. Colman, 10 Mill Street, Drummore, Wigtownshire DG9 9PS • Tel: 01776 840631 or visit our website at www.harbourrow.co.uk

See also Colour Advertisement

SCOTLAND

Self-Catering Holiday Cottages by the Sea in Galloway, South-West Scotland

Four houses – **Craig Cottage** (sleeps 5), **Milncroft Cottage** (sleeps 2/4), **Braeview Cottage** (sleeps 6) and **Barlocco House** (sleeps 10) – in a stunning coastal location.
Borgue 2 miles, Kirkcudbright and Gatehouse-of-Fleet 7 miles.
Beaches within walking distance; good sea fishing, walking, golf. Babysitting, cooking, bike and boat hire are all available by prior arrangement.

Details from: Lindsey Brown, Roberton, Borgue, Kirkcudbright DG6 4UB
Tel: 01557 870217
e-mail: cottages@roberton.sol.co.uk   STB ★★/★★★★ Self-Catering

See also Colour Advertisement

DALBEATTIE

10 Copeland Street, Dalbeattie. Midway Dumfries, Castle Douglas, By Galloway Coast. Small detached cottage with one family bedroom (one double bed, one single bed) and living room with bed settee. Electric fire and storage heaters, colour TV. Shower room, toilet and washbasin; kitchen/diner with cooker, fridge, microwave, washing machine. Fully equipped. Small rear garden and car parking. Holiday complex, golf, beautiful scenic walks (guided walks available) nearby. Sandy beach four miles, shops, post office, park, banks within easy walking distance. Electricity included in rental, bed linen not provided. Small dogs allowed. Terms from £120 weekly. Short breaks available. Telephone: **Mr M Bailey (017683 51466 or 07850 711411).**

PORTPATRICK

Mr A.D. Bryce, "Alinn", 25 Main Street, Portpatrick DG9 8JW (01776 810277). Sea front situation with unrestricted views of harbour and boats, overlooking small sandy beach with safe bathing. Golf, bowling, tennis and sea angling, scenic cliff walks and ideal country roads for touring. Shops and restaurants nearby. Area is of great historical and archaeological interest and enjoys a mild climate. Self-catering flats, three bedrooms; cottage, two bedrooms. Electric heating, cooking, etc. Prepayment coin meter. Terms from £150 to £215 per week. Parking at door. Please write or phone for further details.

10% off admission prices at
CREETOWN GEM ROCK MUSEUM
See our READERS' OFFER VOUCHER for details.

DUNBARTONSHIRE

SCOTLAND

GARTOCHARN

Claire and Gavin MacLellan, The Lorn Mill Cottages, Gartocharn G83 8LX (01389 753074). The MacLellans have converted the 18th century mill providing three stylish, modern and well-equipped cottages/apartments. Hidden down a private drive in a secluded hollow, the property has some of the best views of Loch Lomond, Ben Lomond and the Arrochar Alps - a unique location! This is very much a country setting yet Glasgow Airport is only 30 minutes away and trains from nearby Balloch take you to Glasgow city centre in just 40 minutes. The Lorn Mill offers an ideal base for outdoor pursuits or for touring. Come and relax and soak up the beauty of Loch Lomond. Each cottage sleeps two to four, has en suite bathroom/ shower room, TV, video and CD player. Linen and electricity included in price. Dogs accepted only by arrangement. Prices from £225 to £375. Open all year. Short Breaks available. Please look at our website for further details or telephone us for availability. **STB ★★★★** *SELF-CATERING.*
e-mail: gavmac@globalnet.co.uk   **website: www.lornmill.com**

Loch Lomond and Ben Lomond seen from Luss

DUNDEE & ANGUS

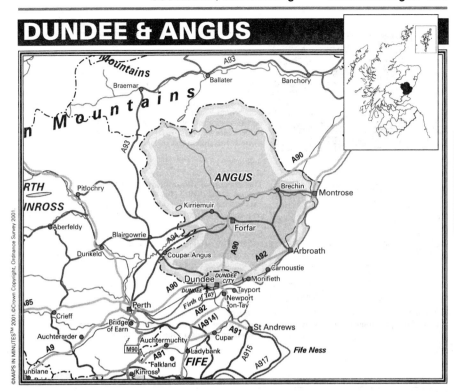

SCOTLAND

BROUGHTY FERRY

Kingennie Lodges, Kingennie, Broughty Ferry, By Dundee DD5 3RD (01382 350777; Fax: 01382 350400). Luxurious self-catering lodges (4) set amidst a delightful woodland setting, overlooking three trout fishing lochans. New coarse fishing lake for 2003. All lodges furnished to the highest standards and are open plan and centrally heated. Each has a double and twin bedroom as well as a folding sofa bed in the lounge; bathroom with shower over bath; fully-equipped kitchen with dishwasher, microwave and washer/dryer. Our "Clova" Lodge has full disabled facilities. Bed linen and towels provided, cot and highchair available upon request. Pets welcome. New lodge has three bedrooms, all en suite. Lodge terms weekly from £245. **STB ★★★★** *SELF CATERING.* Further details contact **Neil Anderson.**
e-mail: kingennie@easynet.co.uk
website: www.kingennie-fishings.com

SCOTLAND

CARNOUSTIE

Balhousie Farm Cottages, Balhousie Farm, Carnoustie DD7 6LG. Balhousie Farm Holiday Cottages are situated on a family-run farm off A92 Dundee to Arbroath. The Bothy, Gardener's, Orramans and Balfour are stone-built farm workers cottages in a group, each with enclosed gardens and parking space. Each cottage has two bedrooms sleeping five, living room with old-style open fire, kitchen fully equipped. The Bothy and Gardener's feature a shower with toilet and Orraman's and Balfour a bathroom. Oil-fired central heating throughout each cottage. Bed linen supplied, electricity coin meter. Rates from £190. Please contact **Mrs E. Watson on 01241 853533.**
e-mail: balhousie@msn.com

KIRRIEMUIR

The Welton of Kingoldrum, Welton Farm, By Kirriemuir, Angus DD8 5HY (Tel & Fax: 01575 574743). Three comfortable, warm and welcoming properties, all ground floor and well equipped, on a secluded working farm in a spectacular setting with panoramic views over the Vale of Strathmore. Ideal base for outdoor pursuits including golf, fishing, riding, skiing and shooting, and for touring the Angus glens, coastline, castles (including Glamis) and gardens. Peaceful and relaxing. Central heating, hot water, linen and towels included in rental. Facilities include microwave, laundry and ironing facilities, colour TV/video player, cot and highchair, garden furniture, BBQ, parking. Open all year. Short breaks available. Walkers and Cyclists welcome. For further information and brochure contact **Jenny Scott.** Rates from £170 to £335 (excl. Christmas and New year). *ASSC MEMBER.* **STB ★★★** *SELF-CATERING.*
e-mail: jennyscott@easicom.com   **websites: www.cottageguide.co.uk/thewelton**
www.angusanddundee.co.uk/members/562htm

FIFE

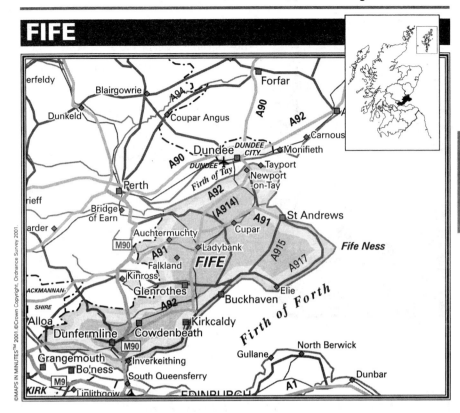

SCOTLAND

ANSTRUTHER

Mr & Mrs R. Sparrow, Old Bank House Restaurant & Apartments, 23-25 High Street East, Anstruther KY10 3DQ (01333 310189/310168). Overlooking its own beach just west of the harbour at Anstruther, the Old Bank House is centrally situated in the heart of the town. Wine and dine in our intimate restaurant or drop in for a drink and a selection of Tapas in the cosy bar; games room with pool table, darts and an inviting log fire. Four letting apartments, all with en suite facilities, central heating, telephone and fully equipped kitchens. All linen and towels are supplied, and a laundry service is available on request. Apartment One sleeps 4-8 and overlooks the garden. Apartment Two is for two people and has twin beds, garden and sea view. Apartment Three has disabled access and facilities and sleeps 2-8. Apartment Four sleeps 4-8 persons. In each apartment one child under seven may stay free of charge. Dogs permitted in apartments One and Two only. Breakfast available on request. Terms from £20 per person per night, based on two sharing. *ASSC MEMBER.*

e-mail: ricardosrest@hotmail.com   www.undiscoveredscotland.co.uk/anstruther/oldbank

SCOTLAND

NEWPORT-ON-TAY

Mr and Mrs Ramsay, Balmore, 3 West Road, Newport-on-Tay DD6 8HH (01382 542274; Fax: 01382 542927). Sleeps 5/6. Situated on the southern shore of the Tay Estuary, Thorndene is the secluded and self-contained west wing of a large Listed house situated in a three-acre walled garden. On the ground floor, it has entry through a paved courtyard, and has its own garden. It is bright and sunny, equipped to a high standard, carpeted throughout, with central heating. There are two double bedrooms – one with a shower en suite, a single bedroom, large sittingroom, diningroom, sun lounge, tiled bathroom with bath and shower, fitted kitchen with washing machine, dishwasher, microwave and breakfast bar. Terms from £200 to £420. Brochure available. **STB ★★★** *SELF-CATERING, ASSC MEMBER.*
e-mail: Allan.Ramsay@ukgateway.net

ST ANDREWS

28 Auldburn Park. Clean, comfortable, well appointed first floor flat overlooking the bowling green, only five minutes' walk from the town centre. Three bedrooms sleeping four, linen supplied. Lounge and fully equipped kitchen including electric oven, gas hob, fridge, washing machine, microwave and toaster. Carpeted throughout, with gas central heating and double glazing. There is a garden with drying green. Available from June until September. Fixed rate of £200 inclusive per week. Contact: **Mr A. Whiteford, The Manse, Ardersier, Inverness IV2 7SX (01667 462224)**
e-mail: revwhiteford@cs.com

• • *Some Useful Guidance for Guests and Hosts* • •

Every year literally thousands of holidays, short breaks and overnight stops are arranged through our guides, the vast majority without any problems at all. In a handful of cases, however, difficulties do arise about bookings, which often could have been prevented from the outset.

It is important to remember that when accommodation has been booked, both parties – guests and hosts – have entered into a form of contract. We hope that the following points will provide helpful guidance.

GUESTS:
- When enquiring about accommodation, be as precise as possible. Give exact dates, numbers in your party and the ages of any children.
- State the number and type of rooms wanted and also what catering you require – bed and breakfast, full board etc. Make sure that the position about evening meals is clear – and about pets, reductions for children or any other special points.
- Read our reviews carefully to ensure that the proprietors you are going to contact can supply what you want. Ask for a letter confirming all arrangements, if possible.
- If you have to cancel, do so as soon as possible. Proprietors do have the right to retain deposits and under certain circumstances to charge for cancelled holidays if adequate notice is not given and they cannot re-let the accommodation.

HOSTS:
- Give details about your facilities and about any special conditions. Explain your deposit system clearly and arrangements for cancellations, charges etc. and whether or not your terms include VAT.
- If for any reason you are unable to fulfil an agreed booking without adequate notice, you may be under an obligation to arrange suitable alternative accommodation or to make some form of compensation.

While every effort is made to ensure accuracy, we regret that FHG Publications cannot accept responsibility for errors, omissions or misrepresentations in our entries or any consequences thereof. Prices in particular should be checked because we go to press early. We will follow up complaints but cannot act as arbiters or agents for either party.

HIGHLANDS

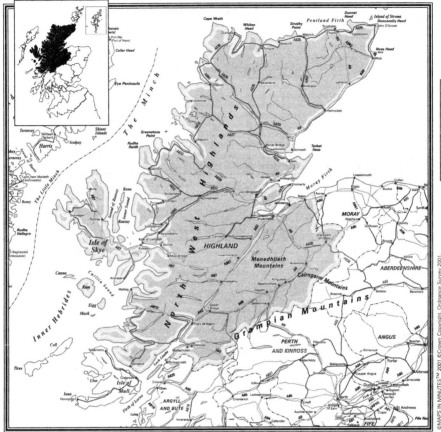

SCOTLAND

©MAPS IN MINUTES™ 2001. ©Crown Copyright, Ordnance Survey 2001.

One FREE adult or child with adult paying full entrance price at
Highland and Rare Breeds Farm
See our READERS' OFFER VOUCHER for details.

One FREE child with each child paying the full admission price at
Highland Folk Museum
See our READERS' OFFER VOUCHER for details.

**Readers are requested to mention this guidebook when seeking
accommodation (and please enclose a stamped addressed envelope).**

SCOTLAND

HIGHLANDS (North)

Superb redwood chalets, set in their own well-kept grounds overlooking Lochinver Bay. Spectacular views of the sea loch and of the majestic mountains of Canisp, Suilven, Cul Mhor and Stac Pollaidh. Very well appointed, quality accommodation with excellent standards of cleanliness. Choice of a one-bedroom chalet with king-size double bed and en suite bathroom with corner jacuzzi bath and corner power shower, or a two-bedroom chalet/house sleeping up to four persons. Fully equipped, with a ceramic hob cooker, microwave, dishwasher, washing machine/dryer, colour TV, video recorder, etc, making this an ideal 'home from home'. An ideal setting to unwind on golden sands; explore an unspoiled landscape; go walking, climbing, fishing or birdwatching – for a truly memorable holiday. A warm welcome awaits you.

Caisteal Liath Chalets

Tel & Fax: 01571 844457

e-mail: **caisteal_liath@compuserve.com**
web: **www.scottishhighlandholidays.co.uk**

Contact: Mrs Sue MacLeod, Caisteal Liath Chalets, Baddidarrach, Lochinver, Sutherland IV27 4LP

See also Colour Advertisement

ARDGAY

Mrs M.C. MacLaren, The Poplars, Ardgay, Sutherland IV24 3BG (01863 766302). Sleeps 6. Detached cottage standing in its own grounds with private parking. Fully furnished except for linen, accommodation comprises one double, one king and one bedroom with bunk beds (all with duvets and covers); sitting room with open fire, electric fire and TV; bathroom with shower; kitchen/dining room with electric cooker, washing machine, refrigerator, microwave, kettle, toaster and iron, together with cutlery, pans, crockery and radio. The cottage is clean and comfortable. Immersion heater for hot water; electric fires in all rooms. Dornoch Cathedral (where Madonna and Guy Ritchie were married), Royal Dornoch Golf Course and beautiful safe sandy beaches only 14 miles away. Skibo Castle, Tain, Brora and Golspie golf courses all within easy reach. Angling, mountain biking, hill walking, wildlife and forest walks all available locally. Tariff £150 to £220 per week..

See also Colour Display Advertisement

LOCHINVER

Clashmore Holiday Cottages, Lochinver. Sleeps 2-5. Our three croft cottages at Clashmore are the ideal base for a holiday in the Highlands. They are cosy and fully equipped, with linen provided. Nearby there are sandy beaches, mountains and lochs for wild brown trout fishing. Children welcome, but sorry – no pets. Open all year. Terms from £160 to £340. **STB ★★★** *SELF-CATERING.* Contact: **Mr and Mrs H. Mackenzie, Lochview, 216 Clashmore, Stoer, Lochinver, Sutherland IV27 4JQ (Tel & Fax: 01571 855226).** *ASSC MEMBER.* e-mail: **clashcotts@supanet.com**

STRATHNAVER

Mrs C.M. MacLeod, Achnabourin, Strathnaver, Near Bettyhill KW11 6UA (01641 561210). Comfy country cottage situated beside the River Naver in the lovely Strathnaver Valley, six miles from coast and village of Bettyhill, 14 miles from Tongue, both with lovely sandy beaches. An ideal base for touring the rugged north coast of Scotland or for just enjoying the local walks and scenery. Trout fishing available. Two double and one twin-bedded rooms, sitting room with open or electric fire, kitchen with electric cooker, fridge, deep freeze, microwave, automatic washing machine, toaster, etc; bathroom. Fully equipped except linen. Open March to October. Rates from £150 to £180 per week. Electricity extra. For full details send SAE.

WICK

SEE ENTRY UNDER ABERDEEN – HOLIDAY FLAT.

HIGHLANDS (Mid)

ACHILTIBUIE

Chalet. Sleeps 4. Norwegian-style log chalet to sleep four persons, situated overlooking the sea and the Summer Isles in Lochbroom in Wester Ross, with magnificent views of islands and mountains. This tranquil area has lots to offer - walking, climbing, fishing, birdwatching, golf and much more. The chalet has electric heating in all rooms by slot meter, electric cooker, microwave, washing machine, colour TV, radio. Bath with shower, everything supplied except linen and towels. Lawned garden with chairs. Ample parking. Shops and eating out facilities in the area. Please ring for full details and brochure. **M.W. MacLeod, Dornie House, Achiltibuie, By Ullapool, Wester Ross IV26 2YP (Tel & Fax: 01854 622271).**
e-mail: dorniehouseBandB@aol.com

AULTBEA

Mrs Peggy MacRae, 'Cove View', 36 Mellon Charles, Aultbea, Wester Ross IV22 2JL (01445 731351). Wester Ross is ideal for a quiet, restful holiday. Detached chalet has two small bedrooms, bathroom and sitting area with mini kitchen. Ideal for two or three persons. Terms from £150 to £200 per week. Bed and Breakfast also available from £16. Open March to September. Your dog is welcome free of charge.

GAIRLOCH

The Old School, Opinan, Gairloch IV21 2AT. Built in the 1870s and in use as a village school until 1964, the Old School was converted to a dwelling house in 1981/82. It lies 100 metres back from the main road and only five minutes from a safe, sandy beach, with splendid views over the Minch to Skye and the Outer Isles. Accommodation comprises sun lounge; large lounge with dining area, colour TV, VCR, CD/radio and piano; fully equipped kitchen with fridge/freezer, microwave, auto washer/dryer and comfortable eating area; small cloak room with WC and wash hand basin; one double and two twin bedrooms. Linen and towels provided. Gas and electric cooking and central heating. Pay phone. Ample parking area. Large enclosed garden with furniture. Terms from £185 to £380 per week. Gas and electricity inclusive. Well controlled pets welcome. **STB ★★★** *SELF-CATERING*. Contact: **Helen & Syd Garrioch (01445 741206).**
website: www.scotia-sc.com/51.htm.

LAIDE

Mrs A. MacIver, "The Sheiling", Achgarve, Laide IV22 2NS (Tel & Fax: 01445 731487). Self-contained, fully equipped apartment on a traditional croft in a small, peaceful village amidst breathtaking scenery on the Gruinard Peninsula on the rugged north west coast. Laide (Post Office, stores) two miles, Gairloch 16 miles, Ullapool and the ferry to the Western Isles 45 miles. Ideal outdoor activities - sandy beaches, wildlife, fishing, sailing, walking, climbing, pony-trekking, golf and bowls. Also restaurants, swimming pool, local arts and crafts, Inverewe Gardens and Gairloch Heritage Museum. Terms from £180 to £260 per week. **STB ★★★★** *SELF-CATERING*. Self-contained, fully equipped caravan also available on the croft, with two double bedrooms and bathroom. STB Inspected. Terms from £120 to £160 per week.
e-mail: maciver@thesheilingholidays.com
website: www.thesheilingholidays.com

LOCHCARRON

The Cottage, Stromecarronach, Lochcarron West, Strathcarron. Working croft. Sleeps 2. The small, stone-built Highland cottage is fully equipped and has a double bedroom, shower room and open plan kitchen/living room (with open fire). It is secluded, with panoramic views over Loch Carron and the mountains. River, sea and loch fishing are available. Hill-walking is popular in the area and there is a small local golf course. Nearby attractions include the Isle of Skye, Inverewe Gardens, the Torridon and Applecross Hills and the historic Kyle Railway Line. Visitors' dogs are welcome provided they are kept under control at all times. For full particulars write, or telephone, **Mrs A.G. Mackenzie, Stromecarronach, Lochcarron West, Strathcarron IV54 8YH (01520 722284). website: www.lochcarron.org**

POOLEWE

"Seabank", Poolewe, By Achnasheen. Sleeps 7. Beautifully situated cottage with large garden on seafront. Three bedrooms (two double and one with double and single beds), two with washbasins; bathroom; shower; sittingroom with electric fire and colour TV; kitchen equipped with electric cooker, fridge/freezer, washing machine, etc. Dimplex wall panel heaters fitted in all rooms. Ideally situated for hill walking, sandy beaches; Inverewe Gardens 10 minutes' walk; hotels, shop and heated swimming pool in village. Families and pets welcome. Available April to October. Terms from £120 to £220 per week. Child's cot available £5 per week. Contact: **Mrs Doreen Robertson, 174 Culduthel Road, Inverness IV2 4BH (01463 238901).**

POOLEWE

See also Colour Display Advertisement

Innes Maree Bungalows, Poolewe IV22 2JU (Tel & Fax 01445 781454). Only a few minutes' walk from the world-famous Inverewe Gardens in magnificent Wester Ross. A purpose-built complex of six superb modern bungalows, all equipped to the highest standards of luxury and comfort. Each bungalow sleeps six with main bedroom en suite. Children and pets welcome. Terms from £190 to £425 inclusive of bed linen and electricity. Brochure available. **STB ★★★★** *SELF-CATERING.* **ASSC MEMBER.**
e-mail: fhg@poolewebungalows.com   **website: www.poolewebungalows.com**

ULLAPOOL

Mrs P.E. Campbell, 5 Custom House Street, Ullapool, Ross-shire IV26 2XF (01854 612107). Two self-catering houses to let. In No.4 (sleeping four/six) the accommodation is: entrance hall, sitting room, kitchen with dining area, utility room. First floor: bathroom, bedroom with double bed, bedroom with twin beds. In No.3 (sleeping two/four) the accommodation consists of entrance hall, sitting room with dining area with concealed fold down double bed, fitted kitchen, shower room with toilet, bedroom with twin beds. Duvets and bed linen provided. In each house fitted carpets throughout, electric cooker, fridge, washing machine, kettle, iron and electric towel rail. Colour TV. Gardens at rear. Ample parking space. Towels provided at extra charge per person. Lets generally for full weeks only from Saturday to Saturday. **STB ★★** *SELF-CATERING.* Bookings contact **Mrs P.E. Campbell (01854 612107).**
website: www.ullapool.co.uk/customhouse

PLEASE NOTE

All the information in this book is given in good faith in the belief that it is correct. However, the publishers cannot guarantee the facts given in these pages, neither are they responsible for changes in policy, ownership or terms that may take place after the date of going to press. Readers should always satisfy themselves that the facilities they require are available and that the terms, if quoted, still apply.

HIGHLANDS (South)

CAIRNGORM HIGHLAND BUNGALOWS

Glen Einich, 29 Grampian View,
Aviemore, Inverness-shire PH22 1TF
Tel: 01479 810653 • Fax: 01479 810262
e-mail: linda.murray@virgin.net
website: www.cairngorm-bungalows.co.uk

Beautifully furnished and well-equipped bungalows ranging from one to four bedrooms. All have colour TV, video, microwave, cooker, washer-dryer, fridge and patio furniture. Some have log fires. Leisure facilities nearby include golf, fishing on the River Spey, swimming, sauna, jacuzzi, tennis, skating and skiing. Within walking distance of Aviemore. Ideal touring base. Children and pets welcome. Phone for colour brochure. Open all year.

See also Colour Display Advertisement

ARISAIG

Arisaig House Cottages. Luxurious, secluded accommodation in mature woodland. Set in an area of breathtaking coastal and hill scenery, and wonderful sandy beaches. Mountain bike hire, clay pigeon shooting, and fishing on Loch Morar can be arranged. Golf seven miles, swimming pool 13 miles. Day trips to the Small Isles and to Skye. Various properties, sleeping from two to eight persons. Details from: **Andrew Smither, Arisaig House, Beasdale, Arisaig, Inverness-shire PH39 4NR (Tel & Fax: 01687 450399).** *ASSC MEMBER.*
e-mail: enquiries@arisaighouse-cottages.co.uk
www.arisaighouse-cottages.co.uk

CARRBRIDGE

Crannich House & Lodges, Carrbridge PH23 3AA (01479 841620). Three wooden lodges set in the large garden of our guest house in the Highland village of Carrbridge. Each lodge has parking for two cars and picnic tables and barbecues are provided on the large grass area surrounding the lodges. To one side is an extensive forested area with numerous paths for walking and cycling. Carrbridge is a friendly village with shops and post office. Local activities include golf, bowls, pony trekking, ski-school and Landmark Centre. There is a choice of places to eat out including coffee shops, family restaurants, licensed bistros, hotels and pubs. Brochure available.

See also Colour Display Advertisement   ### CULLODEN (By Inverness)

Blackpark Farm, Westhill, Inverness IV2 5BP (01463 790620; Fax: 01463 794262). This newly built holiday home is located one mile from Culloden Battlefield with panoramic views over Inverness and beyond. Fully equipped with many extras to make your holiday special, including oil fired central heating to ensure warmth on the coldest of winter days. Ideally based for touring the Highlands including Loch Ness, Skye etc. Extensive information is available on our website. A Highland welcome awaits you. *ASSC MEMBER.*
e-mail: i.alexander@blackpark.co.uk   website: www.blackpark.co.uk

---

10% DISCOUNT for pet owners. FREE admission for pets at
Landmark Forest Heritage Park
See our READERS' OFFER VOUCHER for details.

SCOTLAND

DALCROSS
Easter Dalziel Farm Holiday Cottages, Dalcross IV2 7JL (Tel & Fax: 01667 462213). Three cosy, traditional stone-built cottages in a superb central location, ideal for touring, sporting activities and observing wildlife. Woodland and coastal walks. The cottages are fully equipped including linen and towels. Pets by arrangement. Terms from £135 low season to £430 high season per cottage per week. Recommended in 'The Good Holiday Cottage Guide'. Open all year for long or short breaks. Brochure on request. STB ★★★ and ★★★★ *SELF CATERING. ASSC MEMBER.*
e-mail: fhg@easterdalzielfarm.co.uk
website: www.easterdalzielfarm.co.uk

DRUMNADROCHIT (By Loch Ness)

Allan & Agnes Spence, Drumnadrochit Lodges, Upper Achmony, Drumnadrochit, By Loch Ness, IV63 6UX (Tel: 01456 450467; Tel & Fax: 01456 459049). Lodges sleep 2/6. Come stay with us and enjoy the scenic beauty of the Loch Ness area at any time of year. Spacious quality holiday lodges set in an idyllic location on the hillside above Drumnadrochit and Loch Ness but only 17 miles from the city of Inverness, providing comfortable accommodation for a refuge of peace and tranquillity or a convenient centre for touring (car essential), walking, bird watching, fishing or golfing. Drumnadrochit has several hotels, restaurants, shops, exhibition centres, pony trekking and boat trips on Loch Ness. Our terms range from £200 to £540 per week depending on season and number in party. STB ★★★★ *SELF CATERING.*
e-mail: drumnadrochit-lodges@tiscali.co.uk   **website: www.drumnadrochit-lodges.co.uk**

FORT WILLIAM
Dalaraban, Fort William. Dalaraban is a large comfortable centrally heated house built to accommodate eight people. High on top of the hill three-quarters of a mile from Fort William, it has an unrivalled position with panoramic views of Loch Linnhe and the Morven mountains to the front and Ben Nevis to the rear. All power, bed linen and towels included. Electric blankets on all beds. Off-road parking. One pet welcome. Open all year. £250–£680 per week. STB ★★★ *SELF-CATERING.* Brochure on request, contact **Malcolm or Eileen, Strone Farm, Banavie, by Fort William PH33 7PB (Tel & Fax: 01397 712733).**
e-mail: eilean@stronefarm.co.uk
website: www.stronefarm.co.uk

INVERGARRY
Miss J. Ellice, Taigh-an-Lianach, Aberchalder Estate, Invergarry PH35 4HN (01809 501287). Three self catering properties, all ideal for hill walkers and country lovers. Salmon and trout fishing available. ABERCHALDER LODGE: traditional Highland shooting lodge extensively modernised to give a high standard of comfort, sleeps 12. TAIGH AN LIANACH: modern self contained bed-sit, secluded and peaceful, sleeps two. LEAC COTTAGE: a secluded cottage which combines old world charm with a high standard of comfort, sleeps three. Children and dogs welcome. Please phone or fax **01809 501287.**

KINCRAIG
Loch Insh Log Chalets, Kincraig PH21 1NU (01540 651272). Just six miles south of Aviemore these superb log chalets are set in 14 acres of woodland in the magnificent Spey Valley, surrounded on three sides by forest and rolling fields with the fourth side being half a mile of beach frontage. Free watersports hire for guests, 8.30-10am/4-5.30pm daily. Sailing, windsurfing, canoeing, salmon fishing, archery, dry ski slope skiing. Hire/instruction available by the hour, day or week mid-April to end of October. Boathouse restaurant on the shore of Loch Insh offering coffee, home-made soup, fresh salads, bar meals, children's menu and evening à la carte. Large gift shop and bar. New children's adventure areas, three kilometres lochside/woodland walk/interpretation trail, ski slope, mountain bike hire and stocked trout lochan are open all year round. Ski, snowboard hire and instruction available December to April. *ASSC MEMBER.*
e-mail: office@lochinsh.com   **website: www.lochinsh.com**

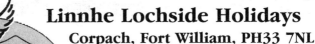

NEWTONMORE

Croft Holidays, Newtonmore PH20 1BA (01540 673504). Thoughtfully renovated cottages in quiet, picturesque surroundings, on outskirts of lovely Highland village in 'Monarch of the Glen' country. Central heating, TV, fridge/freezer, microwave, washer, drying room, disabled access. Way-marked trails, golf course, restaurants, pubs, shops, museums in village. Newtonmore is easy to find, just one mile from A9. Central for touring, many tourist attractions, great area for walking (guided walk included), bird watching, cycling, pony trekking, water sports. Short breaks or long stays welcome all year. Cottages sleeping up to four from £140 to £310 per week including heating and bed linen. Well behaved pets welcome. For brochure/special offers contact Mary Mackenzie. **STB ★★★** *SELF-CATERING. WALKERS WELCOME, CYCLISTS WELCOME. ASSC MEMBER.*
e-mail: FHG@croftholidays.co.uk   website: www.croftholidays.co.uk

See also Colour Display Advertisement

ONICH

Cuilcheanna Cottages and Caravans, Onich, Fort William PH33 6SD. Three cottages and eight caravans (6 x 2003 models) situated on a small peaceful site. The cottages are built to the highest standards with electric heating, double glazing and full insulation. Tastefully furnished and fully equipped, each cottage has a large picture window in the main living area which look out over Loch Leven and Glencoe. Adjacent car parking. Laundry room and phone box on site. Only a short walk from the centre of Onich and an ideal base from which to explore the West Highlands. Paradise for hillwalkers. The caravans also have full facilities. Whether your stay with us is a long one, or just a few days, we shall do our best to ensure that it is enjoyable. Weekend Breaks available, winter rates, off season discounts. *ASSC MEMBER*. For further details please telephone **01855 821526** or **01855 821310**.

LANARKSHIRE

See also Colour Display Advertisement **BIGGAR (Clyde Valley)**

Carmichael Country Cottages, Carmichael Estate Office, Westmains, Carmichael, Biggar ML12 6PG (01899 308336; Fax: 01899 308481). Working farm, join in. Sleep 2/7. These 200-year-old stone cottages nestle among the woods and fields of our 700-year-old family estate. Still managed by the descendants of the original Chief of Carmichael. We guarantee comfort, warmth and a friendly welcome in an accessible, unique, rural and historic time capsule. We farm deer, cattle and sheep and sell meats and tartan – Carmichael of course! Children and pets welcome. Open all year. Terms from £190 to £535. 15 cottages with a total of 32 bedrooms. We have the ideal cottage for you. Private tennis court and fishing loch; cafe, farm shop and visitor centre. Off-road driving course. **STB ★★/★★★★** *SELF-CATERING. ASSC MEMBER. FHB MEMBER.*
e-mail: chiefcarm@aol.com   website: www.carmichael.co.uk/cottages

THE FHG DIPLOMA

HELP IMPROVE BRITISH TOURIST STANDARDS

You are choosing holiday accommodation from our very popular FHG Publications. Whether it be a hotel, guest house, farmhouse or self-catering accommodation, we think you will find it hospitable, comfortable and clean, and your host and hostess friendly and helpful.

Why not write and tell us about it?

As a recognition of the generally well-run and excellent holiday accommodation reviewed in our publications, we at FHG Publications Ltd. present a diploma to proprietors who receive the highest recommendation from their guests who are also readers of our Guides. If you care to write to us praising the holiday you have booked through FHG Publications Ltd. – whether this be board, self-catering accommodation, a sporting or a caravan holiday, what you say will be evaluated and the proprietors who reach our final list will be contacted.

The winning proprietor will receive an attractive framed diploma to display on his premises as recognition of a high standard of comfort, amenity and hospitality. FHG Publications Ltd. offer this diploma as a contribution towards the improvement of standards in tourist accommodation in Britain. Help your excellent host or hostess to win it!

FHG DIPLOMA

We nominate ....

....

Because

Name ....

Address...

....

Telephone No..

PERTH & KINROSS

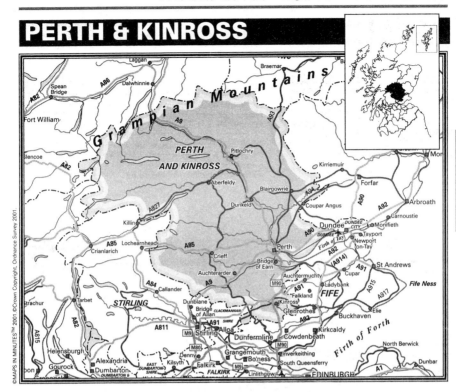

©MAPS IN MINUTES™ 2001. ©Crown Copyright. Ordnance Survey 2001.

SCOTLAND

ABERFELDY

Loch Tay Lodges, Acharn. Lodges sleep 2/8. These lodges are in a recently converted stone-built terrace listed as of special historic and architectural interest, situated on farm on the outskirts of the picturesque Highland village of Acharn on the shores of Loch Tay. There is free trout fishing on the loch; salmon and other fishing by arrangement. Special facilities for sailing: many scenic walks. Golf at Taymouth one and a half miles and five other courses within 20 miles. The lodges are fully equipped to the highest modern standard, including colour TV. Four of the units have log fires. Open all year, with terms from £195 to £510. **STB ★★★★** *SELF-CATERING.* For free brochure, please apply to **Mrs F. Millar, Remony, Acharn, Aberfeldy PH15 2HR (01887 830209; Fax: 01887 830802).**
e-mail: remony@btinternet.com
website: www.lochtaylodges.co.uk

COMRIE

Mrs Pauline Booth, Loch View Farm, Mill of Fortune, Comrie, Crieff PH6 2JE (Tel & Fax: 01764 670677). There is a south facing lodge and a residential caravan situated separately on the edge of a privately owned loch at Loch View farm, in idyllic surroundings, with beautiful scenery, two miles from the village of Comrie and six miles from the town of Crieff. Ideally situated for a quiet holiday, away from it all, with fishing, walking and birdwatching in abundance. Also centrally situated for touring. Wallace Lodge sleeps up to eight and is equipped to a very high standard. The residential caravan sleeps four. **STB ★★★★** *SELF-CATERING.*

DUNKELD (By)

Laighwood Holidays, Butterstone, By Dunkeld PH8 0HB (01350 724241; Fax: 01350 724212). Properties sleep 2/8. A de luxe detached house, comfortably accommodating eight, created from the West Wing of a 19th century shooting lodge with panoramic views. Two popular cottages sleeping four to six, situated on our hill farm, with beautiful views. Two well-equipped apartments adjoining Butterglen House near Butterstone Loch. Butterstone lies in magnificent countryside (especially Spring/Autumn), adjacent to Nature Reserve (ospreys). Central for walking, touring, historic houses, golf and fishing. Private squash court and hill loch (wild brown trout) on the farm. Sorry no pets. Terms: House £424 to £660; Cottages and Apartments £165 to £375 per week. **STB ★★★ to ★★★★** *SELF-CATERING. ASSC MEMBER.*
e-mail: holidays@laighwood.co.uk
website: www.laighwood.co.uk

RENFREWSHIRE

LOCHWINNOCH

Mrs J. Anderson, East Lochhead Country House and Cottages, Largs Road, Lochwinnoch PA12 4DX (Tel & Fax: 01505 842610; mobile: 07885 565131). Four self-catering cottages carefully restored from old byres arranged around a courtyard. Furnished to a high standard with gas central heating, colour TV, fridge, cooker, microwave and bed linen (laundry facilities also available).The property is set within 25 acres of farmland grazed by our own Jacob sheep and Highland cattle and has two acres of lovely gardens.The Glasgow to Carlisle cycle track (Sustrans national route No.7) passes the property and provides access to walks and cycle rides. Cycle hire is available close by. Ideal centre for exploring Ayrshire and Clyde coast, Loch Lomond and the Trossachs, close to ferries to islands of Arran,

Bute and Cumbrae.The cultural, shopping and social attractions of Glasgow are only 25 minutes by car or 15 by rail. Reservations normally Saturday to Sunday; Short Breaks available except July/August. **STB ★★★★** *SELF-CATERING. FINALIST MACALLAN TASTE OF SCOTLAND 2002/3. THISTLE AWARD 2002/3 FOR CUSTOMER CARE, GREEN TOURISM BUSINESS SCHEME GOLD AWARD, INVESTORS IN PEOPLE AWARD 2002. ASSC MEMBER.*
e-mail: eastlochhead@aol.com   **website: www.eastlochhead.co.uk**

SCOTTISH ISLANDS – Isle of Skye

BREAKISH

Tigh Holm Cottages, Sculamus Moss, Breakish IV42 8QB (01471 822848; Fax: 01471 822328). Situated only one mile from Broadford, these cottages are furnished to a very high standard. Their location and comfort are perfect to make your holiday home ideal for exploring the Misty Isle. Open plan ground floor comprises a very spacious lounge/dining room with TV and video; kitchen with all modern appliances and utility room with automatic washing machine. Upper level comprises bathroom with shower, one twin and one double bedroom. All bedding and linen is supplied and electricity is included. Restaurants and bars are within walking distance. Terms from £190 to £425. Please contact for further details.
e-mail: tighholm@lineone.net

WALES
Self-catering Holidays

ANGLESEY & GWYNEDD

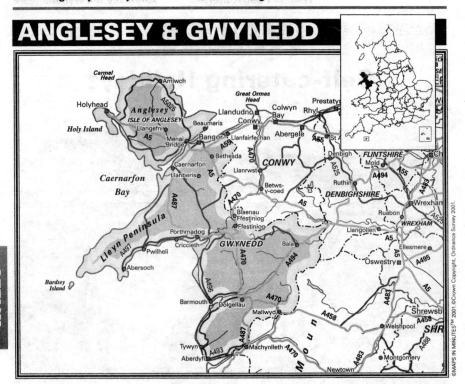

*Q*UALITY COTTAGES

AROUND THE MAGNIFICENT WELSH COAST
Away from the Madding Crowd • Near safe sandy beaches

A small specialist agency with over 40 years experience of providing quality self-catering, offers privacy, peace and unashamed luxury. The first Wales Tourist Board Self-Catering Award Winner. Highest residential standards. *Dishwashers, Microwaves, Washing Machines, Central Heating. No Slot meters.*

LOG FIRES • LINEN PROVIDED • PETS WELCOME FREE!

All in coastal areas famed for scenery, walks, wild-flowers, birds, badgers and foxes.

Free colour brochure from F.G. Rees "Quality Cottages", Cerbid, Solva, Haverfordwest, Pembrokeshire SA62 6YE

Telephone: (01348) 837871 • Website: www.qualitycottages.co.uk

Terms quoted in this publication may be subject to increase if rises in costs necessitate

BEDDGELERT *Bron Eifion, Rhyd Ddu, Beddgelert*

Semi-detached house sleeping 6 in village in National Park. Walks from house including path to summit of Snowdon. Steam railway to village expected to open spring 2003. Seaside, gardens, historic buildings, lakes, riding, fishing, golf within easy reach. Three bedrooms, 2 livingrooms, bathroom, new kitchen; well equipped. Mountain view, terrace, rough garden. Inn (serving meals) nearby. No pets. High season £160 - £320 per week; low season £70 - £150. Short breaks. Open all year.

Contact: PAUL JOHNSON,
20 PLASTURTON AVE, CARDIFF CF11 9HH
079 7030 1198

BRYN BRAS CASTLE

Welcome to beautiful Bryn Bras Castle – enchanting castle Apartments, elegant Tower-House within unique romantic turreted Regency Castle (Listed Building) in the gentle foothills of Snowdonia. Centrally situated amidst breathtaking scenery, ideal for exploring North Wales' magnificent mountains, beaches, resorts, heritage and history. Near local country inns/restaurants, shops. Each spacious apartment is fully self-contained, gracious, peaceful, clean, with distinctive individual character, comfortable furnishings, generously and conveniently appointed from dishwasher to fresh flowers, etc. Inclusive of VAT. Central heating, hot water, linen. All highest WTB grade. 32 acres of tranquil landscaped gardens, sweeping lawns, woodland walks of natural beauty, panoramic hill walks overlooking the sea, Anglesey and Mount Snowdon. Mild climate. Enjoy the comfort, warmth, privacy and relaxation of this castle of timeless charm in truly serene surroundings. Open all year, including for Short Breaks. Sleep 2-4 persons. **Regret no young children. Brochure sent with pleasure**

Llanrug, Near Caernarfon, North Wales LL55 4RE
Tel & Fax: Llanberis (01286) 870210
E-mail: holidays@brynbrascastle.co.uk • Website: www.brynbrascastle.co.uk

ANGLESEY (Beaumaris)

Quality Cottages. Around the magnificent Welsh Coast. Away from the madding crowd. Near safe, sandy beaches. A small specialist agency offering privacy, peace and unashamed luxury. The first WTB Self Catering Gold Medal Award Winners. Residential standards - dishwashers, microwaves, washing machines, central heating, log fires. No slot meters. Linen provided. Pets welcome free. All in coastal areas famed for scenery, walks, wild flowers, birds, badgers and foxes. Free colour brochure **S.C. Rees, "Quality Cottages", Cerbid, Solva, Haverfordwest, Pembrokeshire SA62 6YE (01348 837871).** See also our full colour advertisement on the Inside Back Cover.
website: www.qualitycottages.co.uk

CAERNARFON

Mrs M. Hughes, Glan Llyn, Llanfaglan, Caernarfon LL54 5RD (01286 674700). Sleeps 4. Glan Llyn is a two bedroomed semi-detached cottage, situated in a quiet area, yet only two miles from historic town of Caernarfon and within easy distance of Caernarfon Golf Course and Caernarfon Bay for sea fishing. Ideally situated for touring North Wales, just seven miles from Snowdon and Anglesey and within easy reach of many seaside resorts. Accommodation comprises two double bedrooms; bathroom; lounge with TV; kitchen/diner with fridge, electric stove, electric fires or open fire. Bed linen supplied. Parking space. Cottage available all year round. Mid-week Breaks and Weekend Breaks available during off season. Reduction for winter breaks and weekend bookings during off season period; summer terms and full details on request.

CAERNARFON

Plas-Y-Bryn Chalet Park, Bontnewydd, Near Caernarfon LL54 7YE (01286 672811). Our small park is situated two miles from the historic town of Caernarfon. Set into a walled garden it offers safety, seclusion and beautiful views of Snowdonia. It is ideally positioned for touring the area. Shop and village pub nearby. A selection of chalets and caravans available at prices from £95 to £370 per week for the caravans and £95 to £290 per week for the chalets. Well behaved pets always welcome. **WTB ★★★** *SELF-CATERING.*

CRICCIETH

Quality Cottages. Around the magnificent Welsh Coast. Away from the madding crowd. Near safe, sandy beaches. A small specialist agency offering privacy, peace and unashamed luxury. The first WTB Self Catering Gold Medal Award Winnners. Residential standards - dishwashers, microwaves, washing machines, central heating, log fires. No slot meters. Linen provided. Pets welcome free. All in coastal areas famed for scenery, walks, wild flowers, birds, badgers and foxes. Free colour brochure **S.C. Rees, "Quality Cottages", Cerbid, Solva, Haverfordwest, Pembrokeshire SA62 6YE (01348 837871).** See also our full colour advertisement on the Inside Back Cover.
website: www.qualitycottages.co.uk

HARLECH

Quality Cottages. Around the Welsh Coast. Away from the madding crowd. Near safe, sandy beaches. A small specialist agency offering privacy, peace and unashamed luxury. The first WTB Self Catering Gold Medal Award Winners. Residential standards - dishwashers, microwaves, washing machines, central heating, log fires. No slot meters. Linen provided. Pets welcome free. All in coastal areas famed for scenery, walks, wild flowers, birds, badgers and foxes. Free colour brochure **S.C. Rees, "Quality Cottages", Cerbid, Solva, Haverfordwest, Pembrokeshire SA62 6YE (01348 837871).** See also our full colour advertisement on the Inside Back Cover.
website: www.qualitycottages.co.uk

LLANBEDROG

Mrs K.J. Williams, Bodwrog, Llanbedrog, Pwllheli LL53 7RE (01758 740341). Modernised all-electric farmhouse accommodation to let without attendance. The 80 acre mixed farm offers stupendous views over the bays and headlands towards Snowdonia. Lleyn Peninsula is exceptionally mild - ideal for out of season holidays. Shooting is available on farm. Double glazing. Three double bedrooms accommodating six (cot provided); lounge, colour TV; kitchen with mahogany units, dining room, microwave, Parker Knoll suite. Bathroom and toilet. Linen supplied. Cleanliness assured. One house-trained pet welcome. Car preferable, ample concreted parking area. Shopping less than one mile away. Also available, 37 ft, three bedroomed caravan (shower, flush toilet, fridge, colour TV, microwave, etc). Glorious sandy beach one- and-a-half miles away by car but only one mile across fields. Village pub with Les Routiers listed restaurant three-quarters -of-a-mile, leisure centre five miles. Farmhouse terms from £180 to £330 weekly inclusive of electricity and bed linen. Mid-week or weekend bookings accepted during winter period and possibly March to May and in October. Caravan from £150 per week inclusive of electricity, gas and pillowcases. SAE for prompt reply. **WTB ★★★★** *SELF-CATERING.*

PORTHMADOG

Quality Cottages. Around the magnificent Welsh Coast. Away from the madding crowd. Near safe, sandy beaches. A small specialist agency offering privacy, peace and unashamed luxury. The first WTB Self Catering Gold Medal Award Winners. Residential standards - dishwashers, microwaves, washing machines, central heating, log fires. No slot meters. Linen provided. Pets welcome free. All in coastal areas famed for scenery, walks, wild flowers, birds, badgers and foxes. Free colour brochure **S.C. Rees, "Quality Cottages", Cerbid, Solva, Haverfordwest, Pembrokeshire SA62 6YE (01348 837871).** See also our full colour advertisement on the Inside Back Cover.
website: www.qualitycottages.co.uk

TREARDDUR BAY

Cliff Cottages and Plas Darien Apartments, Plas Darien, The Cliff, Trearddur Bay LL65 2TZ (01407 860789; Fax: 01407 861150). All year round holidays and short breaks in a choice of centrally heated apartments with wonderful sea views or stone-built cottages in village-like situation very near the sea. Own private indoor leisure complex with adults' pool and childrens' pool, saunas, solarium, gym, snooker, bowls, table tennis. Outdoor heated pool, tennis court, badminton, small golf, bowls, croquet. Adjacent 18 hole golf course, horse riding, windsurfing, canoeing, fishing. Phone or write for brochure. Short break details on request.

NORTH WALES

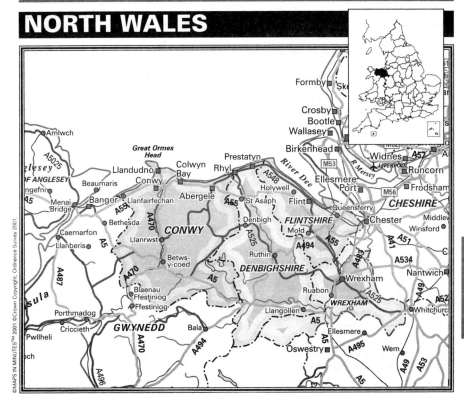

Visit the **FHG** website

www.holidayguides.com

for details of the wide choice of accommodation
featured in the full range of FHG titles

WALES

BETWS-Y-COED

Mrs E. Thomas, Bryn Farm, Nebo, Llanrwst LL26 0TE (01690 710315). Sleeps 2. Self-contained fully equipped farmhouse flat sleeping two on a beef and sheep farm. Situated in the Snowdonia National Park and approximately five miles from Betws-y-Coed with beautiful rural views. The accommodation comprises small double bedroom and large bathroom upstairs. Ground floor has a kitchen/diner/lounge including microwave, fridge/freezer, TV and video. Central heating in winter. Small patio with garden furniture at front of property. Ideally situated for peace and quiet. Excellent base for country walks. Sorry no pets. Terms from £90 to £160 including electricity and all linen. Short Breaks available out of season. Open all year except Christmas and New Year.

BETWS-Y-COED

Jim and Lilian Boughton, Bron Celyn, Lôn Muriau, Llanrwst Road, Betws-y-Coed LL24 0HD (01690 710333; Fax: 01690 710111). Our cosy 200 year-old converted coach house has been tastefully refurbished and offers accommodation for up to four persons. Upstairs: one double room with space for a cot and one bunk-bedded room with full length/width bunk beds. All bed linen is provided but not towels. Downstairs: lounge with colour TV/video and wood burning stove (ample supply of chopped timber available), kitchen with fridge, electric cooker, microwave, toaster and water heater. Shower room and toilet. Electric storage heaters fitted throughout. Open all year. Ideal centre for walking, climbing, fishing or simply just relaxing! Terms: £150 to £325 per week. Short Breaks available.
e-mail: welcome@broncelyn.co.uk
website: http://www.broncelyn.co.uk

CONWY

BRONGAIN, Ty'n-y-Groes. Homely Victorian stone cottage in picturesque Conwy valley. Mountain views. Enjoy walking, mountains, beaches, bird watching. Bodnant Gardens, RSPB reserve and Conwy castle, harbour and marina close by. Victorian Llandudno, Betws-y-Coed, Anglesey, Caernarfon and Snowdon easy distance. Good local food and pubs. Enclosed garden, patio, furniture. Parking. Gas fired central heating. Lounge with gas fire, dining room, kitchen, utility. Two double bedded rooms, one small single; blankets/duvet provided. Bathroom with bath, toilet and basin. Colour TV, electric cooker, fridge, microwave, washing machine and tumbler dryer. Terms £145-£300; heating, electricity included. Linen extra. Pets welcome. Open all year. Short low season breaks. **Mrs G. Simpole 105 Hay Green Road, Terrington-St-Clement, Kings Lynn, Norfolk PE34 4PU (01553 828897; mobile 07989 08665).**

LLANDONNA

Quality Cottages. Around the magnificent Welsh Coast. Away from the madding crowd. Near safe, sandy beaches. A small specialist agency offering privacy, peace and unashamed luxury. The first WTB Self Catering Gold Medal Award Winners. Residential standards - dishwashers, microwaves, washing machines, central heating, log fires. No slot meters. Linen provided. Pets welcome free. All in coastal areas famed for scenery, walks, wild flowers, birds, badgers and foxes. Free colour brochure **S.C. Rees, "Quality Cottages", Cerbid, Solva, Haverfordwest, Pembrokeshire SA62 6YE (01348 837871).** See also our full colour advertisement on the Inside Back Cover.
website: www.qualitycottages.co.uk

LLANGYNHAFAL

Y Bwthyn, Llangynhafal, Denbigh. This farm cottage is set in the picturesque hamlet of Llangynhafal between the historic towns of Ruthin and Denbigh with superb views of the Vale and beyond. Ideal base for walking Offa's Dyke and touring North Wales coast – Rhyl, Llandudno, Conway, etc. The cottage has two bedrooms, one double and one twin, bathroom with shower above the bath, lounge with oak beams, open fire and colour television. Kitchen/diner with cooker, microwave, fridge, toaster, iron and ironing board. Oil-fired central heating and double glazed. Parking for two cars in driveway. Garden and patio area with garden furniture. Clean linen and electricity included in price. Cleanliness guaranteed. No smoking. Terms £120 to £300. Bed and Breakfast available from £20 per person per night. **Mrs E. Morris, Carneddau, Llangynhafal, Denbigh LL16 4LN (01824 790460).**

Readers are requested to mention this guidebook when seeking accommodation (and please enclose a stamped addressed envelope).

MORFA NEFYN

Quality Cottages. Around the magnificent Welsh Coast. Away from the madding crowd. Near safe, sandy beaches. A small specialist agency offering privacy, peace and unashamed luxury. The first WTB Self Catering Gold Medal Award Winners. Residential standards - dishwashers, microwaves, washing machines, central heating, log fires. No slot meters. Linen provided. Pets welcome free. All in coastal areas famed for scenery, walks, wild flowers, birds, badgers and foxes. Free colour brochure **S.C. Rees, "Quality Cottages", Cerbid, Solva, Haverfordwest, Pembrokeshire SA62 6YE (01348 837871).** See also our full colour advertisement on the Inside Back Cover.
website: www.qualitycottages.co.uk

OSWESTRY

Mrs Glenice Jones, Lloran Ganol Farm, Llansilin, Oswestry SY10 7OX (01691 791287). Working farm. Sleeps 5. A luxury self-catering bungalow on mixed farm in quiet valley. Farm and bungalow are situated over the border in the Welsh hills in Clwyd. Five people accommodated in two double and one single bedrooms; bathroom, toilet; sittingroom, diningroom; colour TV; long kitchen with dining area; automatic washing machine, tumble dryer, dishwasher, microwave, freezer and fridge. Linen supplied. Extra charge for pets. Two and a half miles from the shops. Car essential - parking. Trout fishing on farm; horse riding locally, golf and trekking in surrounding area. Open all year round, the bungalow is suitable for partially disabled guests. Storage heaters, fitted carpets and garden furniture provided. Glass conservatory.
Weekly terms from £100. Bed and Breakfast (en suite) also available with family in house adjoining from £18 per night, Bed, Breakfast and Evening Meal (by arrangement) from £30 per night. **WTB ★★★★** *SELF-CATERING.*

CARMARTHENSHIRE

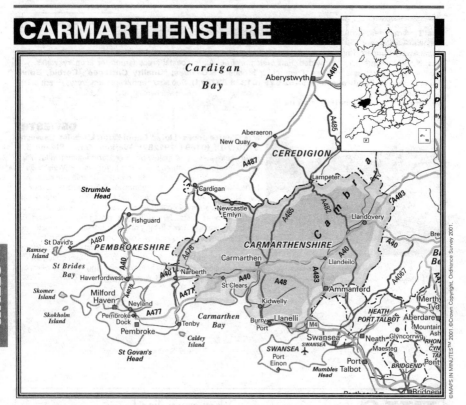

WALES

PENDINE

Mrs Sara Ellis, Sunnybank Cottage, Pendine SA33 4PS (01994 453431). Sleeps up to 5. A semi-detached cottage set down a mile long farm track and really tucked away from it all. The owner has an organic garden, an area of rough pasture and a tree-planting area. Pendine Sands is just a ten minute drive away and Marros Beach a mile and a half walk. The cottage is fully equipped and consists of a kitchen, living/dining area, two bedrooms (one double, one bunkbeads) and bathroom. Night storage heaters and log burning stove for those cold winter nights. Room for parking. Pets allowed. Pub two miles. Shops ten-minute drive. Rates from £200 to £400 including fuel, power and linen. Open all year. Short breaks available. **WTB ★★★** *SELF-CATERING*.

FHG PUBLICATIONS

publish a large range of well-known accommodation guides. We will be happy to send you details or you can use the order form at the back of this book.

CEREDIGION

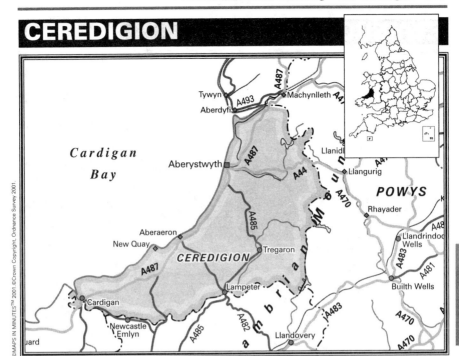

QUALITY COTTAGES

AROUND THE MAGNIFICENT WELSH COAST

Away from the Madding Crowd • Near safe sandy beaches

A small specialist agency with over 40 years experience of providing quality self-catering, offers privacy, peace and unashamed luxury. The first Wales Tourist Board Self-Catering Award Winner. Highest residential standards. *Dishwashers, Microwaves, Washing Machines, Central Heating. No Slot meters.*

LOG FIRES • LINEN PROVIDED • PETS WELCOME FREE!

All in coastal areas famed for scenery, walks, wild-flowers, birds, badgers and foxes.

Free colour brochure from F.G. Rees "Quality Cottages", Cerbid, Solva, Haverfordwest, Pembrokeshire SA62 6YE

Telephone: (01348) 837871 • Website: www.qualitycottages.co.uk

ABERPORTH

Quality Cottages. Around the magnificent Welsh Coast. Away from the madding crowd. Near safe, sandy beaches. A small specialist agency offering privacy, peace and unashamed luxury. The first WTB Self Catering Gold Medal Award Winners. Residential standards - dishwashers, microwaves, washing machines, central heating, log fires. No slot meters. Linen provided. Pets welcome free. All in coastal areas famed for scenery, walks, wild flowers, birds, badgers and foxes. Free colour brochure **S.C. Rees, "Quality Cottages", Cerbid, Solva, Haverfordwest, Pembrokeshire SA62 6YE (01348 837871).** See also our full colour advertisement on the Inside Back Cover.   **website: www.qualitycottages.co.uk**

LLANGRANNOG

Quality Cottages. Around the magnificent Welsh Coast. Away from the madding crowd. Near safe, sandy beaches. A small specialist agency offering privacy, peace and unashamed luxury. The first WTB Self Catering Gold Medal Award Winners. Residential standards - dishwashers, microwaves, washing machines, central heating, log fires. No slot meters. Linen provided. Pets welcome free. All in coastal areas famed for scenery, walks, wild flowers, birds, badgers and foxes. Free colour brochure **S.C. Rees, "Quality Cottages", Cerbid, Solva, Haverfordwest, Pembrokeshire SA62 6YE (01348 837871).** See also our full colour advertisement on the Inside Back Cover.   **website: www.qualitycottages.co.uk**

PEMBROKESHIRE

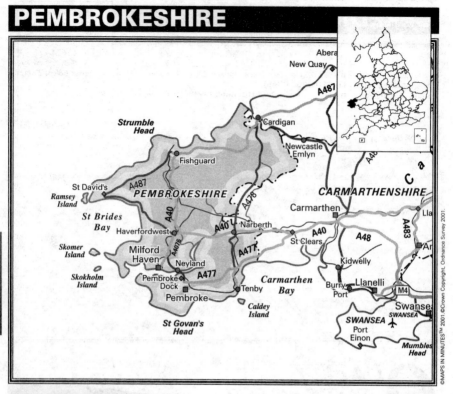

WALES

AMROTH

Carol Lloyd, East Llanteg Farm, Llanteg, Amroth SA67 8QA (01834 831336). Two charming cottages privately situated and ideally located for exploring Pembrokeshire. The resorts of Saundersfoot and Tenby are close at hand with the seaside resort of Amroth and the coastal path just minutes away. Each cottage sleeps four to five adults; cots and highchairs are also provided. All facilities including a fully fitted kitchen, central heating, colour television, etc. are included. There is ample private parking plus a lawned garden area and patio with garden furniture provided. **WTB ★★★★★** *SELF-CATERING*.
e-mail: john@pembrokeshireholiday.co.uk
website: www.pembrokeshireholiday.co.uk

BOSHERTON

Quality Cottages. Around the magnificent Welsh Coast. Away from the madding crowd. Near safe, sandy beaches. A small specialist agency offering privacy, peace and unashamed luxury. The first WTB Self Catering Gold Medal Award Winners. Residential standards - dishwashers, microwaves, washing machines, central heating, log fires. No slot meters. Linen provided. Pets welcome free. All in coastal areas famed for scenery, walks, wild flowers, birds, badgers and foxes. Free colour brochure **S.C. Rees, "Quality Cottages", Cerbid, Solva, Haverfordwest, Pembrokeshire SA62 6YE (01348 837871).** See also our full colour advertisement on the Inside Back Cover.
website: www.qualitycottages.co.uk

The FHG Directory of Website Addresses

on pages 243 – 272 is a useful quick reference guide for holiday accommodation with e-mail and/or website details

BROAD HAVEN

4 Timber Hill, Broad Haven, Pembrokeshire National Park. Sleeps 6. Cedarwood holiday home at Timber Hill Farm. Three-quarters of a mile walk by woodland path to wide sandy beach. A few hundred yards from the Coastal Footpath. Ideal centre for family holidays, walking, windsurfing, bird watching, etc. Situated on a south-facing slope, overlooking a valley, well equipped. Three bedrooms, sleeping six, plus a cot if required, livingroom, kitchen, bathroom, balcony and patio. Parking within a few yards. Electricity is included in the rental. Pets allowed, by arrangement. Terms £100 to £285 per week. Please apply to **Mrs L.E. Ashton, 10 St Leonards Road, Thames Ditton, Surrey KT7 0RJ (020 8398 6349).**
e-mail: lejash@aol.com   website: http://members.aol.com/lejash/thindex.htm

NEWGALE

Quality Cottages. Around the magnificent Welsh Coast. Away from the madding crowd. Near safe, sandy beaches. A small specialist agency offering privacy, peace and unashamed luxury. The first WTB Self Catering Gold Medal Award Winnners. Residential standards - dishwashers, microwaves, washing machines, central heating, log fires. No slot meters. Linen provided. Pets welcome free. All in coastal areas famed for scenery, walks, wild flowers, birds, badgers and foxes. Free colour brochure **S.C. Rees, "Quality Cottages", Cerbid, Solva, Haverfordwest, Pembrokeshire SA62 6YE (01348 837871).** See also our full colour advertisement on the Inside Back Cover.
website: www.qualitycottages.co.uk

NEWPORT

Quality Cottages. Around the magnificent Welsh Coast. Away from the madding crowd. Near safe, sandy beaches. A small specialist agency offering privacy, peace and unashamed luxury. The first WTB Self Catering Gold Medal Award Winnners. Residential standards - dishwashers, microwaves, washing machines, central heating, log fires. No slot meters. Linen provided. Pets welcome free. All in coastal areas famed for scenery, walks, wild flowers, birds, badgers and foxes. Free colour brochure **S.C. Rees, "Quality Cottages", Cerbid, Solva, Haverfordwest, Pembrokeshire SA62 6YE (01348 837871).** See also our full colour advertisement on the Inside Back Cover.
website: www.qualitycottages.co.uk

ST DAVID'S

Quality Cottages. Around the magnificent Welsh Coast. Away from the madding crowd. Near safe, sandy beaches. A small specialist agency offering privacy, peace and unashamed luxury. The first WTB Self Catering Gold Medal Award Winnners. Residential standards - dishwashers, microwaves, washing machines, central heating, log fires. No slot meters. Linen provided. Pets welcome free. All in coastal areas famed for scenery, walks, wild flowers, birds, badgers and foxes. Free colour brochure **S.C. Rees, "Quality Cottages", Cerbid, Solva, Haverfordwest, Pembrokeshire SA62 6YE (01348 837871).** See also our full colour advertisement on the Inside Back Cover.
website: www.qualitycottages.co.uk

ST DAVID'S

Liz Stiles, Swn-y-Don, Tregwynt, Castle Morris, Haverfordwest SA62 5UX (Tel & Fax: 01348 891616). Sleep 2-12. Pembrokeshire Coast – Newport to Little Haven. Charming, individual cottages situated near sandy beaches, rocky bays and spectacular cliff walks. Traditional stone-built cottages or modern properties, many with central heating and wood-burning stoves. All furnished to high residential standards, fully equipped and personally supervised. Watersports, golf, birdwatching and wild flowers. Boat trips to the islands. Explore the Preseli Mountains, castles, cromlechs and Iron Age forts. Visit art galleries and craft workshops, relax in country pubs and quality restaurants. Pets and children welcome.
e-mail: lizstiles@onetel.net.uk
website: www.pembrokeshireholidays.co.uk

SOLVA

Quality Cottages. Around the magnificent Welsh Coast. Away from the madding crowd. Near safe, sandy beaches. A small specialist agency offering privacy, peace and unashamed luxury. The first WTB Self Catering Gold Medal Award Winnners. Residential standards - dishwashers, microwaves, washing machines, central heating, log fires. No slot meters. Linen provided. Pets welcome free. All in coastal areas famed for scenery, walks, wild flowers, birds, badgers and foxes. Free colour brochure **S.C. Rees, "Quality Cottages", Cerbid, Solva, Haverfordwest, Pembrokeshire SA62 6YE (01348 837871).** See also our full colour advertisement on the Inside Back Cover.
website: www.qualitycottages.co.uk

TENBY

Quality Cottages. Around the magnificent Welsh Coast. Away from the madding crowd. Near safe, sandy beaches. A small specialist agency offering privacy, peace and unashamed luxury. The first WTB Self Catering Gold Medal Award Winners. Residential standards - dishwashers, microwaves, washing machines, central heating, log fires. No slot meters. Linen provided. Pets welcome free. All in coastal areas famed for scenery, walks, wild flowers, birds, badgers and foxes. Free colour brochure **S.C. Rees, "Quality Cottages", Cerbid, Solva, Haverfordwest, Pembrokeshire SA62 6YE (01348 837871).** See also our full colour advertisement on the Inside Back Cover.
website: www.qualitycottages.co.uk

WHITLAND

Mrs Angela Colledge, Gwarmacwydd, Llanfallteg, Whitland SA34 0XH (01437 563260; Fax: 01437 563839). Gwarmacwydd is a country estate of over 450 acres including two miles of riverbank. Come and see a real farm in action; the hustle and bustle of harvest, newborn calves and lambs. Children are welcomed. On the estate are five character stone cottages. Each cottage has been lovingly converted from traditional farm buildings, parts of which are over 200 years old. Each cottage is fully furnished and equipped with all modern conveniences. All electricity and linen included. All cottages are heated for year-round use. Colour brochure available. **WTB ★★★★** *SELF-CATERING.*
e-mail: info@a-farm-holiday.org
website: www.a-farm-holiday.org

St Catherine's Island, off the coast at Tenby, Pembrokeshire

POWYS

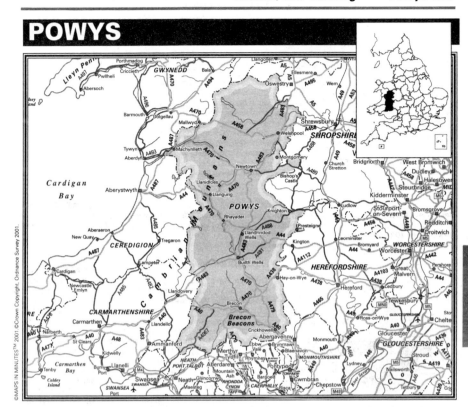

WALES

See also Colour Display Advertisement

GARTHMYL

Phillip and Daphne Jones, Penllwyn Lodges, Garthmyl SY15 6SB (Tel & Fax: 01686 640269). Set in a 30 acre woodland, all our lodges are individually designed and fully fitted throughout, including colour TV, microwave and all bedding. 19 lodges, sleeping two to eight people, and one cottage which sleeps six. On arrival, meet our Vietnamese pigs, Tilley the Llama and Noddy the donkey. Fishing is available on our lake, the canal and River Severn at no extra charge. Relax in the landscaped gardens and feed the ducks and swans, or walk in the woodland which is teeming with wildlife. Near to pony trekking, quad biking, castles and lakes. Open all year round. Brochure available on request.
e-mail: penllwynlodges@supanet.com
website: www.penllwynlodges.co.uk

KNIGHTON

Mrs J. M. Morgan, Selley Hall, Llanfair Waterdine, Knighton LD7 1TR (01547 528429). Sleeps 6 plus cot. A warm welcome awaits guests to this well-furnished and comfortable self-catering accommodation on a working farm overlooking Offa's Dyke. The surrounding countryside is very peaceful with beautiful views; quiet lanes and roads make it an ideal centre for walking and touring. The accommodation comprises two double and one twin-bedded rooms; bathroom, toilet; large lounge with colour TV; diningroom/kitchen, fully fitted, all electric. Ample parking and garden for guests' use. Linen may be hired. Midweek and Short Break bookings taken out of season. Trout fishing in private pool. Many local historic places to visit. Sorry, no pets. Children welcome. Terms from £90 to £230 per week.

LLANDRINDOD WELLS

**Pippins at Neuadd Farm, Penybont, Llandrindod Wells.
Sleeps 4.** Pippins is a superb converted Granary set in the grounds of Neuadd Farm, overlooking the lovely Ithon Valley in the heart of the scenic Mid-Wales. Furnished to a high standard with comfy sofas, Pippins is well-equipped with all modern facilities and full central heating. The accommodation sleeps four in a double en suite room and a twin-bedded room with separate shower room. Linen and towels provided, full electric cooker, microwave, washer/dryer, fridge/freezer, TV and video. Private garden with furniture and barbecue. Ideally situated for walking, golf, fishing, horse riding, bowls and wildlife. **WTB ★★★★★** *SELF-CATERING*. Contact: **Peter and Jackie Longley, Neuadd Farm, Penybont, Llandrindod Wells, Powys LD1 5SW**

(01597 851032; Fax: 01597 851034).
e-mail: jackie@neuaddfarm.fsnet.co.uk website: www.neuaddfarm.co.uk

LLANIDLOES

Barn View Cottage, Llanidloes SY18 6PD . A stone and timber-clad barn converted into three self-contained holiday cottages. Idyllic hillside position overlooking magnificent views through the Severn Valley. Contact: **Mr and Mrs Knight (01656 413527).**
e-mail: wendy_robert_barn_view@supanet.com

LLANWRTHWL

**Dyffryn Barn, Llanwrthwl, Llandrindod Wells LD1 6NU.
Sleeps 5.** Idyllically situated in the Cambrian Mountains above the Upper Wye Valley with its magnificent scenery and close to the Elan Valley with its spectacular dams. Wonderful hill walking, cycling, fishing and bird watching (red kites; RSPB reserves) in this unspoilt area of "Wild Wales". Attached to barn and owners' home, the three-bedroomed, centrally heated cottage comprises: double bedroom, twin-bedded room, single with washbasin, comfortable upstairs sitting room with TV/video and a lovely view, shower room with toilet. Downstairs cloakroom. Well-equipped kitchen/diningroom. No smoking. Heating and electricity included and bed linen supplied. Rates £155 to £300. Bed and Breakfast also available. Details from **Mrs G. Tyler, Dyffryn Farm, Llanwrthwl, Llandrindod Wells LD1 6NU (01597 811017; Fax: 01597 810609).**
e-mail: dyffrynfm@cs.com   website: www.dyffrynfarm.co.uk

MID WALES

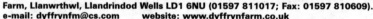

Clyn, Elan Valley, Rhayader LD6 5HP. A remote and peaceful smallholding set high on the edge of open moorland with wonderful views overlooking wooded valleys and heatherclad hillsides, offering holiday accommodation in the cottage (sleeping seven), and the Granary (sleeping four). It is ideally situated for walking, mountain biking, fishing, birdwatching and nature-lovers generally. Children of all ages are catered for with an outside play area (sandpit, swing, etc.), friendly farmyard animals and unlimited space; while inside there is a games room with table tennis/snooker table. Both properties are fully equipped, including woodburners. Homegrown organic produce available, pets by arrangement. Rates per week: £170 to £335 all inclusive. Short breaks available. Contact: **Jan Jenkins (01597 810120).**
e-mail: theclyn@freezone.co.uk

NEWTOWN

Mrs D. Pryce, Aberbechan Farm, Newtown SY16 3BJ (01686 630675). Working farm, join in. Sleeps 10. This part of quaint Tudor farmhouse with its lovely oak beams is situated in picturesque countryside on a mixed farm with trout fishing and shooting in season. Newtown three miles, Welshpool, Powis Castle and Llanfair Light Railway, 14 miles; 45 miles to coast. The accommodation sleeps ten persons in four double and two single bedrooms, also cot. Two bathrooms, two toilets. Sitting/diningroom with colour TV. Fully fitted oak kitchen with fridge, electric cooker, washing machine and dishwasher. Log fires and off-peak heaters. Electricity on meter. Large lawn with pool and swing. Everything supplied for visitors' comfort. Linen available for overseas guests at extra cost. Car essential to obtain the best from the holiday. Village shop one-and-a-half miles away. Open all year. Children welcome. SAE please.

TALYBONT-ON-USK

1 Caerfanell Place, Talybont-on-Usk, Brecon. Talybont-on-Usk is a small village nestling below the Beacons in the National Park. Cottage is built of traditional Welsh slate and stone, situated in the centre of village with garden leading to River Caerfanell. Three bedrooms sleep seven; bathroom and toilet upstairs and shower room and toilet downstairs; comfortable lounge with colour TV and cosy wood/coal stove for winter or chilly nights. A washing machine, dryer, dishwasher, fridge, freezer and microwave are complemented by a full range of smaller kitchen essentials. Roadside parking. Excellent village pubs serve a wide selection of beers. Short Breaks available out of season. Canal trips available nearby as are many other sporting activities. Terms from £215 to £450 per week. Winter fuel supplement of £20 October to April, payable with rent. Linen and duvets provided. No pets. Apply: **Mrs F.I. Smith, Holt's Farm House, Coopers Lane, Fordcombe, Near Tunbridge Wells, Kent TN3 0RN (01892 740338).**

WALES

• • *Some Useful Guidance for Guests and Hosts* • •

Every year literally thousands of holidays, short breaks and overnight stops are arranged through our guides, the vast majority without any problems at all. In a handful of cases, however, difficulties do arise about bookings, which often could have been prevented from the outset.

It is important to remember that when accommodation has been booked, both parties – guests and hosts – have entered into a form of contract. We hope that the following points will provide helpful guidance.

GUESTS:

• When enquiring about accommodation, be as precise as possible. Give exact dates, numbers in your party and the ages of any children.

• State the number and type of rooms wanted and also what catering you require – bed and breakfast, full board etc. Make sure that the position about evening meals is clear – and about pets, reductions for children or any other special points.

• Read our reviews carefully to ensure that the proprietors you are going to contact can supply what you want. Ask for a letter confirming all arrangements, if possible.

• If you have to cancel, do so as soon as possible. Proprietors do have the right to retain deposits and under certain circumstances to charge for cancelled holidays if adequate notice is not given and they cannot re-let the accommodation.

HOSTS:

• Give details about your facilities and about any special conditions. Explain your deposit system clearly and arrangements for cancellations, charges etc. and whether or not your terms include VAT.

• If for any reason you are unable to fulfil an agreed booking without adequate notice, you may be under an obligation to arrange suitable alternative accommodation or to make some form of compensation.

While every effort is made to ensure accuracy, we regret that FHG Publications cannot accept responsibility for errors, omissions or misrepresentations in our entries or any consequences thereof. Prices in particular should be checked because we go to press early. We will follow up complaints but cannot act as arbiters or agents for either party.

REPUBLIC OF IRELAND – Co. Clare

IRELAND

BALLYVAUGHAN

Ballyvaughan Village and Country Holiday Homes. Offering a wide range of top quality self-catering holiday accommodation in the charming village of Ballyvaughan on the southern shores of Galway Bay in the heartland of the world famous Burren district of County Clare. You can choose from our four star houses, which sleep four or six, or one of our apartments, which sleep two or three. All our village accommodation is located in the centre of the village. There is a good choice of restaurants and pubs in the area. Our location is an ideal base to explore the unique Burren landscape or tour the west coast of Ireland. All our accommodation is available all year and are very suitable for off-season bookings. Terms from 200 euros to 800 euros. Ring or write for our full colour brochure: **Mr George Quinn, Frances Street, Kilrush, Co.Clare (00353 659 051977; Fax: 00353 659 052370).**
e-mail: vchh@iol.ie   **website: www.ballyvaughan-cottages.com**

FOREIGN – Malta

MALTA

Holiday Complex - Malta

Winston

Self-catering apartments, ideal for families and couples, centrally located and a few metres from the sea and the beautiful promenade. The Aparthotel has all the facilities for an enjoyable holiday close at hand, with a variety of shops, bars, restaurants, food stores, cinema, night life entertainment, water sports, and a casino.

Hotel Facilities • choice of 1/2/3 bedrooms • parking • bar and restaurant • swimming pool • lounge and luggage room • hotel doctor • babysitting • transport from airport (extra) • car hire • cots and sunbeds free.

Short Lets: From £88 per week for 2 persons
Long Lets: From November 2002 to 30th April 2003
£248 monthly for two persons.
For brochures and prices apply
**WINSTON APARTHOTEL, IMREJKBA STREET, BUGIBBA SPB 13 MALTA
TELEPHONE: +356 21572039 • FAX: +356 21577419**
e-mail: info@winstonmalta.com • website: www.winstonmalta.com

---

The **FHG**

**GOLF
GUIDE**

*Where to Play
Where to Stay*

Available from most bookshops, THE GOLF GUIDE (published annually) covers details of every UK golf course – well over 2800 entries – for holiday or business golf. Hundreds of hotel entries offer convenient accommodation, accompanying details of the courses – the 'pro', par score, length etc.

In association with 'Golf Monthly' and including Holiday Golf in Ireland, France, Portugal, Spain, The USA, South Africa and Thailand

£9.99 from bookshops or from the publishers (postage charged outside UK) • FHG Publications, Abbey Mill Business Centre, Paisley PA1 1TJ

CARAVAN & CAMPING HOLIDAYS

ENGLAND

CORNWALL

ST IVES

**G. & H. Rogers, Hellesveor Caravan and Camping Site,
Hellesveor Farm, St Ives TR26 3AD (01736 795738).** Six-
berth caravans for hire on small secluded approved farm site, one
mile from St Ives town centre and nearest beaches, five minutes
from bus route on Land's End Road (B3306). Coastal and
countryside walks nearby. Shop and laundry facilities on site.
Special terms for early and late season. Campers and touring
caravans welcome. Electrical hook-ups available. Dogs allowed
under strict control. Nearby horse riding, pony trekking, golf
course, bowling greens and leisure centre. SAE for further details.

WADEBRIDGE

**Gunvenna Touring Caravan and Camping Park, St Minver
PL27 6QN (01208 862405).** The Park is a well drained site of
level grassland on 10 acres commanding uninterrupted views of
the countryside within five minutes' drive of safe, golden, sandy
beaches. Local activities include golf, fishing, tennis, surfing and
swimming, etc. Site facilities include two modern toilet and
shower blocks, launderette and ironing room, children's play
area, children's games room (9am to 10pm), barbecue area, dog
exercise area, shop, telephone, etc. We also have a licensed Bar
with indoor heated swimming pool. Please send for our colour
brochure and tariff.

CUMBRIA

KESWICK
Burns Caravan & Camping Site, St Johns in the Vale CA12 4RR (01768 779225). Quiet family-run caravan and camping site, situated two-and-a-half miles east of Keswick-on-Derwentwater. Beautiful views of the surrounding fells. Ideal centre for walking and touring the Lake District. Touring caravans, motor caravans and tents are welcome. Electric hook-ups are available. Toilet block with hot showers etc. Prices from £7.50 per caravan and from £6 per tent, enquiries with S.A.E. please to **Mrs Linda Lamb.**
e-mail: llamb@callnetuk.com

KESWICK
Scotgate Chalet, Camping and Caravan Holiday Park, Braithwaite, Keswick CA12 5TF (017687 78343). Careful thought and years of experience have gone into the planning of Scotgate. The result is a spacious and comfortable holiday park, superbly placed between Derwentwater and Bassenthwaite Lake. All our chalets and caravans are maintained to the same high standard. We are always happy to welcome touring caravans and all types of tents. The ground has the double advantage to campers of being level and well drained. There is a licensed shop selling groceries, newspapers and snacks and also a licensed cafe. Laundry room with washing machines, tumble dryers and ironing facilities. Showers, shaver points and hair dryers are also provided in the toilet blocks. The site has its own games room with pool table and video machines. Please telephone or write for further details.

LITTLE ASBY

Mrs L.M. Watson, Whygill Head Farm, Little Asby, Appleby-in-Westmorland CA16 6QD (017683 71531). Two six-berth caravans on their own private site in half-acre sheltered copse near farm. Fully-equipped except for bed linen. Electricity and running water in both vans. Heating and cooking by Calor gas (no extra charge). Flush toilet, shower and telephone nearby. Children welcome; also pets under control. Ideal centre for walkers and naturalists. Golf, fishing, swimming and pony trekking; interesting market towns and villages. Ideal for relaxation, fell walking, touring Yorkshire Dales and Lake District. Price from £85 per week low season, £90 high season; weekends £14 per night.

DERBYSHIRE

ASHBOURNE

Mrs Louie Tatlow, Ashfield Farm, Calwich, Near Ashbourne DE6 2EB (01335 324279 or 324443). Working farm. Five modern six-berth caravans, fully equipped, each with gas cooker, fridge, TV; shower and flush toilet; mains electricity. Ashfield Farm overlooks the peaceful Dove Valley and is convenient for the Peak District. The old market town of Ashbourne is only two miles away, with golf courses, swimming pool, squash and bowling. Within easy reach of stately homes like Haddon Hall and Chatsworth, with the Potteries and Lichfield 25 miles distant, Uttoxeter 10 miles away while Alton Towers Theme Park is under five miles away. Prices and brochure on request. Write or telephone for further information.

DEVON

ASHBURTON

Parkers Farm Holiday Park, Ashburton TQ13 7LJ (01364 652598; Fax: 01364 654004). A friendly, family-run farm site, set in 400 acres and surrounded by beautiful countryside. 12 miles to the sea and close to Dartmoor National Park. Ideal for touring Devon/Cornwall. Perfect for children and pets with all farm animals, play area and plenty of space to roam, also large area for dogs. Holiday cottages and caravans fully equipped except for linen. Level touring site with some hard standings. Electric hook-up. Free showers in fully tiled block, laundry room and games room. Small family bar, restaurant, shop and phone. Prices start from £90 Low Season to £480 High Season. Good discounts for couples. To find us: From Exeter take A38 to Plymouth till you see "26 miles Plymouth" sign; take second left at Alston Cross signposted to Woodland and Denbury *ETC* ★★★★, *AA ✓✓✓✓. BRITISH FARM TOURIST AWARD. 2000 GOLD AWARD FOR QUALITY & SERVICE. SILVER DAVID BELLAMY CONSERVATION AWARD. PRACTICAL CARAVAN TOP 100 PARKS 2000.*
e-mail: parkersfarm@btconnect.com   **website: www.parkersfarm.co.uk**

KINGSBRIDGE

Mounts Farm Touring Park, The Mounts, Near East Allington, Kingsbridge TQ9 7QJ (01548 521591). Mounts Farm is a family-run site in the heart of south Devon. On site facilities include FREE hot showers, flush toilets, FREE hot water in washing-up room, razor points, laundry and information room, electric hook-ups and site shop. We welcome tents, touring caravans and motor caravans. Large pitches in level, sheltered fields. No charges for awnings. Children and pets welcome. Situated three miles north of Kingsbridge, Mounts Farm is an ideal base for exploring Dartmouth, Salcombe, Totnes, Dartmoor and the many safe, sandy beaches nearby. Please telephone or write for a free brochure. Self-catering cottage also available.

THE SALTER FAMILY WELCOMES YOU

HALDON LODGE FARM
Kennford, Near Exeter, Devon
*20 minutes from Dawlish
and Teignmouth Beaches*

Freedom and safety for all the family

Central for South Devon coast and Exeter in an attractive setting, three modern six-berth holiday caravans and log cabin in a private and friendly park. Excellent facilities including picnic tables and farm shop. Weekly barbecues plus hay-ride, with 'sounds of the sixties' at a friendly country inn nearby, subject to demand during school holidays. Set in glorious rural Devon, the site offers freedom and safety for all the family. Very reasonable prices. Pets accepted/exercising area. Open all year.

Relax and enjoy the scenery or stroll along the many forest lanes. Famous country inns nearby. Three coarse fishing lakes close to the Park and the attraction of ponies and horse riding at a nearby farm.

Large six-berth caravans, two bedrooms, lounge with TV, bathroom/toilet (H/C); rates from £70 to £195 High Season.

Personal attention and welcome by David & Betty Salter.
For brochure telephone 01392 832312.

Mr & Mrs V Tomkins,
*GL41 **Bideford Bay Holiday Park,***
Bucks Cross, Near Bideford,
Devon EX39 5DU
Tel: 0771 971 7121
e-mail: mariposa@tesco.net

Attractive privately owned, fully equipped, elegant 3 bedroom/6 berth caravan. Situated on a quiet secluded spot at Bideford Bay Holiday Park – a Park Resorts site – with beautiful sea views. Full amenities and entertainment included in the price. Linen also supplied. Small pets welcome by arrangement. Bideford Bay/Clovelly area ideal for hikers and ramblers. Nearby are beaches, shopping and local attractions for families with children. Open March to October from £200 p/w low season. Brochure and further information available on request.

See also Colour Display Advertisement

SEATON
Axevale Caravan Park, Seaton EX12 2DF (0800 0688816).
A quiet, family-run park with 68 modern and luxury caravans for hire. The park overlooks the delightful River Axe Valley, and is just a 10 minute walk from the town with its wonderfully long, award-winning beach. Children will love our extensive play area, with its sand pit, paddling pool, swings and slide. Laundry facilities are provided and there is a wide selection of goods on sale in the park shop which is open every day. All of our caravans have a shower, toilet, fridge and TV. Also, with no clubhouse, a relaxing atmosphere is ensured. Prices from £75 per week; reductions for three or fewer persons early/late season. ✓✓✓
website: www.axevale.co.uk

TEIGN VALLEY

S. and G. Harrison-Crawford, Silver Birches, Teign Valley, Trusham, Newton Abbot TQ13 0NJ (01626 852172). Two 23ft and 29ft four-berth caravans in an attractive two acre garden on the bank of the River Teign. Each has mains water, electricity, shower/bath, flush toilet, washbasin, immersion heater, Calor gas cooker, fridge; TV. Ideally situated two miles from A38 on B3193. Dartmoor, Exeter, Torquay easily accessible. Sea 12 miles. Car essential, ample parking. Excellent centre for fishing (river and reservoir), bird-watching, forest walks; 70 yards private salmon and trout fishing. Golf courses and horse riding within easy reach. Shops two-and-a-half miles. Pets by arrangement. Dogs free of charge. Open March to October. Terms from £135 to £185 per week. Bed and Breakfast available in bungalow from £25 per person per night, £168 per week per person

DORSET

WAREHAM

Manor Farm Caravan Park, East Stoke, Wareham BH20 6AW (Tel & Fax: 01929 462870). David and Gillian Topp (resident proprietors) look forward to welcoming you to their clean, quiet, secluded, level touring park - in total 50 pitches some of which are for seasonal pitches. We are in the River Frome valley in an Area of Outstanding Natural Beauty central for most of Dorset. On site you will find clean showers & toilets, play area, public telephone, 16 amp electric hook-ups, gas exchange, short and long term storage for caravans and boats, plus seasonal pitches. Find us mid-way between Wareham and Wool half a mile south from East Stoke Church off A352. Or off B3070 into Holme Lane or from Wool take Bindon Lane. Sorry no groups. SAE or dial a brochure. **AA** *THREE PENNANTS*, **RAC** *APPOINTED, ALAN ROGERS QUALITY SITE GUIDE.*

e-mail: info@manorfarmcp.co.uk
websites: www.manorfarmcp.co.uk   or   **www.caravan-sitefinder.co.uk**

See also Colour Display Advertisement

WIMBORNE

Woolsbridge Manor Farm Caravan Park, Three Legged Cross, Wimborne, Dorset BH21 6RA (01202 826369). Situated approximately three-and-a-half-miles from the New Forest market town of Ringwood – easy access to the south coast. Seven acres level, semi-sheltered, well-drained spacious pitches. Quiet country location on a working farm, ideal and safe for families. Showers, mother/baby area, laundry room, washing up area, chemical disposal, payphone, electric hook-ups, battery charging. Children's play area on site. Site shop. Dogs welcome on leads. Fishing adjacent. Moors Valley Country Park golf course one mile. Pub and restaurant 10 minutes' walk. **AA** *THREE PENNANTS*, **ETC** ★★★

ESSEX

CLACTON-ON-SEA

Highfield Holiday Park, London Road, Clacton-on-Sea CO16 9QY (0870 442 9287; Fax: 01255 689 805). The ultimate in holiday venues. Highfield enjoys high levels of repeat business and being located on the famous Essex sunshine coast it's easy to see why. Within easy reach of golden beaches and bustling, colourful promenades on the one hand and gentle Essex countryside on the other, it's a region of contrasts. Enjoy the superb entertainment and range of facilities on offer at Highfield and enjoy a drink at the pool's edge whilst your children amuse themselves for hours on the new flume and slide. Large outdoor pools with amazing new flume and slide. Outdoor adventure play area. Children's entertainment with Dylan the Dinosaur. Well-stocked convenience store. Solarium. Wide-screen satellite TV. Amusement centre featuring some of the latest electronic games. Organised outdoor games (football, rounders, baseball). Fantastic beaches nearby. Pony trekking available locally. Pool-side bar for snacks and beverages. GREAT BRITISH HOLIDAY PARKS.

e-mail: highfield@gbholidayparks.co.uk   **web: www.gbholidayparks.co.uk**

MERSEA ISLAND

Coopers Beach, East Mersea, Mersea Island, Near Colchester, Essex CO5 8TN (Tel: 0870 442 9288; Fax: 01206 385 483). Discover an island that will capture your imagination. Coopers Beach is located on Mersea Island, whose only link with the mainland is an ancient causeway known as The Strood. West Mersea is a small resort and sailing centre. At East Mersea, beautiful leafy lanes wind their way towards the seafront, where you will find the park. Here the clubhouse with adjacent pool is an ideal place to relax, and offers great sea views. We think you will agree, this park has it all. Popular outdoor heated pool (open May-Sept). Beach access. Adventure playground. Dylan the Dinosaur's Children's Club. Golf courses nearby. Pony trekking nearby (7 miles). Fast food takeaway. Adult beach club. Fishing trips nearby. Nightlife. Countryside walks. Multi-sports centre. Tennis court. Launderette. Family clubroom (suitable for children) with outdoor beach terrace and fantastic sea views. GREAT BRITISH HOLIDAY PARKS.

e-mail: coopersbeach@gbholidayparks.co.uk   **web: www.gbholidayparks.co.uk**

ST LAWRENCE BAY

Waterside Holiday Park, St Lawrence Bay, Near Southminster CM0 7LY (0870 442 9298; Fax: 01621 778106). Leisurely pursuits in an idyllic countryside setting. Waterside is an attractive park with leafy, tree-lined avenues. Situated by the River Blackwater, the park enjoys fine estuary views towards Mersea Island. With a modern, quality fleet of hire caravans and excellent facilities that include an indoor pool, sauna and jacuzzi, the park is well equipped for holidaymakers. The surrounding district has varied attractions and several nature reserves and footpaths, or for shopping there's Maldon, an attractive riverside town. Indoor leisure pool with adjacent children's splash pool and slide. Relaxing sauna and jacuzzi. Amusement Centre. Outdoor play area. Sheltered beach nearby. Waterside Country Club. Lovely tree-lined walks. Golf (9 & 18-hole) and fishing nearby. Café/take-away. Horse riding available locally. Well-stocked mini-market. Lake feature. GREAT BRITISH HOLIDAY PARKS.

e-mail: waterside@gbholidayparks.co.uk   **website: www.gbholidayparks.co.uk**

WALTON-ON-THE-NAZE

Naze Marine Holiday Park, Hall Lane, Walton-on-the-Naze CO14 8HL (0870 442 9292; Fax: 01255 682427). Lazy days at the Naze. The Essex coast is dotted with colourful seaside resorts and Naze Marine sits alongside one of these. Walton-on-the-Naze boasts golden beaches, a nature reserve and pier. Take time to explore the many shops selling seaside specialities and when you're ready head back to the park where the emphasis is on relaxation. This delightful park offers a friendly, country club together with superb heated outdoor pool complex. Outdoor swimming pool. Sea fishing trips. Adjacent Nature Reserve. Children's amusements and play area. Well-stocked convenience store. Naze Armada Country Club. Golf, horse riding and fishing locally. Crabbing off the jetty. Attractive Marina close-by. Café/take-away. Sandy beaches. GREAT BRITISH HOLIDAY PARKS.

e-mail: nazemarine@gbholidayparks.co.uk   **website: www.gbholidayparks.co.uk**

GLOUCESTERSHIRE

TEWKESBURY

Mill Avon Holiday Park, Gloucester Road, Tewkesbury GL20 5SW (01684 296876). As the name suggests, our Park is bordered on one side by the river Mill Avon and has pleasant views across the Severn Ham to the Malvern Hills. The historic town of Tewkesbury is on the doorstep and a few minutes' walk takes you through picturesque streets past the magnificent 12th century Abbey to the busy shopping centre. The park comprises an area for 24 privately owned holiday caravans and two areas for touring caravans - one accommodates 24 pitches, the other is smaller, accommodating six tourers. All pitches have mains hook-up and awnings are accepted. Modern toilet block, laundry room and chemical toilet point on site. Dogs welcome if kept on lead. Please send for our brochure giving further information and tariffs. Seasonal pitches available.

HAMPSHIRE

ENGLAND

KENT

DOVER (Near)

St Margaret's Holiday Park, Reach Road, St Margaret's at Cliffe, Near Dover CT15 6AE (0870 442 9286; Fax: 01304 853434). A breath of fresh air! St. Margaret's is an exclusive 4 star park perched high on the white cliffs and close to the bustling port of Dover. There are spectacular views over the English channel towards the hazy distant shores of France and the gentle rolling countryside is typical of rural Kent. The park itself has well manicured lawns and houses a superb leisure complex with indoor pools, gymnasium, reflexology and massage clinic, sauna, spa pool and solarium. Two indoor heated pools. Alternative therapy clinic. Fully equipped gymnasium. Dylan the Dinosaur Children's Club at peak times. Outdoor play area. Spa pool, sauna and solarium. Garden restaurant and Bistro bar. Horse riding nearby. Superb walking opportunities. Quality golf courses nearby (incl. Royal St. George's at Sandwich). GREAT BRITISH HOLIDAY PARKS.

e-mail: stmargarets@gbholidayparks.co.uk   website: www.gbholidayparks.co.uk

NEW ROMNEY

Romney Sands Holiday Park, The Parade, Greatstone-on-Sea, New Romney TN28 8RN (0870 442 9285; Fax: 01797 367497). A park designed for families. Romney Sands is a popular 4 star park that sits opposite one of the finest sandy beaches on the Kent coast and is surrounded by the mysterious Romney Marsh, past haunt of smugglers. Straddling the Sussex/Kent border there's lush countryside, pretty villages, colourful seaside resorts and a legacy of historic castles and stately homes. All this and a park offering fabulous facilities and quality entertainment makes for a memorable holiday experience. Bistro restaurant. Well-conditioned, outdoor bowling green. Celebrities Club for live entertainment. Dylan the Dinosaur Children's Club and outdoor play area. Large indoor pool complex. Ideal area for cycling. Tennis courts. Pool and darts. Karting and Golf nearby. Well-stocked mini-market. Crazy golf. Pub snacks in Tavern bar. Nearest town one mile. GREAT BRITISH HOLIDAY PARKS.

e-mail: romneysands@gbholidayparks.co.uk   website: www.gbholidayparks.co.uk

---

PLEASE NOTE

All the information in this book is given in good faith in the belief that it is correct. However, the publishers cannot guarantee the facts given in these pages, neither are they responsible for changes in policy, ownership or terms that may take place after the date of going to press. Readers should always satisfy themselves that the facilities they require are available and that the terms, if quoted, still apply.

FHG

Visit the ～ website
www.holidayguides.com
for details of the wide choice of accommodation
featured in the full range of FHG titles

LINCOLNSHIRE

GRANTHAM

Woodland Waters, Willoughby Road, Ancaster, Grantham NE32 3RT (Tel & Fax: 01400 230888). Set in 72 acres of parkland. Five fishing lakes. Luxury holiday lodges. Large touring and camping site with electric hook-ups. Excellent toilets; shower block with disabled facilities. Bar/restaurant on site. Children's play area. Dogs welcome. Four golf courses nearby. Rallies welcome. Open all year.
e-mail: info@woodlandwaters.co.uk
website: www.woodlandwaters.co.uk

See also Colour Display Advertisement

SALTFLEET

Sunnydale Holiday Park, Sea Lane, Saltfleet LN11 7RP (0870 442 9293; Fax: 01507 339 100). Sun, sea and sand on the Lincolnshire coast. Sunnydale sits on the edge of the beautiful Lincolnshire coastline in a region that is incredibly popular with holidaymakers. There are the lively seaside resorts of Skegness and Cleethorpes but Sunnydale nestles in an area more renowned for its rural beauty and picturesque market towns like Louth. The park itself has quality written all over it – modern, well equipped caravans, a superb leisure complex incorporating indoor pool and well-maintained park grounds. Indoor heated pool. Windmill Lounge Bar. Convenience store. Golf courses nearby. Children's amusements centre. Play zone with multi-activity play equipment and outdoor play area. Attractive spacious beer garden. Sun terrace. Family entertainment. Cabaret Bar. Well-stocked fishing pond. Nearby beach.
GREAT BRITISH HOLIDAY PARKS
e-mail: sunnydale@gbholidayparks.co.uk   **website: www.gbholidayparks.co.uk**

NORFOLK

See also Colour Display Advertisement

THETFORD

Lowe Caravan Park, Thetford. Small, friendly country park. Primarily a touring park, we now have four luxury holiday homes for hire in peaceful surroundings. Ideal for touring East Anglia or a quiet relaxing break. More suited to over 50's but children are welcome. Touring caravans also available for hire. Please contact: **May Lowe, Ashdale, Hills Road, Saham Hills (Nr Watton), Thetford IP25 7EZ (01953 881051).**

The FHG Directory of Website Addresses
on pages 243-272 is a useful quick reference guide for holiday accommodation with e-mail and/or website details

ENGLAND

NORTHUMBERLAND

See also Colour Display Advertisement

MORPETH (Near)

Cresswell Towers Holiday Park, Cresswell, Near Morpeth NE61 5JT (0870 422 9311; Fax: 01670 860 226). Total relaxation in a natural setting. Cresswell Towers is a highly attractive park in a natural woodland setting that lends the park much of its charm. You cannot help but be taken by the lush leafy lanes. This area does have spectacular beaches, and Druidge Bay with its huge sand dunes is worth a visit. On the park the emphasis is on relaxation, and a friendly bar, welcoming holiday caravans, pleasant walks and attractive outdoor pool make this easy to achieve. Sun terrace. Popular golf courses nearby. Café offering meals throughout the day. Watersport opportunities locally. Well-stocked shop. Sandy beaches with amazing sand dunes. Multi-sports court. Children's amusement arcade and play area. Sea fishing locally. Outdoor heated pool. Norseman Club. GREAT BRITISH HOLIDAY PARKS.

e-mail: cresswelltowers@gbholidayparks.co.uk   website: www.gbholidayparks.co.uk

SOMERSET

See also Colour Advertisement on Inside Front Cover

STAFFORDSHIRE

COTTON

Star Caravan and Camping Park, Near Alton Towers, Stoke-on-Trent ST10 3DW (01538 702256/702219). Situated off the B5417 road, between Leek and Cheadle, within 10 miles of the market towns of Ashbourne and Uttoxeter, with Alton Towers just three-quarters-of-a-mile away. A family-run site where your enjoyment is our main concern. Site amenities include large children's play area, shop, toilet block with free showers, etc., laundry room with drying and ironing facilities, electric hook-ups, etc. Dogs welcome but must be kept on leash. Open 1st March to 31st October. £8 per night for two persons. Special rates for groups and parties of campers (Scouts, schools, etc). Static caravans for hire. Brochure and further details available. **ETC ★★★, AA** *THREE PENNANTS*
website: www.starcaravanpark.co.uk

EAST SUSSEX

BODIAM

Lordine Court Holiday Park, Ewhurst Green, Robertsbridge TN32 5TS (01580 830209; Fax: 01580 830091). A well known and established holiday caravan park. Situated in the heart of the Sussex countryside, yet only 10 miles from the ancient historic towns of Hastings, Battle and Rye, on the doorstep of Bodiam Castle and a short drive from Battle Abbey. The Park's facilities include; outdoor swimming pool, restaurant and cafe with take-away service, clubhouse with bars (one child friendly) and amusements room. Dogs are permitted in designated areas. Holiday caravans for hire and purchase. New holiday lodge development. **Contact 01580 830209 for bookings and brochure.**

See also Colour Display Advertisement

RYE (Near)

Camber Sands, Camber, Near Rye TN31 7RT (0870 442 9284; Fax: 01797 225 756). Top fun in a fantastic seaside setting. Camber Sands faces 7 miles of award-winning Blue Flag golden beach in East Sussex. This beautiful region is steeped in history with unspoilt Sussex towns like Rye and historic Hastings and is jam-packed with top attractions. The park itself has wonderful leisure facilities including four indoor pools, sauna, spa bath and solarium and presents a first-rate entertainment programme. Is it any wonder guests return to Camber year after year – one visit and you'll be hooked. Four fun pools with amazing whirlpool. Sauna, spa bath and solarium. Amusements centre. Dylan the Dinosaur children's club and outdoor play area. Family Fun Bar. Indoor games, competitions, pool and satellite TV. Bouncy castle. Well-stocked convenience store. Fast-food cafe. Fishing nearby. Golf driving range nearby. Windsurfing lessons and Karting nearby. GREAT BRITISH HOLIDAY PARKS.
e-mail: cambersands@gbholidayparks.co.uk   website: www.gbholidayparks.co.uk

TYNE & WEAR

See also Colour Display Advertisement

GREAT BRITISH *Holiday Parks*

WHITLEY BAY

The Links, Whitley Bay, Tyne and Wear NE26 4RR (0870 442 9282; Fax: 0191 297 1033). Premier Park in a prime location. Whitley Bay is an immensely popular park that sits on the edge of a well-known seaside resort with a whole array of restaurants, cafes and bars. The walk from the park through to the resort is along a pleasant promenade with lovely views out towards St Mary's Lighthouse and long stretch of beach. The park itself has well appointed holiday caravans and facilities that include a lovely indoor pool and inviting bars. Indoor heated swimming pool. Dylan the Dinosaur children's club and outdoor play area. Popular indoor pub games. Local sea fishing opportunities. Fish & Chips take-away. Nearby golf courses. Multi-sports court. Well-stocked convenience store. Ten-pin bowling, roller skating and ice skating locally. Café. Adult and Family Clubs offering entertainment. GREAT BRITISH HOLIDAY PARKS.
e-mail: whitleybay@gbholidayparks.co.uk   **website: www.gbholidayparks.co.uk**

EAST YORKSHIRE

Set on the spectacular heritage coast with unrivalled coastal scenery. Six-berth caravans and chalets for hire. Tents and tourers welcome. Bars, entertainment, shop, pool and gym on site.

Thornwick & Sea Farm... Holiday Centre

Flamborough, East Yorks
Tel 01262 850369
www.thornwickbay.co.uk
e-mail: enquiries@thornwickbay.co.uk

NORTH YORKSHIRE

ACASTER MALBIS

Moor End Farm,(Established 1965), York YO23 2UQ (Tel & Fax: 01904 706727). Moor End Farm is a small, family-run caravan and camping site four miles south-west of York. The Tourist Board graded site has 10 touring pitches and five static caravans. Two of the static caravans are available for holiday lets starting from £37 a night or £165 a week. The hire caravans have colour TV, shower, wc, fridge, two bedrooms, kitchen, dining/living area and accommodate up to six persons. Touring facilities available are electric hook-ups, hot showers, toilets, dish-washing sink, fridge/freezer and microwave oven. There are picnic tables around the site for our guests to use. Moor End Farm is on a bus route to York and is five minutes' walk from the popular river bus service and the local inn. We are also very close to the York/Selby cycle track and the York park & ride scheme. **AA** *TWO PENNANTS,* **ETC** ★★★★ *CAMPING & TOURING PARK RAC, BH & HPA.*

See also Colour Display Advertisement

RUDDING
HOLIDAY PARK

HARROGATE

Rudding Holiday Park, Follifoot, Harrogate HG3 1JH (01423 870439; Fax: 01423 870859). These superior holiday cottages and lodges are set in picturesque surroundings near Harrogate. The luxury cottages have been completely restored retaining many of their original features (sleep 2-10 persons). The Timber Lodges are situated in beautiful parkland, many overlooking a small lake (sleep 2-6 persons). All are centrally heated and fully equipped. Facilities within the private country estate include; heated swimming pool and paddling pool, children's adventure playground, licensed bar, games room and bicycle hire, 18 hole Pay and Play golf course plus floodlit driving range. Please send for free illustrated brochure. **ETC** ★★★★★ Lodges, ★★★ Cottages.

MASHAM

Mr J. McCourt, Black Swan Holiday Park, Fearby, Masham, Ripon HG4 4NF (01765 689477). A small, family-run park in an Area of Outstanding Natural Beauty designated by the Countryside Commission. Ideal for walking. Six miles from Lightwater Valley Theme Park, two miles from Masham, famous for its two breweries - Theakstons and Blacksheep, both of which have visitor centres. Pub on site serving food. First class restaurant. Luxury caravans for hire. Ideal place for that quiet, relaxing, family holiday.
e-mail: Blackswanholidaypark@fsmail.net
website: http://www.geocities.com/theblackswan_uk/

SCARBOROUGH

Mrs Carol Croft, Cayton Village Caravan Park Ltd (Dept 19), Mill Lane, Cayton Bay, Scarborough YO11 3NN. Situated three miles south of Scarborough, four miles from Filey, half a mile from sandy beach at Cayton Bay. Attractive, sheltered, level, landscaped park adjoining Cayton Village Church with footpath 150 yards to two village inns, fish and chip shop and bus service. New luxurious shower, toilet, disabled toilet, dishwashing and laundry facilities. Central heating plus Super Saver and OAP weeks for early and late season bookings. Four acre floodlit dog walk, children's adventure playground. Seasonal pitches available Easter to October. Separate rally field. Min/Max touring caravans and tents £7.50 to £15.00 covers two adults and two children, £2 awnings, £1 dogs. **Telephone: 01723 583171 or Winter: 01904 624630** for brochure and booking details. **ETC** ★★★★
e-mail: info@caytontouring.co.uk **website: www.caytontouring.co.uk**

WHITBY

Middlewood Farm Holiday Park, Robin Hood's Bay, Near Whitby YO22 4UF (01947 880414; Fax: 01947 880871). Small, peaceful, family park. A walkers', artists' and wildlife paradise, set amidst the beautiful North Yorkshire Moors National Park, Heritage Coast and 'Heartbeat Country'. Relax and enjoy the magnificent panoramic views of our spectacular countryside. Five minutes' walk to the village PUB and shops. Ten minutes' walk to the BEACH and picturesque Robin Hood's Bay. SUPERIOR LUXURY HOLIDAY HOMES FOR HIRE, equipped to the highest standards (1 March - 4 January). TOURERS and TENTS: level, sheltered park with electric hook-ups. Superb heated facilities, free showers and dishwashing. Laundry. Gas. Children's adventure playground. Adjacent dog walk and cycle route. Credit cards accepted. Signposted. A warm welcome awaits you. **ETC** ★★★★★ *HOLIDAY PARK, ROSE AWARD, WELCOME HOST,* **AA** *THREE PENNANTS, DAVID BELLAMY GOLD AWARD.*
e-mail: info@middlewoodfarm.com **website: www.middlewoodfarm.com**

Why Yorkshire?

With ruined abbeys and castles, great houses and gardens framed by high moors and wooded hills, Yorkshire is a place of great natural beauty. This beauty is conserved in three national parks: the Yorkshire Dales, the Peak District and the North York Moors. In contrast to nature, Yorkshire is also home to The West Yorkshire Playhouse, The Yorkshire Sculpture Park and The National Museum of Photography, Film & Television. The Millennium Galleries, the new multi-million MAGNA and The Deep all make it a worthwhile place to visit.
For further information contact the Yorkshire Tourist Board,
Tel: **01904 707070** or visit **www.yorkshirevisitor.com**

Ratings You Can Trust

ENGLAND

The **English Tourism Council** (formerly the English Tourist Board) has joined with the **AA** and **RAC** to create a new, easily understood quality rating for serviced accommodation, giving a clear guide of what to expect.

HOTELS are given a rating from One to Five **Stars** – the more Stars, the higher the quality and the greater the range of facilities and level of services provided.

GUEST ACCOMMODATION, which includes guest houses, bed and breakfasts, inns and farmhouses, is rated from One to Five **Diamonds**. Progressively higher levels of quality and customer care must be provided for each one of the One to Five Diamond ratings.

HOLIDAY PARKS, TOURING PARKS and CAMPING PARKS are now also assessed using **Stars**. Standards of quality range from a One Star (acceptable) to a Five Star (exceptional) park.

Look out also for the new **SELF-CATERING** Star ratings. The more **Stars** (from One to Five) awarded to an establishment, the higher the levels of quality you can expect. Establishments at higher rating levels also have to meet some additional requirements for facilities.

SCOTLAND

Star Quality Grades will reflect the most important aspects of a visit, such as the warmth of welcome, efficiency and friendliness of service, the quality of the food and the cleanliness and condition of the furnishings, fittings and decor.

THE MORE STARS,
THE HIGHER THE STANDARDS.

The description, such as Hotel, Guest House, Bed and Breakfast, Lodge, Holiday Park, Self-catering etc tells you the type of property and style of operation.

WALES

Places which score highly will have an especially welcoming atmosphere and pleasing ambience, high levels of comfort and guest care, and attractive surroundings enhanced by thoughtful design and attention to detail

STAR QUALITY GUIDE FOR

HOTELS, GUEST HOUSES AND FARMHOUSES

SELF-CATERING ACCOMMODATION
(Cottages, Apartments, Houses)

CARAVAN HOLIDAY HOME PARKS
(Holiday Parks, Touring Parks, Camping Parks)

★★★★★ *Exceptional quality*
★★★★ *Excellent quality*
★★★ *Very good quality*
★★ *Good quality*
★ *Fair to good quality*

In England, Scotland and Wales, all graded properties are inspected annually by Tourist Authority trained Assessors.

SCOTLAND
Caravan & Camping Holidays

ARGYLL & BUTE

ROSNEATH CASTLE PARK
SO NEAR... YET SO FAR AWAY

Rosneath Castle Park, Rosneath,
Nr Helensburgh, Argyll G84 0QS

For a brochure call
01436 831208

ROSNEATH CASTLE PARK

Scottish
TOURIST BOARD
★★★★★
HOLIDAY
PARK

See also Colour Advertisement on Outside Back Cover

SCOTLAND

AYRSHIRE & ARRAN

AYR (By)

Mr & Mrs McCormack, Crofthead Holiday Park, By Ayr KA6 6EN (01292 263516). Crofthead Holiday Park is located two miles east of Ayr town centre. The park, of approximately 10 acres, nestles in a sheltered, tranquil hollow amidst rolling farmland, with the Annfield burn flowing alongside. Crofthead Park is privately owned, family-run, short on formality and long on quiet enjoyment. Facilities include clean toilets, washbasins and showers, fully equipped launderette and well stocked shop with off-licence. The recreation building has TV lounge and games rooms with pool table and amusements. Pets are welcome. Touring sites and tenting pitches are mainly on grass, with hardstanding available. Electric hook-ups for tourers and motorhomes. Ayr is an ideal location for touring south west Scotland and there is a wide variety of local activities including golf, riding, fishing, swimming pool and many sites of historic interest. Please call or write for our brochure.

BORDERS

See also Colour Display Advertisement

e-mail: eyemouth@gbholidayparks.co.uk

EYEMOUTH

Eyemouth Holiday Park, Fort Road, Eyemouth, Berwickshire TD14 5BE (0870 442 9280; Fax: 01890 751 462). Relaxation in an area of outstanding scenic beauty. Eyemouth is a beautiful 4-star park situated on the Berwickshire coastline with commanding views over two of Scotland's finest bays. Situated by a unique marine nature reserve, the park has its own beach with some of the best rock pools in the British Isles. The holiday letting accommodation is of a high standard, some with unrivalled sea views. Ideally situated for visiting Edinburgh, Berwick upon-Tweed and the Scottish Borders, this holiday location has it all. Beaches nearby. Outdoor play area. Indoor pool nearby. Satellite TV in bar. Family bar. Golf nearby.Coastal countryside walks. GREAT BRITISH HOLIDAY PARKS.
web: www.gbholidayparks.co.uk

DUNDEE & ANGUS

BRECHIN

Scott Murray, Eastmill Caravan Park, Brechin DD9 7EL (01356 622810; out of season 01356 622487; Fax: 01356 623356). Beautifully situated on flat grassy site along the River South Esk, within easy access of scenic Angus Glens, local walks and 10 miles from sandy east coast beaches; midway between Dundee and Aberdeen. Shop, gas supplies, shower block, laundry and hook-ups on site; licensed premises nearby. Open April to October. Six-berth caravans with mains services available to rent. Facilities for tourers, caravanettes and tents. Dogs welcome.

Visit the FHG website
www.holidayguides.com
for details of the wide choice of accommodation
featured in the full range of FHG titles

HIGHLANDS

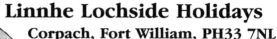

Linnhe Lochside Holidays
Corpach, Fort William, PH33 7NL

Tel: 01397 772376 • Fax: 01397 772007
e-mail: holidays@linnhe.demon.co.uk
website: www.linnhe-lochside-holidays.co.uk

"Best Park in Scotland 1999 Award"

Almost a botanical garden and stunningly beautiful. Wonderful views and ideal for touring or simply relaxing and soaking up the scenery. Licensed shop, private beach and free fishing.

Colour Brochure sent with pleasure

★ **Deluxe pine chalets** from £325/week.
★ **Luxury holiday caravans** from £180/week.
★ **Tourers** from £12.50/night.
★ **Camping** from £9.50/night.

ACHNASHEEN

Gruinard Bay Caravan Park. Situated just a stone's throw from the beach, Gruinard Bay Caravan Park offers the perfect setting for a holiday or a stop over on the West Coast of Scotland. Family-owned and personally operated, the park boasts magnificent views across Gruinard Bay. Sea-front touring pitches; electric hook-ups; no charge for awnings; camping pitches; free toilet and shower facilities; shop gas available on site; laundry facilities by request; static holiday homes available; pets welcome (not in holiday homes). **Tony & Ann Davis, Gruinard Bay Caravan Park, Laide, Wester Ross IV22 2ND (Tel & Fax: 01445 731225).**

FREE entry to 'Heather Story' exhibition at
Speyside Heather Garden & Visitor Centre
See our READERS' OFFER VOUCHER for details.

The FHG Directory of Website Addresses
on pages 243-272 is a useful quick reference guide for holiday accommodation with e-mail and/or website details

FORTROSE

Royal Hotel, Union Street, Fortrose IV10 8TD (Tel & Fax: 01381 620236). The hotel is located within the small town of Fortrose immediately adjacent to the historic Cathedral dating back to the 9th century. There are 15 bedrooms ranging from singles to family rooms for 5, all are well appointed and start from £25 per person. Food is served usually from 12 noon to 2 pm and 5 pm to 9 pm, but be prepared to wait a little as it is popular with locals as well as visitors. All is prepared to order using local grown produce including the beef, lamb and especially the wild boar. Vegetables are grown organically in the hotel's own garden. Two bars cater for varying types of guest and children are welcome in the non-smoking dining room as well as the lounge bar. Real ale is available during Summer months depending on availability and choice. The hotel is only a five minute walk away from the **Fortrose Caravan and Camp Site** and can be contacted on **01381 620236.**

LAIRG

Dunroamin Caravan Park, Main Street, Lairg IV27 4AR (01549 402447). Lew Hudson, his wife Margaret and their family welcome you to Dunroamin Caravan Park. A small family-run park situated in the picturesque village of Lairg by Loch Shin, this is the ideal base for touring the whole of Sutherland and Caithness. Pony trekking, fishing, walking and water sports all nearby, with golf just 15 miles away. Outstandingly well maintained grounds with Crofters licensed restaurant on site. Electric hook-ups. 200 yards from pub, bank, shops, post office, etc. Holiday caravans for hire, tourers and tents welcome. **STB** ★★★★ *HOLIDAY PARK*, **AA** *THREE PENNANTS*.

WALES
Caravan & Camping Holidays

ANGLESEY & GWYNEDD

CRICCIETH

Mrs D. J. Hughes, Bryn-Efail-Uchaf, Garndolbenmaen, Gwynedd LL51 9LQ (01766 530232). Comfortable six-berth caravan in peaceful rural setting on livestock farm. Local attractions include Italianate village of Portmeirion, Ffestiniog Railway, Criccieth and Caernarfon castles. Ideal for walkers or for touring the whole of Snowdonia. Nearest beach Criccieth five miles away. Safe open space for children to play, ample parking. Pub/restaurant within walking distance. Accommodation: lounge/diner with colour TV and gas fire, convertible double bed settee. Kitchen - microwave, gas cooker, fridge. Bathroom - sit in shower/bath, toilet and wash basin. Bedrooms - one double, one twin. Electricity by £1 meter. Gas included in price. Bed linen by arrangement. No pets. Terms from £160 - £190.

MERIONETH

Islawrffordd Caravan Park, Tal-y-Bont, Merioneth LL43 2BQ (01341 247269; Fax: 01341 242639). Within the Snowdonia National Park and adjoining a clean, safe bathing beach, we offer for hire a choice of caravans. All come with colour TV, fridge, integral shower and toilet, electricity and gas included in price. For the camper and touring caravans we offer our large camping field and 25 tourer pitches both offering a limited number of hook-ups. Facilities include self service shop, laundry room, pub with children's room, amusements and HEATED INDOOR SWIMMING POOL. Booking facility for touring caravans. For enquiries about the above and/or caravan sales telephone or write to **John Billingham**.
e-mail: info@islawrffordd.co.uk
website: www.islawrffordd.co.uk

WALES

NORTH WALES

ABERGELE

Mr and Mrs T.P. Williams, Pen Isaf Caravan Park, Llangernyw, Abergele LL22 8RN (01745 860276). This small caravan site in beautiful unspoilt countryside is ideal for touring North Wales and is situated 10 miles from the coast and 12 miles from Betws-y-Coed. The eight-berth caravans are fully equipped except for linen and towels and have shower, flush toilet, hot and cold water, Calor gas cooker, electric light and fridge. Fresh eggs and milk can be obtained from the farm on which this 20 caravan site is situated. Children especially will enjoy a holiday here, there being ample space and facilities for fishing and pony riding. Pets are allowed but must be kept under control. Open March to October. Terms on application with SAE, please.

CEREDIGION

See also Colour Display Advertisement

NEW QUAY

The Village Holiday Park, Cross Inn, New Quay SA44 6LW (01545 560624/561446). Set just outside New Quay in the centre of Cross Inn, The Village is just the place to relax or to discover the whole of the West Wales coast. The park offers its own children's play area, as well as our fabulous heated swimming pool; the village pub, restaurant and shops are only yards from the park. We offer Dragon Award caravans for up to seven people. Caravans have heating in all rooms, as well as a microwave, colour TV and a Play Station.
website: www.villageholidaypark.com

PLEASE NOTE

All the information in this book is given in good faith in the belief that it is correct. However, the publishers cannot guarantee the facts given in these pages, neither are they responsible for changes in policy, ownership or terms that may take place after the date of going to press. Readers should always satisfy themselves that the facilities they require are available and that the terms, if quoted, still apply.

FHG PUBLICATIONS publish a large range of well-known accommodation guides. We will be happy to send you details or you can use the order form at the back of this book.

DIRECTORY OF WEBSITE AND E-MAIL ADDRESSES

A quick-reference guide to holiday accommodation with an e-mail address and website, conveniently arranged by country and county, with full contact details.

•LONDON

B & B

Mrs Anne Scott, Holiday Hosts
(London) Ltd, 59 Cromwell Road,
Wimbledon, LONDON SW19 8LF
020 8540 7942
• e-mail: holiday.hosts@btinternet.com
• website: www.holidayhosts.free-online.co.uk

Guesthouse

MacDonald Hotel, 45-46 Argyle Square,
LONDON WC1H 8AL
020 7837 3552
• e-mail: fhg@macdonaldhotel.com
• website: www.macdonaldhotel.com

Hotel / B & B

Lincoln House Hotel, 33 Gloucester Place,
LONDON W1V 8HY
020 7486 7630
• e-mail: reservations@lincoln-house-hotel.co.uk
• website: www.lincoln-house-hotel.co.uk

Hotel

Gower Hotel, 129 Sussex Gardens,
Hyde Park, LONDON W2 2RX
020 7262 2262
• e-mail: gower@stavrouhotels.co.uk
• website: www.stavrouhotels.co.uk

Hotel

Athena Hotel, 110-114 Sussex Gardens,
Hyde Park, LONDON W2 1UA
020 7706 3866
• e-mail: athena@stavrouhotels.co.uk
• website: www.stavrouhotels.co.uk

B & B / Guesthouse

Barry House Hotel, 12 Sussex Place,
Hyde Park, LONDON W2 2TP
020 7723 7340
• e-mail: hotel@barryhouse.co.uk
• website: www.barryhouse.co.uk

Hotel

Shakespeare Hotel, 22-28 Norfolk Square,
LONDON W2 1RS
020 7402 4646
• e-mail: info@shakespearehotel.co.uk
• website: www.shakespearehotel.co.uk

Hotel

Adria Hotel, 44 Glenthorne Road,
Hammersmith, LONDON W6 0LS
020 7602 6386
• e-mail: george@adria.demon.co.uk
• website: www.dalmacia-hotel.co.uk

Hotel

Dalmacia Hotel, 71 Shepherds Bush Road,
Hammersmith, LONDON W6 7LS
020 7603 2887
• e-mail: george@adria.demon.co.uk
• website: www.dalmacia-hotel.co.uk

B & B

Sohel & Anne Armanios, 67 Rannoch Road,
Hammersmith, LONDON W6 9SS
020 7385 4904
• website: www.thewaytostay.co.uk

Hotel

Queens Hotel, 33 Anson Road,
Tufnell Park, LONDON N7
020 7607 4725
• e-mail: queens@stavrouhotels.co.uk
• website: www.stavrouhotels.co.uk

B & B

Hanover Hotel, 30 St George's Drive
LONDON SW1V 4BN
020 7834 0367
• e-mail: reservations@hanoverhotel.co.uk
• website: www.hanoverhotel.co.uk

Please mention SELF-CATERING HOLIDAYS IN BRITAIN when enquiring about accommodation

•BERKSHIRE

Guest House

Mrs Sue Chapman, Lyndrick House,
The Avenue, ASCOT, Berkshire SL5 7ND
01344 883520
• e-mail: mail@lyndrick.com
• website: www.lyndrick.com

Inn

Swan Inn, INKPEN, Hungerford,
Berkshire RG17 9DX
01488 668326
• e-mail: enquiries@theswaninn-organics.co.uk
• website: www.theswaninn-organics.co.uk

•CAMBRIDGESHIRE

Guest House

Dykelands Guest House, 157 Mowbray
Road, CAMBRIDGE,
Cambridgeshire CB1 7SP
01223 244300
• e-mail: dykelands@fsbdial.co.uk
• website: www.dykelands.com

B & B

J & R Farndale, Cathedral House,
17 St Mary's Street, ELY,
Cambridgeshire CB7 4ER
01353 662124
• e-mail: farndale@cathedralhouse.co.uk
• website: www.cathedralhouse.co.uk

B & B

Mrs Linda Peck, Sharps Farm, Twenty Pence
Road, Wilburton, ELY,
Cambridgeshire CB6 3PX
01353 740360
• e-mail: sharpsfarm@yahoo.com

•CHESHIRE

Hotel

Frogg Manor Hotel & Restaurant,
Fullers Moor, Nantwich Road, Broxton,
CHESTER, Cheshire CH3 9JH
01829 782629
• e-mail: info@froggmanorhotel.co.uk
• website: www.froggmanorhotel.co.uk

> **Please mention**
> **Self Catering Holidays in Britain**
> **when enquiring about**
> **accommodation**

B & B / Self-Catering

Mrs Angela Smith, Mill House and Granary,
Higher Wych, MALPAS,
Cheshire SY14 7JR
01948 780362
• e-mail: angela@videoactive.co.uk
• website: www.millhouseandgranary.co.uk

B & B

Mrs Jean E. Callwood, Lea Farm,
Wrinehill Road, Wybunbury,
NANTWICH, Cheshire CW5 7NS
01270 841429
• e-mail: contactus@leafarm.co.uk

•CORNWALL

Self-Catering

Fiona & Martin Nicolle,
Classy Cottages, Cornwall
07000 423000
• e-mail: nicolle@classycottages.co.uk
• website: www.classycottages.co.uk

Self-Catering

Cornish Traditional Cottages, Blisland,
BODMIN, Cornwall PL30 4HS
01208 821666
• e-mail: info@corncott.com
• website: www.corncott.com

Self-Catering / Caravan & Camping

Ruthern Valley Holidays, Ruthernbridge
BODMIN, Cornwall PL30 5LU
01208 831395
• e-mail: ruthernvalley@hotmail.com
• website: www.self-catering-ruthern.co.uk

Self-Catering

Mr Charles Tippet, Mineshop Holiday
Cottages, Crackington Haven, BUDE,
Cornwall EX23 0NR
01840 230338
• e-mail: tippett@mineshop.freeserve.co.uk
• website: www.cornwall-online.co.uk/mineshop

Self-Catering / Caravan & Camping

Willow Valley Holiday Park,
Bush, BUDE, Cornwall EX23 9LB
01288 353104
• e-mail: willowvalley@talk21.com
• website: www.caravansitecornwall.co.uk

Caravan & Camping
Cornish Coasts Caravan & Camping Park,
Middle Penlean, Poundstock,
Widemouth Bay, BUDE, Cornwall EX23 0EE
01288 361380
• e-mail: info@cornishcoasts.co.uk
• website: www.cornishcoasts.co.uk

Guest House
Harvey Jay, Wringford Down Motel,
CAWSAND, Cornwall PL10 1LE
01752 822287
• e-mail: ramehols@aol.com
• website: www.cornwallholidays.co.uk

Guest House
Mrs C. Carruthers, The Clearwater,
59 Melvill Road, FALMOUTH,
Cornwall TR11 4DF
01326 311344
• e-mail: clearwater@lineone.net
• website: www.theclearwater.co.uk

Guest House
Miss Fannin, Trevaylor, 8 Pennance Road,
FALMOUTH, Cornwall TR11 4EA
01326 316899
• e-mail: stay@trevaylor.co.uk
• website: www.trevaylor.co.uk

Self-Catering / Caravan Park
Mr Christopher Harvey, St Ives Bay Chalet &
Caravan Park, HAYLE, Cornwall TR27 5BH
01736 752274
• e-mail: stivesbay@dial.pipex.com
• website: www.stivesbay.co.uk

Caravan & Camping
Mrs J. Jenkin, Mudgeon Farm,
St Martin, HELSTON, Cornwall TR12 6BZ
01326 231202
• e-mail: jenkin@mudgeon.fsnet.co.uk

Self-Catering
Mrs S. Trewhella, Mudgeon Vean,
St Martin, HELSTON, Cornwall TR12 6DB
01326 231341
• e-mail: mudgeonvean@aol.com
• website:
www.cornwall-online.co.uk/mudgeon-vean/ctb.htm

Caravan & Camping
Boscrege Caravan & Camping Park,
Ashton, HELSTON, Cornwall TR13 9TG
01736 762231
• e-mail: enquiries@caravanparkcornwall.com
• website: www.caravanparkcornwall.com

Guest House
Greystones Guest House, 40 West End,
Porthleven, HELSTON TR13 9JL
01326 565583
• e-mail: neilvwoodward@hotmail.com

Self-Catering
Trewalla Farm Cottages, Trewalla Farm,
Minions, LISKEARD, Cornwall PL14 6ED
01579 342385
• e-mail: cotter.trewalla@virgin.net

B & B
Mrs S. Rowe, Tregondale Farm, Menheniot,
LISKEARD, Cornwall PL14 3RG
01579 342407
• e-mail: tregondale@connectfree.co.uk
• website: www.tregondalefarm.co.uk

Self-Catering
Sue Jewell, Boturnell Farm Cottages,
St Pinnock, LISKEARD, Cornwall PL14 4QS
01579 320880
• e-mail: boturnell-barns@breathemail.net
• website: www.dogs-holiday.co.uk

Caravan & Camping
Tregoad Farm Touring Caravan & Camping
Park, St Martins, LOOE, Cornwall PL13 1PB
01503 262718
• e-mail: tregoadfarmtccp@aol.com
• website: www.cornwall-online.co.uk/tregoad

B & B / Self-Catering
Paul Brumpton, Talehay Holiday Cottages,
Pelynt, near LOOE, Cornwall PL13 2LT
01503 220252
• e-mail: paul@talehay.co.uk
• website: www.talehay.co.uk

Small Hotel / Guest House
Mr G.J. & Mrs P.E. Hope, Seavista Hotel,
MAWGAN PORTH, Newquay,
Cornwall TR8 4AL
01637 868276
• e-mail: seavista@btopenworld.com
• website: www.seavista.co.uk

B & B
Mrs Dawn Rundle, Lancallan Farm,
MEVAGISSEY, St Austell,
Cornwall PL26 6EW
01726 842284
• e-mail: dawn@lancallan.fsnet.co.uk

Hotel
White Lodge Hotel, Mawgan Porth Bay,
near NEWQUAY, Cornwall TR8 4BN
01637 860512
• e-mail: adogfriendly@aol.com
• website: www.dogfriendlyhotel.co.uk

Hotel
Mrs M.G. Waldron, Golden Bay Hotel,
Pentire Avenue, Pentire, NEWQUAY,
Cornwall TR7 1PD
01637 873318
• e-mail: enquiries@goldenbayhotel.co.uk
• website: www.goldenbayhotel.co.uk

Guest House / Self-Catering
Trewerry Mill Guest House, Trewerry Mill,
Trerice, St Newlyn East, NEWQUAY,
Cornwall TR8 5GS
01872 510345
• e-mail: trewerry.mill@which.net
• website: www.trewerrymill.co.uk

Guest House
Mrs C. Lavery, Pensalda, 98 Henver Road,
NEWQUAY, Cornwall TR7 3BL
01637 874601
• e-mail: carol@pensalda.fsnet.co.uk
• website: www.pensalda-guesthouse.co.uk

Self-Catering
Trevose Golf Club, Constantine Bay,
PADSTOW, Cornwall PL28 8JB
01841 520208
• e-mail: info@trevose-gc.co.uk
• website: www.trevose-gc.co.uk

Guest House
Mr & Mrs J.A. Leggatt, Cornerways Guest
House, 5 Leskinnick Street, PENZANCE,
Cornwall TR18 2HA
01736 364645
• e-mail: LEGGATT6@aol.com
• website: www.penzance.co.uk/cornerways

Farm / B & B
Mrs Hall, Treen Farmhouse, Treen,
St Levan, PENZANCE, Cornwall TR19 6LF
01736 810253
• e-mail: paulachrishall@treenfarm.fsnet.co.uk

Caravan & Camping
Roselands Caravan Park, Dowran,
St Just, PENZANCE, Cornwall TR19 7RS
01736 788571
• e-mail: camping@roseland84.freeserve.co.uk
• website: www.roselands.co.uk

Hotel
Boscean Country Hotel, St Just,
PENZANCE, Cornwall TR19 7QP
01736 788748
• e-mail: Boscean@aol.com
• website: www.bosceancountryhotel.co.uk

Hotel / Inn
Mrs J. Treleaven, Driftwood Spars Hotel,
Trevaunance Cove, ST AGNES,
Cornwall TR5 0RT
01872 552428 / 553323
• e-mail: driftwoodspars@hotmail.com
• website: www.driftwoodspars.com

B & B
Ted and Jeanie Ellis, Cleaderscroft Hotel,
16 British Road, ST AGNES,
Cornwall TR5 0TZ
01872 552349
• e-mail: tedellis@btinternet.com

B & B
Mrs Liz Berryman, Polegreen Farm,
London Apprentice, ST AUSTELL,
Cornwall PL26 7AP
01726 75151
• e-mail: polgreen.farm@btclick.com

Hotel
Dalswinton House, ST MAWGAN,
near Newquay, Cornwall TR8 4EZ
01637 860385
• e-mail: dalswinton@bigwig.net
• website: www.dalswinton.com

Self-Catering
Mr & Mrs C.W. Pestell, Hockadays,
Tregenna, near Blisland, ST TUDY,
Cornwall PL30 4QJ
01208 850146
• website: www.hockadaysholidaycottages.co.uk

Self-Catering
Mrs Sandy Wilson, Salutations, Atlantic
Road, TINTAGEL, Cornwall PL34 0DE
01840 770287
• e-mail: sandyanddave@tinyworld.co.uk
• website: www.tintagelsalutations.co.uk

Small Hotel
The Penallick Hotel, Treknow,TINTAGEL,
Cornwall PL34 0EJ
01840 770296
• website: www.penallickhotel.co.uk

Self-Catering
Mrs Sue Zamaria, Colesent Cottages,
St Tudy, WADEBRIDGE, Cornwall PL30 4QX
01208 850112
• e-mail: welcome@colesent.co.uk
• website: www.colesent.co.uk

•CUMBRIA

Hotel
Anne-Marie O'Neill, Rothay Manor, Rothay Bridge, AMBLESIDE, Cumbria LA22 0EH
015394 33605
- e-mail: **hotel@rothaymanor.co.uk**
- website: **www.rothaymanor.co.uk**

B & B
Malcolm & Margaret MacFarlane, Borwick Lodge, Outgate, Hawkshead, AMBLESIDE, Cumbria LA22 0PU
015394 36332
- e-mail: **borwicklodge@talk21.com**
- website: **www.borwicklodge.com**

Self-Catering
Lakelovers, Belmont House, Lake Road, BOWNESS-ON-WINDERMERE, Cumbria LA23 3BJ
015394 88855
- e-mail: **bookings@lakelovers.co.uk**
- website: **www.lakelovers.co.uk**

Farmhouse B & B
Anne Taylor, Russell Farm, BURTON-IN-KENDAL, Carnforth, Lancashire LA6 1NN
01524 781334
- e-mail: **miktaylor@farming.co.uk**

Hotel
Hazel Thompson, New House Farm, Lorton, BUTTERMERE, near Cockermouth, Cumbria CA13 9UU
01900 85404
- e-mail: **hazel@newhouse-farm.co.uk**
- website: **www.newhouse-farm.co.uk**

Guest House
Dalegarth Guest House, Hassness Estate, BUTTERMERE, Cumbria CA13 9XA
01768 770233
- e-mail: **dalegarth.buttermere@rdplus.net**
- website: **www.dalegarthguesthouse.co.uk**

B & B
Mr & Mrs A. Savage, Swaledale Watch, Whelpo, CALDBECK, Cumbria CA7 8HQ
016974 78409
- e-mail: **nan.savage@talk21.com**

Half Board / Self-Catering / B & B
J. Elwen, New Pallyards, Hethersgill, CARLISLE, Cumbria CA6 6HZ
01228 577308
- e-mail: **info@newpallyards.freeserve.co.uk**
- website: **www.newpallyards.freeserve.co.uk**

Farm
Mrs L. Lawson, Craigburn Farm, Penton, CARLISLE, Cumbria CA6 5QP
01228 577214
- e-mail: **louiselawson@hotmail.com**
- website: **www.craigburnfarmhouse.co.uk**

Self-Catering
Loweswater Holiday Cottages, Scale Hill, Loweswater, COCKERMOUTH, Cumbria CA13 9UX
01900 85232
- e-mail: **mike@loweswaterholidaycottages.co.uk**
- website: **www.loweswaterholidaycottages.co.uk**

Guest House
George & Isobel Kerr, Link House, Bassenthwaite Lake, COCKERMOUTH, Cumbria CA13 9YD
017687 76291
- e-mail: **linkhouse@lineone.net**
- website: **www.link-house.com**

Self-Catering
Mr P. Johnston, The Coppermines and Lakes Cottages, The Estate Office, The Bridge, CONISTON, Cumbria LA21 8HX
015394 41765 (24 hours)
- website: **www.coppermines.co.uk**
- website: **www.lakescottages.info**

Self-Catering
Mrs J. Hall, Fisherground Farm Cottages, Fisherground, ESKDALE, Cumbria, CA19 1TF
01946 723319
- e-mail: **holidays@fisherground.co.uk**
- website: **www.fisherground.co.uk**

Self-Catering
Margaret & William Beck, Brunt Knott Farm, Staveley, KENDAL, Cumbria LA8 9QX
01539 821030
- e-mail: **margaret@bruntknott.demon.co.uk**
- website: **www.bruntknott.demon.co.uk**

Self-Catering
Keswick Cottages, Kentmere, How Lane,
KESWICK, Cumbria CA12 5RS
017687 73895
• e-mail: info@keswickcottages.co.uk
• website: www.keswickcottages.co.uk

Self-Catering
Barrowside & Swinside Cottages,
c/o Mrs Walker, 15 Acorn Street, KESWICK,
Cumbria CA12 4EA
01768 774165
• e-mail: info@watendlathguesthouse.co.uk
• website: www.watendlathguesthouse.co.uk

Hotel
Swan Hotel, Thornthwaite, KESWICK,
Cumbria CA12 5SQ
017687 78100
• e-mail: bestswan@aol.com
• website: www.swan-hotel-keswick.co.uk

Guest House
Mr & Mrs Birtwistle, Kalgurli Guest House,
33 Helvellyn Street, KESWICK,
Cumbria CA12 4EP
017687 72935
• e-mail: info@kalgurli.co.uk
• website: www.kalgurli.co.uk

B & B
Val Bradley, Rickerby Grange, Portinscale,
KESWICK, Cumbria CA12 5RH
017687 72344
• e-mail: val@ricor.co.uk
• website: www.ricor.co.uk

Self-Catering
Derwentwater Marina, Portinscale,
KESWICK, Cumbria CA12 5RF
017687 72912
• website: www.derwentwatermarina.co.uk

Guest House
Linda & Stuart Robertson, Clarence House,
14 Eskin Street, KESWICK,
Cumbria CA12 4DQ
017687 73186
• e-mail: enquiries@clarencehousekeswick.co.uk
• website: www.clarencehousekeswick.co.uk

Guest House
Ian & Janice Picken, Lynwood House
(Licensed Guest House),
35 Helvellyn Street, KESWICK,
Cumbria CA12 4EP
017687 72398
• e-mail: info@lynwoodhouse.net
• website: www.lynwoodhouse.net

Caravan & Camping
Linda Lamb, Burns Caravan & Camping Site,
St Johns In the Vale, KESWICK,
Cumbria CA12 4RR
017687 79225
• e-mail: llamb@callnetuk.com

Self-Catering
Liz Webster, Howscales, KIRKOSWALD,
Penrith, Cumbria CA10 1JG
01768 898666
• e-mail: liz@howscales.fsbusiness.co.uk
• website: www.eden-in-cumbria.co.uk/howscales

Self-Catering
Mrs S.J. Bottom, Crossfield Cottages,
KIRKOSWALD, Penrith, Cumbria CA10 1EU
01768 898711
• e-mail: info@crossfieldcottages.co.uk
• website: www.crossfieldcottages.co.uk

Guest House / B & B
Mr & Mrs C. Smith, Mosedale House,
MOSEDALE, Mungrisdale,
Cumbria CA11 0XQ
01768 779371
• e-mail: mosedale@northlakes.co.uk
• website: www.mosedalehouse.co.uk

Guest House
Geoff Mason, Knotts Mill Country Lodge,
Ullswater, Watermillock, PENRITH,
Cumbria CA11 0JN
017684 86699
• e-mail: knottsmill@cwcom.net
• website: www.knottsmill.cwc.net

Self-Catering / Caravan & Camping
Parkfoot Caravan & Camping Park, Howtown
Road, Pooley Bridge, PENRITH,
Cumbria CA10 2NA
017684 86309
• e-mail: park.foot@talk21.com
• website: www.parkfootullswater.co.uk

Self-Catering
Mr & Mrs Dodsworth, Birthwaite Edge,
Birthwaite Road, WINDERMERE,
Cumbria LA23 1BS
015394 42861
• e-mail: lakedge@lakedge.com
• website: www.lakedge.com

Self-Catering
J.R. Benson, High Sett, Sun Hill Lane,
Troutbeck Bridge, WINDERMERE,
Cumbria LA23 1HJ
015394 42731
• e-mail: info@accommodationlakedistrict.com
• website: www.accommodationlakedistrict.com

Guest House
John Dixon, The Beaumont Hotel,
Holly Road, WINDERMERE,
Cumbria LA23 2AF
015394 47075
- e-mail: thebeaumonthotel@btinternet.com
- website: www.lakesbeaumont.co.uk

•DERBYSHIRE

Self-Catering
Derbyshire Cottages, Contact: Mary
01335 300202
- e-mail: info@dogandpartridge.co.uk
- website: www.dogandpartridge.co.uk

Farmhouse B & B / Self-Catering
Mrs M.A. Richardson, Throwley Hall Farm,
Ilam, ASHBOURNE, Derbyshire DE6 2BB
01538 308202
- e-mail: throwleyhall@talk21.com
- website: www.throwleyhallfarm.co.uk

Farm / Board
New House Organic Farm, Kniveton,
ASHBOURNE, Derbyshire DE6 1JL
01335 342429
- e-mail: b&b@newhousefarm.co.uk

Inn
Mrs Stelfox, The Dog & Partridge Country
Inn, Swinscoe, ASHBOURNE,
Derbyshire DE6 2HS
01335 343183
- e-mail: info@dogandpartridge.co.uk
- website: www.dogandpartridge.co.uk

Self-Catering
Cotterill Farm Cottages, Cotterill Farm,
Links Road, BIGGIN-BY-HARTINGTON,
Buxton, Derbyshire SK17 0DJ
01298 84447
- e-mail: enquiries@cotterillfarm.co.uk
- website: www.cotterillfarm.co.uk

Guest House
Mr & Mrs Hyde, Braemar,10 Compton Road,
BUXTON, Derbyshire SK17 9DN
01298 78050
- e-mail: buxtonbraemar@supanet.com
- website: www.cressbrook.co.uk/buxton/braemar

Self-Catering
R.D. Hollands, Wheeldon Trees Farm, Earl
Sterndale, BUXTON, Derbyshire SK17 0AA
01298 83219
- e-mail: hollands@earlsterndale.fsnet.co.uk
- website: www.wheeldontreesfarm.co.uk

Inn
Nick & Fiona Clough, The Devonshire Arms,
Peak Forest, near BUXTON,
Derbyshire SK17 8EJ
01298 23875
- e-mail: fiona.clough@virgin.net
- website: www.devarms.com

Hotel
The Charles Cotton Hotel, Hartington,
near BUXTON, Derbyshire SK17 0AL
01298 84229
- e-mail: info@charlescotton.co.uk
- website: www.charlescotton.co.uk

Hotel
Biggin Hall Hotel, Biggin-by-Hartington,
BUXTON, Derbyshire SK17 0DH
01298 84451
- e-mail: bigginhall@compuserve.com
- website: www.bigginhall.co.uk

Self-Catering
Hartington Cottages,
HARTINGTON, Derbyshire
01298 84447
- e-mail: enquiries@hartingtoncottages.co.uk
- website: www.hartingtoncottages.co.uk

Self-Catering
Field Head Farmhouse Holidays, Calton,
PEAK DISTRICT, Derbyshire
Contact: Janet Hudson
01538 308352
- e-mail: info@field-head.co.uk
- website: www.field-head.co.uk

•DEVON

Self-Catering
Toad Hall Cottages,
DEVON
08700 777345
- website: www.toadhallcottages.com

Self-Catering
Mr Ridge, Braddon Cottages, Ashwater,
BEAWORTHY, Devon EX21 5EP
01409 211350
- e-mail: holidays@braddoncottages.co.uk
- website: www.braddoncottages.co.uk

Self-Catering / B & B
Peter & Lesley Lewin, Lake House Cottages
and B&B, Lake Villa, BRADWORTHY,
Devon EX22 7SQ
01409 241962
- e-mail: info@lakevilla.co.uk
- website: www.lakevilla.co.uk

B & B
Mrs Roselyn Bradford, St Merryn, Higher
Park Road, BRAUNTON, Devon EX33 2LG
01271 813805
• e-mail: ros@st-merryn.co.uk
• website: www.st-merryn.co.uk

Self-Catering
Little Comfort Farm Cottages,
Little Comfort Farm, BRAUNTON,
North Devon EX33 2NJ
01271 812414
• e-mail: jackie.milsom@btclick.com
• website: www.littlecomfortfarm.co.uk

Hotel
The Smugglers Haunt, Church Hill,
BRIXHAM, Devon TQ5 8HH
01803 853050
• e-mail:
enquiries@smugglershaunt-hotel-devon.co.uk
• website:
www.smugglershaunt-hotel-devon.co.uk

Guest House
Mr John Parry, Woodlands Guest House,
Parkham Road, BRIXHAM,
South Devon TQ5 9BU
01803 852040
• e-mail: Diparry@aol.com
• website: www.dogfriendlyguesthouse.co.uk

Self-Catering
Little Farm, Southleigh,
near COLYTON, Devon EX24 6JE
01404 871361
• e-mail: littlefarmhols@madasafish.com
• website: www.littlefarmonline.co.uk

Self-Catering/ Caravan /Board
Mrs Ruth Gould, Bonehayne Farm,
COLYTON, Devon EX24 6SG
01404 871416 / 871396
• e-mail: gould@bonehayne.co.uk
• website: www.bonehayne.co.uk

Hotel
The Lord Haldon Country House Hotel,
DUNCHIDEOCK, near Exeter,
Devon EX6 7YF
01392 832483
• e-mail: enquiries@lordhaldonhotel.co.uk
• website: www.lordhaldonhotel.co.uk

Farm / B & B
Mrs Karen Williams, Stile Farm, Starcross,
EXETER, Devon EX6 8PD
01626 890268
• e-mail: info@stile-farm.co.uk
• website: www.stile-farm.co.uk

B & B
Culm Vale Guest House, Stoke Canon,
EXETER, Devon EX5 4EG
01392 841615
• e-mail: culmvale@talk21.com
• website:
www.SmoothHound.co.uk/hotels/culmvale.html

Self-Catering
Mr F. Wigram, Riggles Farm, Upottery,
HONITON, Devon EX14 4SP
01404 891229
• e-mail: rigglesfarm@farming.co.uk
• website: www.braggscottage.co.uk

Self-Catering
Mr Tromans, Hope Barton Barns,
HOPE COVE, Devon TQ7 3HT
01548 561393
• e-mail: info@hopebarton.co.uk
• website: www.hopebarton.co.uk

Caravan & Camping
John Fowler Holidays, Marlborough Road,
ILFRACOMBE, Devon EX34 8PF
01271 866766
• e-mail: bookings@jfhols.co.uk
• website: www.johnfowlerholidays.com

Farmhouse B&B
Mrs Alison Homa, Mullacott Farm,
Mullacott Cross, ILFRACOMBE,
Devon EX34 8NA
01271 866877
• e-mail: alison@mullacottfarm.co.uk
• website: www.mullacottfarm.co.uk

Farm / Self-Catering
Mrs E. Sansom, Widmouth Farm,
Watermouth, near ILFRACOMBE,
Devon EX34 9RX
01271 863743
• e-mail: holiday@widmouthfarmcottages.co.uk
• website: www.widmouthfarmcottages.co.uk

B & B / Self-Catering
Mrs Stephens, Venn Farm, Ugborough,
IVYBRIDGE, Devon PL21 0PE
01364 73240
• website:
www.SmoothHound.co.uk/hotels/vennfarm

Guest House / Self-Catering
Mrs M. Newsham, Marsh Mills, Aveton
Gifford, KINGSBRIDGE, Devon TQ7 4JW
01548 550549
• e-mail: Newsham@Marshmills.co.uk
• website: www.Marshmills.co.uk

Self-Catering
Dittiscombe Holiday Cottages, Slapton,
near KINGSBRIDGE, Devon TQ7 2QF
01548 521272
• e-mail: info@dittiscombe.co.uk
• website: www.dittiscombe.co.uk

Guest House / Tea Gardens
Mrs J. Parker, Tregonwell, The Olde Sea
Captain's House, 1 Tors Road, LYNMOUTH,
Exmoor National Park, Devon EX35 6ET
01598 753369
• website:
www.SmoothHound.co.uk/hotels/tregonwl.html

Guest House
Tricia & Alan Francis, Glenville House,
2 Tors Road, LYNMOUTH,
North Devon EX35 6ET
01598 752202
• e-mail: tricia@glenvillelynmouth.co.uk
• website: www.glenvillelynmouth.co.uk

Inn
The Crown, Market Street, LYNTON,
Devon EX35 6AG
01598 752253
• website: www.thecrown-lynton.co.uk

Guest House
John McGowan, The Denes, 15 Longmead,
LYNTON, Devon EX35 6DQ
01598 753573
• e-mail: enquiries@thedenes.com
• website: www.thedenes.com

Hotel
Alford House Hotel, Alford Terrace,
LYNTON, North Devon EX35 6AT
01598 752359
• e-mail: enquiries@alfordhouse.co.uk
• website: www.alfordhouse.co.uk

Farm / B & B
Great Sloncombe Farm,
MORETONHAMPSTEAD,
Newton Abbot, Devon TQ13 8QF
01647 440595
• e-mail: hmerchant@sloncombe.freeserve.co.uk
• website: www.greatsloncombefarm.co.uk

Self-Catering
Helen Griffiths, Look Weep Farm Cottages,
Liverton, NEWTON ABBOT,
Devon TQ12 6HT
01626 833277
• e-mail: holidays@lookweep.co.uk
• website: www.lookweep.co.uk

Self-Catering
Christine & Mike Grindrod, Serena Lodge,
15 Cliff Road, PAIGNTON TQ4 6DG
01803 550330
• website: www.serenalodge.com

Guest House
The Lamplighter Hotel, 103 Citadel Road,
The Hoe, PLYMOUTH, Devon PL1 2RN
01752 663855
• e-mail: lamplighterhotel@ukonline.co.uk

Hotel / Inn
The Port Light, Bolberry Down,
near SALCOMBE, South Devon TQ7 3DY
01548 561384
• e-mail: info@portlight-salcombe.co.uk
• website: www.portlight.co.uk

Self-Catering
Boswell Farm Cottages, Boswell Farm,
SIDFORD, Devon EX10 0PP
01395 514162
• e-mail: dillon@boswell-farm.co.uk
• website: www.boswell-farm.co.uk

Farmhouse B & B
Mrs Elizabeth Tancock, Lower Pinn Farm,
Peak Hill, SIDMOUTH, Devon EX10 0NN
01395 513733
• e-mail: liz@lowerpinnfarm.co.uk
• website: www.lowerpinnfarm.co.uk

Farm / Board
Mrs Hilary Tucker, Beera Farm, Milton
Abbot, TAVISTOCK, Devon PL19 8PL
01822 870216
• website: www.beera-farm.co.uk

Hotel
Mr Stevens, The Old Coach House Hotel,
Ottery, near TAVISTOCK, Devon PL19 8NS
01822 617515
• e-mail: eddie@coachhouse1.supanet.com
• website: www.the-coachouse.co.uk

Hotel / Guest House
Rowan & Carole Ward, Green Park Hotel,
25 Morgan Avenue, TORQUAY,
Devon TQ2 5RR
01803 293618
• e-mail: greenpark.torquay@cwcom.net
• website: www.greenparktorquay.co.uk

Self-Catering
South Sands Apartments, Torbay Road,
TORQUAY, Devon TQ2 6RG
01803 293521
- e-mail: southsands.torquay@virgin.net
- website: www.southsands.co.uk

Self-Catering
Atlantis Holiday Apartments, Solsbro Road,
Chelston, TORQUAY, Devon TQ2 6PF
01803 607929
- e-mail: enquiry@atlantistorquay.co.uk
- website: www.atlantistorquay.co.uk

Guest House
Aveland Hotel, Aveland Road, Babbacombe,
TORQUAY, Devon TQ1 3PT
01803 326622
- e-mail: avelandhotel@aol.com
- website: www.avelandhotel.co.uk

Self-Catering
Ashfield Rise Holiday Apartments,
Ruckamore Road, Chelston, TORQUAY,
Devon TQ2 6HF
01803 605156
- e-mail: stay@ashfieldrise.co.uk
- website: www.ashfieldrise.co.uk

Self-Catering
Mrs S. Milsom, Stowford Lodge, Langtree,
TORRINGTON, North Devon, EX38 8NV
01805 601540
- e-mail: stowford@dial.pipex.com
- website: www.stowford.dial.pipex.com

Guest House / Hotel
The Old Forge at Totnes, Seymour Place,
TOTNES, Devon, TQ9 5AY
01803 862174
- e-mail: enq@oldforgetotnes.com
- website: www.oldforgetotnes.com

Hotel
Dartington Hall, TOTNES, Devon TQ9 6EZ
01803 847136
- e-mail: dhcc.ops@dartingtonhall.com
- website: www.dartingtonhall.com

Guest House
Lynda Hunt, Sunnymeade Country Hotel,
Dean Cross, West Down, WOOLACOMBE,
Devon EX34 8NT
01271 863668
- e-mail: info@sunnymeade.co.uk
- website: www.sunnymeade.co.uk

Hotel
Woolacombe Bay Hotel, WOOLACOMBE,
Devon EX34 7BN
01271 870388
- e-mail: woolacombe.bayhotel@btinternet.com
- website: www.woolacombe-bay-hotel.co.uk

Hotel
Crossways Hotel, The Seafront,
WOOLACOMBE, Devon EX34 7DJ
01271 870395
- website:
  www.s-h-systems.co.uk/hotels/crossway.html

B & B
S.R. Seabrook, Torrfields, Sheepstor,
YELVERTON, Devon PL20 6PF
01822 852161
- e-mail: lbsrseabrook@aol.com
- website:
  http://users.eggconnect.net/seabrook/torrfields.htm

Farmhouse
Mrs Gozzard, Stokehill Farmhouse,
Stokehill Lane, Crapstone, YELVERTON,
Devon PL20 7PP
01822 853791
- e-mail: gozzard@btopenworld.com
- website: www.stokehillfarmhouse.co.uk

•DORSET

Hotel
The Anvil Hotel, Salisbury Road, Pimperne,
BLANDFORD, Dorset DT11 8UQ
01258 453431
- e-mail: info@anvilhotel.co.uk
- website: www.anvilhotel.co.uk

Farm / Self-Catering
Mr M. Kayll, Luccombe Farm, Luccombe,
Milton Abbas, BLANDFORD FORUM,
Dorset DT11 0BE
01258 880558
- e-mail: mkayll@aol.com
- website: www.luccombeholidays.co.uk

Hotel
Golden Sovereign Hotel,
97 Alumhurst Road, BOURNEMOUTH,
Dorset BH4 8HR
01202 762088
- e-mail: goldensov@aol.com
- website: www.goldensovereign.co.uk

Guest House
S. Barling, Mayfield, 46 Frances Road,
BOURNEMOUTH, Dorset BH1 3SA
01202 551839
• e-mail: accom@mayfieldguesthouse.com
• website: www.mayfieldguesthouse.com

Hotel / Guest House
Southernhay Hotel, 42 Alum Chine Road,
Westbourne, BOURNEMOUTH,
Dorset BH4 8DX
01202 761251
• e-mail: enquiries@southernhayhotel.co.uk
• website: www.southernhayhotel.co.uk

Hotel
Fircroft Hotel, Owls Road, BOURNEMOUTH,
Dorset BH5 1AE
01202 309771
• e-mail: info@fircrofthotel.co.uk
• website: www.fircrofthotel.co.uk

Self-Catering
Westover Farm Cottages, Wootton
Fitzpaine, BRIDPORT, Dorset DT6 6NE
01297 560451
• e-mail: wfcottages@aol.com
• website:
www.lymeregis.com/westover-farm-cottages/

Caravan & Camping
Martin Cox, Highlands End Holiday Park,
Eype, BRIDPORT, Dorset DT6 6AR
01308 422139
• e-mail: holidays@wdlh.co.uk
• website: www.wdlh.co.uk

B & B
Mrs Jane Greening, New House Farm,
Mangerton Lane, Bradpole, BRIDPORT,
Dorset DT6 3SF
01308 422884
• e-mail: jane@mangertonlake.freeserve.co.uk
• website: www.mangertonlake.co.uk

Hotel
Eypes Mouth Country Hotel, Eype,
near BRIDPORT, Dorset DT6 6AL
01308 423300
• e-mail: eypehotel@aol.com
• website: www.eypehotel.co.uk

Caravan Park
Mr F. Loosmore, Manor Farm Holiday Centre,
CHARMOUTH, Bridport, Dorset DT6 6QL
01297 560226
• website: www.manorfarmholidaycentre.co.uk

B & B / Self-Catering
Mrs S.M. Johnson, Cardsmill Farm Holidays,
Whitchurch Canonicorum, CHARMOUTH,
Bridport, Dorset DT6 6RP
01297 489375
• e-mail: cardsmill@aol.com
• website: www.farmhousedorset.com

B & B
The Old Rectory, Winterbourne Steepleton,
DORCHESTER, Dorset DT2 9LG
01305 889468
• e-mail: trees@eurobell.co.uk
• website: www.trees.eurobell.co.uk

Self-Catering
Lyme Bay Holidays, 44 Church Street,
LYME REGIS, Dorset DT7 3DA
01297 443363
• website: www.lymebayholidays.co.uk

Farm
Mrs Stephenson, Holly Hedge Farm,
Malls Road, Lytchett Matravers, POOLE,
Dorset BH16 6EP
01929 459688
• e-mail: ceri.stephenson@lineone.net
• website: www.hollyhedgefarm.com

Guest House / Self-Catering
White Horse Farm, Middlemarsh,
SHERBORNE, Dorset DT9 5QN
01963 210222
• e-mail: enquiries@whitehorsefarm.co.uk
• website: www.whitehorsefarm.co.uk

Hotel
The Knoll House, STUDLAND BAY,
Dorset BH19 3AW
01929 450450
• e-mail: enquiries@knollhouse.co.uk
• website: www.knollhouse.co.uk

Hotel / Guest House
The Limes Hotel, 48 Park Road, SWANAGE,
Dorset BH19 2AE
01929 422664
• e-mail: info@limeshotel.demon.co.uk
• website: www.limeshotel.demon.co.uk

Farm / Bed & Breakfast
Mrs Justine Pike, Downshay Farm,
Haycrafts Lane, Harmans Cross, SWANAGE,
Dorset BH19 3EB
01929 480316
• e-mail: downshayfarm@farmersweekly.net

Self-Catering
Dorset Cottage Holidays, 11 Tyneham
Close, Sandford, WAREHAM,
Dorset BH20 7BE
01929 553443
• e-mail: enq@dhcottages.co.uk
• website: www.dhcottages.co.uk

Farm B & B / Caravan & Camping
Mrs L.S. Barnes, Luckford Wood House,
East Stoke, WAREHAM, Dorset BH20 6AW
01929 463098
• e-mail: info@luckfordleisure.co.uk
• website: www.luckfordleisure.co.uk

Caravan & Camping
Mrs Savage, Wareham Forest Tourist Park,
North Trigon, WAREHAM, Dorset BH20 7NZ
01929 551393
• e-mail: holiday@wareham-forest.co.uk
• website: www.wareham-forest.co.uk

Self-Catering on Working Farm
Josephine Pearse, Tamarisk Farm Cottages,
WEST BEXINGTON, Dorchester,
Dorset DT2 9DF
01308 897784
• e-mail: tamarisk@eurolink.ltd.net
• website: www.tamariskfarm.co.uk

B & B
Mrs Tory, Hemsworth Farm, Witchampton,
near WIMBORNE, Dorset BH21 5BN
01258 840216
• website: www.ruraldorset.org.uk/bed

•DURHAM

Farmhouse B & B
Mrs Carol Oulton, Newlands Hall,
Frosterley in Weardale, BISHOP AUCKLAND
Co Durham DL13 2SH
01388 529233
• e-mail: carol.oulton@ukonline.co.uk

B & B
David Turner, Bee Cottage Farmhouse,
Castleside, near CONSETT,
Co Durham DH8 9HW
01207 508224
• e-mail:
welcome@beecottagefarmhouse.freeserve.co.uk

•GLOUCESTERSHIRE

Farmhouse
Mrs Ann Cook, Moor's Farmhouse,
32 Beckford Road, ALDERTON,
Gloucestershire GL20 8AL
01242 620 523 / Freephone: 0800 298 9287
• e-mail: annmoorsfarmhouse@talk21.com

Farmhouse B & B / Self-Catering
Box Hedge Farm, Coalpit Heath, BRISTOL,
Gloucestershire BS36 2UW
01454 250786
• e-mail: marilyn@boxhedgefarmbandb.co.uk
• website: www.boxhedgefarmbandb.co.uk

Hotel
Charlton Kings Hotel, London Road,
CHELTENHAM, Gloucestershire GL52 6UU
01242 231061
• e-mail: enquiries@charltonkingshotel.co.uk
• website: www.charltonkingshotel.co.uk

B & B
Mrs G. Jeffrey, Brymbo, Honeybourne Lane,
Mickleton, CHIPPING CAMPDEN,
Gloucestershire GL55 6PU
01386 438890
• e-mail: enquiries@brymbo.com
• website: www.brymbo.com

B & B
Mrs C. Hutsby, Holly House, Ebrington,
CHIPPING CAMPDEN,
Gloucestershire GL55 6NL
01386 593213
• e-mail: hutsby@talk21.com
• website: www.hollyhousebandb.co.uk

Farm / B & B
Mrs D. Gwilliam, Dryslade Farm,
English Bicknor, COLEFORD,
Gloucestershire, GL16 7PA
01594 860259
• e-mail: dryslade@agriplus.net
• website: www.fweb.org.uk/dryslade

Guest House
Gunn Mill Guest House, Lower Spout Lane,
MITCHELDEAN, Gloucestershire GL17 0EA
01594 827577
• e-mail: info@gunnmillhouse.co.uk
• website: www.gunnmillhouse.co.uk

B & B
Mrs F.J. Adams, Aston House,
Broadwell, MORETON-IN-MARSH,
Gloucestershire GL56 0TJ
01451 830475
• e-mail: fja@netcomuk.co.uk
• website:
   www.netcomuk.co.uk/~nmfa/aston_house.html

B & B
Mrs Wendy Swait, Inschdene, Atcombe
Road, SOUTH WOODCHESTER, Stroud,
Gloucestershire GL5 5EW
01453 873254
• e-mail: malcolm.swait@repp.co.uk
• website: www.inschdene.co.uk

•HAMPSHIRE

B & B
Mrs Arnold-Brown, Hilden B&B,
Southampton Road, Boldre,
BROCKENHURST, Hampshire SO41 8PT
01590 623682
• e-mail: aliab@totalise.co.uk
• website: www.newforestbandb-hilden.co.uk

Hotel
The Watersplash Hotel, The Rise,
BROCKENHURST, Hampshire SO42 7ZP
01590 622344
• e-mail: bookings@watersplash.co.uk
• website: www.watersplash.co.uk

Caravan & Camping
Kingfisher Caravan Park, Browndown Road,
Stokes Bay, GOSPORT,
Hampshire PO13 9BE
023 9250 2611
• e-mail: info@kingfisher-caravan-park.co.uk
• website: www.kingfisher-caravan-park.co.uk

Campsite
Hayling Island Family Campsites, Copse
Lane, HAYLING ISLAND, Hampshire
023 9246 2479, 023 9246 4695, 023 9246 3684
• e-mail: lowertye@euphony.net
• website: www.haylingcampsites.co.uk

Farm / B & B
John & Penny Harkinson, Fritham Farm,
Fritham, LYNDHURST,
Hampshire SO43 7HH
023 8081 2333
• e-mail: frithamfarm@supanet.com

Guest House
The Penny Farthing Hotel, Romsey Road,
LYNDHURST, Hampshire SO43 7AA
023 8028 4422
• e-mail: stay@pennyfarthinghotel.co.uk
• website: www.pennyfarthinghotel.co.uk

B & B
Mrs P. Farrell, Honeysuckle House,
24 Clinton Road, LYMINGTON,
Hampshire SO41 9EA
01590 676635
• e-mail: skyblue@beeb.net
• website:
   www.newforest.demon.co.uk/honeysuckle.htm

Hotel
Woodlands Lodge Hotel, Bartley Road,
Woodlands, NEW FOREST,
Hampshire SO40 7GN
023 8029 2257
• e-mail: reception@woodlands-lodge.co.uk
• website: www.woodlands-lodge.co.uk

Self-Catering
Jenny Monger, Little Horseshoes,
South Gorley, RINGWOOD,
Hampshire BH24 3NL
01425 479340
• e-mail: jenny@littlehorseshoes.co.uk
• www.littlehorseshoes.co.uk

Self-Catering
Mrs Thelma Rowe, 9 Cruse Close, SWAY,
near Lymington, Hampshire SO41 6AY
01590 683092
• e-mail: ronrowe@talk21.com
• website: www.tivertonnewforest.co.uk

B & B
Mrs S. Buchanan, "Acacia", 44 Kilham Lane,
WINCHESTER, Hampshire SO22 5PT
01962 852259
• website: www.btinternet.com/~eric.buchanan

Please mention SELF-CATERING HOLIDAYS IN BRITAIN when enquiring about accommodation

•HEREFORDSHIRE

Guest House
Brian Roby, Felton House, FELTON,
Herefordshire HR1 3PH
01432 820366
• e-mail: bandb@ereal.net
• website:
www.SmoothHound.co.uk/hotels/felton.html

B & B
Mrs Gill Andrews, Webton Court
Farmhouse, KINGSTONE,
Herefordshire HR2 9NF
01981 250220
• e-mail: gill@webton.fsnet.co.uk

Farmhouse B & B
Mrs Jane West, Church Farm, Coddington,
LEDBURY, Herefordshire HR8 1JJ
01531 64027
• e-mail: jane@dexta.co.uk
• website: www.dexta.co.uk

B & B
Mrs S.W. Born, The Coach House, Putley,
LEDBURY, Herefordshire HR8 2QP
01531 670684
• e-mail: wendyborn@putley-coachhouse.co.uk
• website: www.putley-coachhouse.co.uk

Small Hotel
Miss G. Benjamin, The New Priory Hotel,
STRETTON SUGWAS, Hereford,
Herefordshire HR4 7AR
01432 760264
• e-mail: newprioryhotel@ukonline.co.uk
• website: www.newprioryhotel.co.uk

•ISLE OF WIGHT

Self-Catering
Island Cottage Holidays, Isle of Wight.
Contact: Honor Vass, The Old Vicarage,
Kingston, Wareham, Dorset BH20 5LH
01929 480080
• e-mail: enq@islandcottageholidays.com
• website: www.islandcottageholidays.com

> *Please mention*
> *Self-Catering Holidays*
> *In Britain*
> *when enquiring about*
> *accommodation*

Caravan Park / Self-Catering
Mrs A.J. Coleman, Sunnycott Caravan Park,
Rew Street, Gurnard, COWES,
Isle of Wight PO31 8NN
01983 292859
• e-mail:
sunnycott2000@sunnycott2000.freeserve.co.uk
• website: www.sunnycott.co.uk

Guest House
Barbara Tubbs, The Hazelwood,
14 Clarence Road, SHANKLIN,
Isle of Wight PO37 7BH
01983 862824
• e-mail:
barbara.tubbs@thehazelwood.free-online.co.uk
• website: www.thehazelwood.free-online.co.uk

Caravan & Camping
The Orchards Holiday Caravan & Camping
Park, Newbridge, YARMOUTH,
Isle of Wight PO41 0TS
01983 531331/350
• e-mail: info@orchards-holiday-park.co.uk
• website: www.orchards-holiday-park.co.uk

•KENT

Hotel / Guest House
Ashford Warren Cottage Hotel,
136 The Street, Willesborough, ASHFORD,
Kent TN24 0NB
01233 621905
• e-mail: general@warrencottage.co.uk
• website: www.warrencottage.co.uk

Farm
Mrs Lewana Castle, Great Field Farm,
Misling Lane, Stelling Minnis,
CANTERBURY, Kent CT4 6DE
01227 709223
• e-mail: greatfieldfarm@aol.com

Guest House
Mr R.D. Linch, Upper Ansdore, Duckpit
Lane, Petham, CANTERBURY, Kent CT4 5QB
01227 700672
• e-mail:
upperansdore@hotels.activebooking.com
• website:
www.SmoothHound.co.uk/hotels/upperans.html

Farmhouse B & B
Nicola Ellen, Crockshard Farmhouse,
Wingham, CANTERBURY Kent CT3 1NY
01227 720464
• e-mail: crockshardbnb@yahoo.com
• website: www.crockshard.com

Guest House
Penny Farthing Guest House, 109 Maison Dieu Road, DOVER, Kent CT16 1RT
01304 205563
• e-mail: pennyfarthingdover@btinternet.com
• website: www.pennyfarthingdover.com

B & B
Bleriot's, 47 Park Avenue, DOVER, Kent CT16 1HE
01304 211394
• website: www.SmoothHound.co.uk

Caravan & Camping
Woodlands Park, Biddenden Road, TENTERDEN, Kent
01580 291216
• e-mail: woodlandsp@aol.com
• website: www.campingsite.co.uk

Self-Catering
Garden of England Cottages, The Mews Office, 189a High Street, TONBRIDGE, Kent TN9 1BX
• e-mail: holidays@gardenofenglandcottages.co.uk
• website: www.gardenofenglandcottages.co.uk

•LANCASHIRE

B & B
Mrs Melanie Smith, Capernwray House, Capernwray, CARNFORTH, Lancashire LA6 1AE
01524 732363
• e-mail: thesmiths@capernwrayhouse.com
• website: www.capernwrayhouse.com

•LEICESTERSHIRE

Guest House
Mrs Indge, The Highbury Guest House, 146 Leicester Road, LOUGHBOROUGH, Leicestershire LE11 2AQ
01509 230545
• e-mail: emkhighbury@supanet.com
• website: www.thehighburyguesthouse.co.uk

Guest House
Mrs Jackson, The Exeter Guest House, Wakerley, OAKHAM, Rutland LE15 8PA
01572 747817
• website: www.exeterguesthouse.co.uk

•LINCOLNSHIRE

B & B
Jubilee House, Waring Street, HORNCASTLE Lincolnshire LN9 6DY
01507 527000
• e-mail: mizpahvilla@aol.com

Farm / Board
Mrs Evans, Willow Farm, THORPE FENDYKES, Wainfleet, Skegness, Lincolnshire PE24 4QH
01754 830316
• website: www.willowfarmholidays.fsnet.co.uk

•NORFOLK

Guest House
Mrs J.A. Bell, Peacock House, Peacock Lane, Old Beetley, DEREHAM, Norfolk NR20 4DG
01362 860371
• e-mail: PeackH@aol.com
• website: www.SmoothHound.co.uk/hotels/peacockh.html

Self-Catering
Winterton Valley Holidays, 15 Kingston Avenue, Caister-on-Sea, GREAT YARMOUTH, Norfolk NR30 5ET
01493 377175
• e-mail: info@wintertonvalleyholidays.fsnet.co.uk
• website: www.wintertonvalleyholidays.co.uk

Self-Catering
Blue Riband Holidays, HEMSBY, Great Yarmouth, Norfolk NR29 4HA
01493 730445
• website: www.BlueRibandHolidays.co.uk

Farmhouse B & B
Mrs Lynda Mack, Hempstead Hall, HOLT, Norfolk NR25 6TN
01263 712224
• website: www.broadland.com/hempsteadhall

Farm / Board
Mrs Davidson, Holmdene Farm, Beeston, KING'S LYNN, Norfolk, PE32 2NJ
01328 701284
• e-mail: holmdenefarm@farmersweekly.net
• website: www.northnorfolk.co.uk/holmdenefarm

Guest House B & B
Mrs Christine Lilah Thrower, Whincliff, Cromer Road, MUNDESLEY-ON-SEA, Norfolk NR11 8DU
01263 721554
• e-mail: whincliff@freeuk.com
• website: http://whincliff.freeuk.com

Guest House
Mrs D. Curtis, Rosedale, 145 Earlhay Road,
NORWICH, Norfolk NR2 3RG
01603 453743
• e-mail: drcbac@aol.com
• website: www.http://members.aol.com/drcbac

Guest House / Self-Catering
L.D. Poore, 3 Wodehouse Road,
OLD HUNSTANTON, Norfolk PE36 6JD
01485 534036
• e-mail: st.crispins@btinternet.com
    or: lesley.cobblerscottage@btinternet.com

Self-Catering
Norfolk Country Cottages, Carlton House,
Market Place, REEPHAM,
Norfolk NR10 4QN
01603 871872
• e-mail: info@norfolkcottages.co.uk
• website: www.norfolkcottages.co.uk

•NORTHUMBERLAND

B & B
Eileen Finn, Thornley House, ALLENDALE,
Northumberland NE47 9NH
01434 683255
• e-mail: e.finn@ukonline.co.uk
• website: web.ukonline.co.uk/e.finn

Self-Catering
Catriona Moore, West Fallodon, Embleton,
ALNWICK, Northumberland NE67 5EB
01665 579357
• e-mail: rn.moore@freeonline.com
• website: www.wfallodon.freeuk.com

Self-Catering
Heritage Coast Holidays,
66 Greensfield Court, ALNWICK,
Northumberland NE66 2DE
01670 787864
• e-mail: office@marishalthompson.co.uk
• website: www.northumberland-holidays.co.uk

Guest House
John & Edith Howliston, North Cottage,
Birling, WARKWORTH, Morpeth,
Northumberland NE65 0XS
01665 711263
• e-mail: edithandjohn@another.com
• website: www.accta.co.uk/north

•OXFORDSHIRE

Farm / Board
Mrs Katherine Brown, Hill Grove Farm,
Crawley Road, MINSTER LOVELL,
Oxfordshire OX29 ONA
01993 703120
• e-mail: kbrown@eggconnect.net

Guest House
Mandy Buck, Elbie House, East End,
Northleigh, near Witney, WOODSTOCK,
Oxfordshire OX8 6PZ
01993 880166
• e-mail: mandy@cotswoldbreak.co.uk
• website: www.cotswoldbreak.co.uk

Inn
Killingworth Castle Inn, Glympton Road,
Wootton, by WOODSTOCK,
Oxfordshire OX20 1EJ
01993 811401
• e-mail: wiggiscastle@aol.com
• website: www.oxlink.co.uk/woodstock/kilcastle

•SHROPSHIRE

Farm B & B
Mrs M. Jones, Acton Scott Farm, Acton
Scott, CHURCH STRETTON,
Shropshire SY6 6QN
01694 781260
• e-mail: edandm@clara.co.uk
• website: http://welcome.to/acton-scott-b&b

Farm / B & B
Mrs Brereton, Brereton's Farm, Woolston,
CHURCH STRETTON, Shropshire SY6 6QD
01694 781201
• e-mail: joanna@breretonhouse.f9.co.uk
• website: www.breretonhouse.f9.co.uk

Guest House
Ron & Jennie Repath, Meadowlands,
Lodge Lane, Frodesley, DORRINGTON,
Shropshire SY5 7HD
01694 731350
• e-mail: meadowlands@talk21.com
• website: www.meadowlands.co.uk

Hotel
Miles Hunter, Pen-y-Dyffryn Country Hotel,
OSWESTRY, Shropshire SY10 7JD
01691 653700
• e-mail: stay@peny.co.uk
• website: www.peny.co.uk

Please mention SELF-CATERING HOLIDAYS IN BRITAIN when enquiring about accommodation

Self-Catering
Mrs Ann Cartwright, Ryton Farm, Ryton,
Dorrington, SHREWSBURY,
Shropshire SY5 7LY
01743 718449
• website: www.rytonfarm.co.uk

Self-Catering
Courtyard Cottages, Lower Springs Farm,
Kenley, SHREWSBURY, Shropshire SY5 6PA
01952 510 841
• e-mail: a-gill@lineone.net

•SOMERSET

B & B / Self-Catering
Jackie & David Bishop, Toghill House Farm,
Wick, BATH, Somerset BS30 5RT
01225 891261
• website: www.toghillhousefarm.co.uk

Guest House
Mrs C. Bryson, Walton Villa, 3 Newbridge
Hill, BATH, Somerset BA1 3PW
01225 482792
• e-mail: walton.villa@virgin.net
• website: www.walton.izest.com

Guest House
Jan Wotley, The Albany Guest House,
24 Crescent Gardens, BATH,
Somerset BA1 2NB
01225 313339
• e-mail: the_albany@lineone.net
• website: www.bath.org/hotel/albany.htm

Hotel
Elaine Sexton, Bailbrook Lodge Hotel,
35-37 London Road West, BATH,
Somerset BA1 7HZ
01225 859090
• e-mail: hotel@bailbrooklodge.co.uk
• website: www.bailbrooklodge.co.uk

Self-Catering
T.M. Hicks, Diamond Farm, Weston Road,
BREAN, Near Burnham-on-Sea,
Somerset TA8 2RL
01278 751263
• e-mail: trevor@diamondfarm42.freeserve.co.uk
• website: www.diamondfarm.co.uk

B & B
Mrs Alexander, Priors Mead, 23 Rectory
Road, BURNHAM-ON-SEA,
Somerset TA8 2BZ
01278 782116
• e-mail: priorsmead@aol.com
• website: www.priorsmead.co.uk

Caravan & Camping Park
Broadway House Holiday Touring Caravan &
Camping Park, CHEDDAR,
Somerset BS27 3DB
01934 742610
• e-mail: enquiries@broadwayhouse.uk.com
• website: www.broadwayhouse.uk.com

B & B
Mrs C. Bacon, Honeydown Farm,
Seaborough Hill, CREWKERNE,
Somerset TA18 8PL
01460 72665
• e-mail: cb@honeydown.freeserve.co.uk
• website: www.honeydown.freeserve.co.uk

Hotel
Jeff Everitt, Lion Hotel, Bank Square,
DULVERTON, Somerset TA22 9BU
01398 323444
• e-mail: jeffeveritt@tiscali.co.uk

Farm / Board
Mrs Humphrey, Highercombe Farm,
DULVERTON, Exmoor, Somerset TA22 9PT
01398 323616
• e-mail: abigail@highercombe.demon.co.uk
• website: www.highercombe.demon.co.uk

Self-Catering
Mrs Joan Atkins, 2 Edgcott Cottage,
EXFORD, Minehead, Somerset TA24 7QG
01643 831564
• e-mail: info@stilemoorexmoor.co.uk
• website: www.stilemoorexmoor.co.uk

B & B / Self-Catering
C.R. Horstmann, Court Farm, EXFORD,
Exmoor, Somerset TA24 7LY
01643 831207
• e-mail: colin@courtfarm.co.uk
• website: www.courtfarm.co.uk

Farm B & B / Self-Catering
Penny Webber, Hindon Organic Farm,
Near Selworthy, Minehead, EXMOOR,
Somerset TA24 8SH
01643 705244
• e-mail: info@hindonfarm.co.uk
• website: www.hindonfarm.co.uk

Hotel / Self-Catering
Simonsbath House Hotel, Simonsbath,
EXMOOR, Somerset TA24 7SH
01643 831259
• e-mail: hotel@simonsbathhouse.co.uk
• website: www.simonsbathhouse.co.uk

Farm / Self-Catering
Mrs Styles, Wintershead Farm, Simonsbath,
EXMOOR, Somerset TA24 7LF
01643 831222
• website: www.wintershead.co.uk

Self-Catering
Mrs N. Hanson, Woodcombe Lodges,
Bratton, MINEHEAD,
Somerset TA24 8SQ
01643 702789
• e-mail: nicola@woodcombelodge.co.uk
• website: www.woodcombelodge.co.uk

Self-Catering
Inner Lype & Goosemoor Farm Cottages,
Wheddon Cross, MINEHEAD,
Somerset TA24 7BJ
01643 841557
• e-mail: om.howe@virgin.net
• website: www.cottageguide.co.uk/innerlype

B & B
Mr P.R. Weir, Slipper Cottage,
41 Bishopston, MONTACUTE,
Somerset TA15 6UX
01935 823073
• e-mail: sue.weir@totalise.co.uk
• website: www.slippercottage.co.uk

Inn
Jackie & Alan Cottrell, The Ship Inn, High
Street, PORLOCK, Somerset TA24 8QD
01643 862507
• e-mail: mail@shipinnporlock.co.uk
• website: www.shipinnporlock.co.uk

Hotel
Mrs Murphy, Farthings Hotel & Restaurant,
Hatch Beauchamp, TAUNTON,
Somerset TA3 6SG
01823 480664
• e-mail: farthing1@aol.com
• website: www.farthingshotel.com

Self-Catering
Croft Holiday Cottages, Anchor Street,
WATCHET, Somerset TA23 0BY
01984 631121
• e-mail: croftcottages@talk21.com
• website: www.cottageguide.co.uk/croft-cottages

Guest House
Infield House, 36 Portway, WELLS,
Somerset BA5 2BN
01749 670989
• e-mail: infield@talk21.com
• website: www.infieldhouse.co.uk

Hotel
Braeside Hotel, 2 Victoria Park,
WESTON-SUPER-MARE,
Somerset BS23 2HZ
01934 626642
• e-mail: braeside@tesco.net
• website: www.braesidehotel.co.uk

•STAFFORDSHIRE

Farm
Mrs M. Hiscoe-James, Offley Grove Farm,
Adbaston, ECCLESHALL,
Staffordshire ST20 0QB
01785 280205
• e-mail: accom@offleygrovefarm.freeserve.co.uk
• website: www.offleygrovefarm.co.uk

Self-Catering
Brookhays, Park Lane, Ipstones,
near LEEK, Staffordshire
01335 344132
• e-mail: KeithLomas@aol.com

Guest House
Mrs Griffiths, Prospect House Guest House,
334 Cheadle Road, Cheddleton, LEEK,
Staffordshire ST13 7BW
01782 550639
• e-mail: prospect@talk21.com
• website:
www.touristnetuk.com/wm/prospect/index.htm

Guest House
Ruth Franks, The Beehive Guest House,
Churnet View Road, OAKAMOOR,
Staffordshire ST10 3AE
01538 702420
• e-mail: thebeehiveoakamoor@btinternet.com
• website: www.thebeehiveguesthouse.co.uk

•SUFFOLK

Hotel
The Cornwallis Country Hotel & Restaurant,
Brome, EYE, Suffolk IP23 8AJ
01379 870326
• e-mail: enquiries@thecornwallis.com
• website: www.thecornwallis.com

Farm B & B / Self-Catering
Mr & Mrs Kindred, High House Farm,
Cransford, WOODBRIDGE, Suffolk IP13 9PD
01728 663461
• e-mail: info@highhousefarm.co.uk
• website: www.highhousefarm.co.uk

Hotel
The Crown and Castle, Orford,
near WOODBRIDGE, Suffolk IP12 2LJ
01394 450205
• e-mail: info@crownandcastlehotel.co.uk
• website: www.crownandcastle.co.uk

Hotel / Inn
The Three Tuns Coaching Inn, Main Road,
Pettistree, WOODBRIDGE, Suffolk IP13 0HW
01728 747979
• e-mail: jon@threetuns-coachinginn.co.uk
• website: www.threetuns-coachinginn.co.uk

•SURREY

Hotel
Chase Lodge Hotel, 10 Park Road, Hampton
Wick, KINGSTON-UPON-THAMES,
Surrey KT1 4AS
020 8943 1862
• e-mail: info@chaselodgehotel.com
• website: www.chaselodgehotel.com

•EAST SUSSEX

Bed & Breakfast / Guest House
Brighton Marina House Hotel, 8 Charlotte
Street, BRIGHTON, East Sussex BN2 1AG
01273 605349
• e-mail: rooms@jungs.co.uk
• website: www.brighton-mh-hotel.co.uk

Hotel
Jonathan Turner, Dale Hill Hotel,
TICEHURST, East Sussex TN5 7DQ
01580 200112
• e-mail: info@dalehill.co.uk
• website: www.dalehill.co.uk

•WEST SUSSEX

Caravan & Camping
Val & Jeff Burrow, Honeybridge Park,
Honeybridge Lane, Dial Post, near
HORSHAM, West Sussex RH13 8NX
01403 710923
• e-mail: enquiries@honeybridgepark.co.uk
• website: www.honeybridgepark.co.uk

B & B
Lady M.R. Milton, Beacon Lodge B&B,
London Road, WATERSFIELD,
West Sussex RH20 1NH
01798 831026
• e-mail: beaconlodge@hotmail.com
• website: www.beaconlodge.co.uk

•WARWICKSHIRE

Guest House / B & B
Julia Downie, Holly Tree Cottage, Pathlow,
STRATFORD-UPON-AVON,
Warwickshire CV37 0ES
01789 204461
• e-mail: john@hollytree-cottage.co.uk
• website: www.hollytree-cottage.co.uk

Self-Catering
Karen Cauvin, Penshurst Guest House,
34 Evesham Place, STRATFORD-UPON-
AVON, Warwickshire CV37 6HT
01789 550197
• e-mail: karen@penshurst.net
• website: www.penshurst.net

Guest House
Mr J. Worboys, Broadlands Guest House,
23 Evesham Place, STRATFORD-UPON-AVON,
Warwickshire CV37 6HT
01789 299181
• e-mail: broadlands.com@virgin.net
• website:
www.stratford-upon-avon.co.uk/broadlands.htm

Guest House
Linhill Guest House, 35 Evesham Place,
STRATFORD-UPON-AVON, Warwickshire
01789 292879
• e-mail: linhill@bigwig.net
• website: www.linhillguesthouse.co.uk

Guest House
Mr & Mrs Learmount, Green Haven Guest
House, 217 Evesham Road, STRATFORD-
UPON-AVON, Warwickshire CV37 9AS
01789 297874
• e-mail: susanlearmount@green-haven.co.uk
• website: www.green-haven.co.uk

Guest House / Self-Catering
Mrs Elizabeth Draisey, Forth House/
Copes Flat, 44 High Street, WARWICK,
Warwickshire CV34 4AX
01926 401512
• e-mail: info@forthhouseuk.co.uk
• website: www.forthhouseuk.co.uk

Guest House
Croft Guest House, Haseley Knob,
WARWICK, Warwickshire CV35 7NL
01926 484447
• e-mail: david@croftguesthouse.co.uk
• website: www.croftguesthouse.co.uk

•WILTSHIRE

Farmhouse / Board

Susan Barnes, Lovett Farm,
Little Somerford, near MALMESBURY,
Wiltshire SN15 5BP
01666 823268
• e-mail: lovettfarm@btinternet.com
• website: www.lovettfarm.co.uk

Guest House

Alan & Dawn Curnow, Hayburn Wyke Guest
House, 72 Castle Road, SALISBURY,
Wiltshire SP1 3RL
01722 412627
• e-mail: hayburn.wyke@tinyonline.co.uk
• website: www.hayburnwykeguesthouse.co.uk

Farm Guest House

Mrs S. Lanham, Newton Farmhouse,
Southampton Road, Whiteparish,
SALISBURY, Wiltshire SP5 2QL
01794 884416
• e-mail: reservations@newtonfarmhouse.co.uk
• website: www.newtonfarmhouse.co.uk

•WORCESTERSHIRE

Farmhouse B & B

Mrs Jane Hill, Lower Field Farm, Willersey,
BROADWAY, Worcestershire WR11 5HF
01386 858273
• e-mail: info@lowerfield-farm.co.uk
• website: www.lowerfield-farm.co.uk

Inn

The Crown & Sandys, Main Road,
Ombersley, DROITWICH, Worcester
Worcestershire WR9 0EW
01905 620252
• e-mail: crown&sandys@evertons.co.uk

Hotel

Joseph Petitjean, Brockencote Hall,
Chaddesley Corbett, KIDDERMINSTER,
Worcestershire
01562 777876
• e-mail: info@brockencotehall.com
• website: www.brockencotehall.com

•EAST YORKSHIRE

B & B

Paws-a-While, KILNWICK PERCY,
East Yorkshire YO42 1UF
01759 301168
• e-mail: paws.a.while@lineone.net
• website: www.pawsawhile.net

•NORTH YORKSHIRE

Guest House

Mr Kingsley, Arbutus Guest House,
Riverside, CLAPHAM, near Settle,
North Yorkshire LA2 8DS
01524 251240
• e-mail: info@arbutus.co.uk
• website: www.arbutus.co.uk

Guest House

Janet and Steve Frankland, Amadeus,
115 Franklin Road, HARROGATE,
North Yorkshire HG1 5EN
01423 505151
• e-mail: amadeushotel@btinternet.com

B & B / Self-Catering

Mrs E.J. Moorhouse, The Courtyard at
Duke's Place, Bishop Thornton,
HARROGATE, North Yorkshire HG3 3JY
01765 620229
• e-mail: jakimoorhouse@onetel.net.uk

Guest House

Phil & Carolyn Smith, Inglenook Guest
House, 20 Main Street, INGLETON,
North Yorkshire LA6 3HJ
01524 241270
• e-mail: inglenook20@hotmail.com
• website: www.nebsweb.co.uk/inglenook

Farm B & B / Self-Catering

John & Felicity Wiles, Sinnington Common
Farm, KIRKBYMOORSIDE, York,
North Yorkshire YO62 6NX
01751 431719
• e-mail: felicity@scfarm.demon.co.uk
• website: www.scfarm.demon.co.uk

Farmhouse B & B

Mrs Julie Clarke, Middle Farm,
Woodale, Coverdale, LEYBURN,
North Yorkshire DL8 4TY
01969 640271
• e-mail: julie-clarke@amserve.com
• website:
    www.yorkshirenet.co.uk/stayat/middlefarm/

Holiday Park

John McCourt, Black Swan Holiday Park,
Rear Black Swan, Fearby, MASHAM, Ripon,
North Yorkshire HG4 4NF
01765 689477
• e-mail: blackswanholidaypark@fsmail.net
• website: www.geocities.com/theblackswan_uk/

Hotel

Mrs Ella Bowes, Banavie, Roxby Road,
Thornton-Le-Dale, PICKERING, North
Yorkshire YO18 7SX
01751 474616
• e-mail: ella@banavie.fsbusiness.co.uk
• website:
www.SmoothHound.co.uk/hotels/banavie

Country House Hotel

Hartforth Hall Hotel, Gilling West,
RICHMOND, North Yorkshire DL10 5JU
01748 825715
• website: www.hartforthhall.com

Farmhouse B & B

Mrs Sandra Gordon, St George's Court, Old
Home Farm, Grantley, RIPON
North Yorkshire HG4 3EU
01765 620618
• e-mail: stgeorgescourt@bronco.co.uk
• website: www.stgeorges-court.co.uk

Guest House

Sue & Tony Hewitt, Harmony Country
Lodge, 80 Limestone Road, Burniston,
SCARBOROUGH,
North Yorkshire YO13 0DG
0800 2985840
• e-mail: tony@harmonylodge.net
• website: www.harmonylodge.net

B & B (Small Hotel)

Mrs M.M Abbott, Howdale Hotel,
121 Queen's Parade, SCARBOROUGH,
North Yorkshire YO12 7HU
0800 056 6622
• e-mail: maria_keith_howdalehotel@yahoo.co.uk
• website: www.howdalehotel.moonfruit.com

Hotel

Ganton Greyhound, Main Street, Ganton,
near SCARBOROUGH,
North Yorkshire YO12 4NX
01944 710116
• e-mail: gantongreyhound@supanet.com
• website: www.gantongreyhound.co.uk

Self-Catering

Mr Donnelly, Gowland Farm, Gowland Lane,
Cloughton, SCARBOROUGH,
North Yorkshire YO13 0DU
01723 870924
• e-mail: gowlandfarm@hotmail.com
• website: www.gowlandfarm.co.uk

Hotel

Coniston Hall Hotel, Coniston Cold,
SKIPTON, North Yorkshire, BD23 4EB
01756 748080
• e-mail: conistonhall@clara.net
• website: www.conistonhall.co.uk

Self-Catering

Mrs Jones, New Close Farm,
Kirkby Malham, SKIPTON,
North Yorkshire BD23 4DP
01729 830240
• e-mail:
brendajones@newclosefarmyorkshire.co.uk
• website: www.newclosefarmyorkshire.co.uk

Self-Catering Cottages

Anne Fawcett, Mile House Farm Country
Cottages, Mile House Farm, Hawes,
WENSLEYDALE, North Yorkshire DL8 3PT
01969 667481
• e-mail: milehousefarm@hotmail.com
• website: www.wensleydale.uk.com

Self-Catering

Mrs Sue Cooper, St Edmunds, The Green,
Crakehall, Bedale, WENSLEYDALE,
North Yorkshire DL8 1HP
01677 423584
• e-mail:stedmundscountrycottages@hotmail.com
• website: www.crakehall.org.uk

Self-Catering

Westclose House (Allaker),
WEST SCRAFTON, North Yorkshire
c/o Mr A Cave,
020 8567 4862
• e-mail: ac@adriancave.com
• website: www.adriancave.com/allaker

Self-Catering

June Roberts, White Rose Holiday Cottages,
5 Brook Park, Sleights, near WHITBY,
North Yorkshire YO21 1RT
01947 810763
• e-mail: enquiries@whiterosecottages.co.uk
• website: www.whiterosecottages.co.uk

Self-Catering

Mrs N. Pattinson, South House Farm,
Fylingthorpe, WHITBY,
North Yorkshire YO22 4UQ
01947 880243
• e-mail: kmp@bogglehole.fsnet.co.uk

FREE or REDUCED RATE entry to Holiday Visits and Attractions see our READERS' OFFER VOUCHERS on pages 49-76

Inn
Flask Inn, Near Robin's Hood Bay, WHITBY,
North Yorkshire YO22 4QH
01947 880305
• e-mail: flaskinn@aol.com
• website: www.flaskinn.com

Self-Catering
Nick Eddleston, Greenhouses Farm Cottage,
Green Houses Farm,
Lealholm, near WHITBY,
North Yorkshire YO21 2AD
01947 897486
• e-mail: n_eddleston@yahoo.com
• website: www.greenhouses-farm-cottages.co.uk

Self-Catering
Jill McNeil, Swallow Holiday Cottages,
The Farm, Stainsacre, WHITBY,
North Yorkshire YO22 4NT
01947 603790
• e-mail: jillian@swallowcottages.co.uk
• website: www.swallowcottages.co.uk

Hotel
Seacliffe Hotel, North Promenade,
West Cliff, WHITBY,
North Yorkshire YO21 3JX
01947 603139
• e-mail: julie@seacliffe.fsnet.co.uk
• website: www.seacliffe.co.uk

Guest House
Mr Gary Hudson, Orillia House,
89 The Village, Stockton on Forest,
YORK, North Yorkshire YO3 9UP
01904 400600
• e-mail: orillia@globalnet.co.uk
• website: www.orilliahouse.co.uk

B & B / Self-Catering / Holiday Caravans
Mr & Mrs Tyerman, Partridge Nest Farm,
Eskdaleside, Sleights, WHITBY,
North Yorkshire YO22 5ES
01947 810450
• e-mail: barbara@partridgenestfarm.com
• website: www.partridgenestfarm.com

Self-Catering
Mrs O. Hepworth, Land of Nod Farm,
Ugthorpe, near WHITBY,
North Yorkshire YO21 2BL
• e-mail:
colin@thecottage-ugthorpe.freeserve.co.uk
• website:
www.thecottage-ugthorpe.freeserve.co.uk

Farm / Self-Catering
Mrs Robinson, Valley View Farm,
Old Byland, Helmsley, YORK,
North Yorkshire YO6 5LG
01439 798221
• e-mail: sally@valleyviewfarm.com
• website: www.valleyviewfarm.com

Farmhouse B & B
High Gaterley Farmhouse, Castle Howard
Estate, YORK, North Yorkshire YO60 7HT
01653 694636
• e-mail: relax@highgaterley.com
• website: www.highgaterley.com

•SCOTLAND

•ABERDEEN, BANFF & MORAY

Self-Catering
Willie Bremner, Bremner of Foggie,
Old School, ABERCHIRDER,
Banffshire AB54 7XS
01466 780260
• website: www.bremnersoffoggie.co.uk

Self-Catering
Mrs J. White, Beechgrove Cottages,
Tomnavoulin, BALLINDALLOCH,
Aberdeenshire AB37 9JA
01807 590220
• e-mail: jaqui154@msn.com
• website: www.beechgrovecottages.co.uk

B & B
Mrs E. Malim, Invercairn House, BRODIE,
by Forres, Moray IV36 2TD
01309 641261
• e-mail: invercairnhouse@supanet.com
• website: www.invercairnhouse.co.uk

B & B
Mrs H. Massie, Milton of Grange Farm,
FORRES, Morayshire IV36 0TR
01309 676360
• website: www.forres-accommodation.co.uk

Farmhouse B & B
Mrs Alice Jane Morrison, Haddoch Farm,
by HUNTLY, Aberdeenshire AB54 4SL
01466 711217
• e-mail: alice.morrison@tinyworld.co.uk

•ARGYLL & BUTE

Inn
Mr D. Fraser, Cairndow Stagecoach Inn,
CAIRNDOW, Argyll PA26 8BN
01499 600286
• e-mail: cairndowinn@aol.com

B & B
Mrs D. MacCormick, Mains Farm,
CARRADALE, Campbeltown,
Argyll PA28 6QG
01583 431216
• e-mail:
  maccormick@mainsfarm.freeserve.co.uk

Self-Catering
Mrs Isabella Crawford, Blarghour Farm,
Loch Awe-side, By DALMALLY,
Argyll PA33 1BW
01866 833246
• e-mail: blarghour@aol.com
• website: www.self-catering-argyll.co.uk

FHG PUBLICATIONS LTD

publish a large range of well-known accommodation guides.
We will be happy to send you details or you can use the order form at the back
of this book.

Self-Catering
David Shaw, Ardbrecknish House,
Ardbrecknish, Loch Awe,
DALMALLY, Argyll PA33 1BH
01866 833223
• e-mail: enquiries@ardbrecknish.com
• website: www.ardbrecknish.com

Guest House
A.J. Burke, Orchy Bank, DALMALLY,
Argyll PA33 1AS
01838 200370
• e-mail: aj.burke@talk21.com
• website:
  www.loch-awe.com/orchybank/c2.htm

Self-Catering
B & M Phillips, Kilbride Croft, Balvicar,
ISLE OF SEIL, Argyll PA34 4RD
01852 300475
• e-mail: kilbridecroft@aol.com
• website: www.kilbridecroft.fsnet.co.uk

Self-Catering
Castle Sween Bay (Holidays) Ltd,
Ellery, LOCHGILPHEAD,
Argyll PA31 8PA
01880 770232
• e-mail: info@ellary.com
• website: www.ellary.com

Hotel
Willowburn Hotel, Clachan Seil,
by OBAN, Argyll PA34 4TJ
01852 300276
• e-mail: willowburn.hotel@virgin.net
• website: www.willowburn.co.uk

•AYRSHIRE & ARRAN

B & B
Mrs J. Clark, Eglinton Guest House,
23 Eglinton Terrace, AYR,
Ayrshire KA7 1JJ
01292 264623
• website: www.eglintonguesthouse.co.uk

Self-Catering
Arran Hideaways, Invercloy House, Brodick,
ISLE OF ARRAN
01770 302303
• e-mail: info@arran-hideways.co.uk
• website: www.arran-hideways.co.uk

Caravan & Camping
Mr Angus McKie, Braemoor Christian
Holiday Village, Torranyard, KILWINNING,
Ayrshire KA13 7RD
01274 850286
• e-mail: info@braemoorchu.com
• website: www.braemoorchu.com

•BORDERS

Guest House
Dunlaverock Guest House, COLDINGHAM
BAY, Berwickshire TD14 5PA
01890 771450
• e-mail: dunlaverockhouse@lineone.net
• website: www.dunlaverock.fsnet.co.uk

Guest House
Mrs Ewen Kenworthy, St Albans, Clouds,
DUNS, Berwickshire TD11 3BB
01361 883285
• e-mail: st_albans@ukf.net
• website: www.scotlandbordersbandb.co.uk

Self-Catering
Mill House, Letterbox and Stockman's
Cottages, c/o Mrs A Fraser, Overwells,
JEDBURGH, Borders TD8 6LT
01835 863020
• website: www.overwells.co.uk

Hotel
The Crook Inn, TWEEDSMUIR,
Borders ML12 6QN
01899 880272
• e-mail: the crookinn@btinternet.com
• website: www.crookinn.co.uk

Self-Catering
Slipperfield House, WEST LINTON,
Peeblesshire EH46 7AA
01968 660401
• e-mail: cottages@slipperfield.com
• website: www.slipperfield.com

•DUMFRIES &
GALLOWAY

Guest House / Self-Catering
Mrs E.M. Bardsley, The Rossan,
Auchencairn, CASTLE DOUGLAS,
Dumfries & Galloway
01556 640269
• e-mail: bardsley@rossan.freeserve.co.uk
• website: www.the-rossan.co.uk

Self-Catering
Mr Ball, Barncrosh Leisure Co Ltd,
Barncrosh, CASTLE DOUGLAS,
Dumfries & Galloway DG7 1TX
01556 680216
• e-mail: enq@barncrosh.co.uk
• website: www.barncrosh.co.uk

Hotel / Guest House
Mrs Nicki Proudlock, Mabie House Hotel,
Mabie, DUMFRIES,
Dumfries & Galloway DG2 8HB
01387 263188
• e-mail: niki@mabiehouse.co.uk
• website: www.mabiehouse.co.uk

Self-Catering
Mrs B. Gilbey, Rusko Holidays,
GATEHOUSE OF FLEET, Castle Douglas,
Dumfries & Galloway DG7 2BS
01557 814215
• e-mail: gilbey@rusko.demon.co.uk
• website: www.ruskoholidays.co.uk

Self-Catering
Mrs S.M.Finlay, Manor Cottage,
Ross Bay, KIRKCUDBRIGHT,
Dumfries & Galloway DG6 4TR
01557 870381
• e-mail: finlay.baycottage@btopenworld.com
• website: www.baycottage.net

B & B
June Deakins, Annandale House, MOFFAT,
Dumfriesshire
01683 221460
• e-mail: june.deakins@virgin.net
• website:
  www.geocities.com/meadowdale/index.html

B & B
Fiona Corlett, Craigie Lodge, Ballplay Road,
MOFFAT, Dumfries & Galloway DG10 9JD
01683 221769
• e-mail: craigielodge@aol.com
• website: www.craigielodge.co.uk

Caravan Park
A & E Mackie, Galloway Point Holiday Park,
Portpatrick, STRANRAER,
Dumfries & Galloway DG9 9AA
01776 810561
• website: www.gallowaypointholidaypark.co.uk

•DUNDEE & ANGUS

Farmhouse B & B
Rosemary Beatty, Brathinch Farm,
by BRECHIN, Angus DD9 7QX
01356 648292
• e-mail: adam.brathinch@btinternet.com

Self-Catering
Jenny Scott, Welton Farm, The Welton of
Kingoldrum, KIRRIEMUIR, Angus DD8 5HY
01575 574743
• e-mail: weltonholidays@btinternet.com
• website: www.cottageguide.co.uk/thewelton

•EDINBURGH & LOTHIANS

B & B
Kenneth Harkins, 78 East Main Street,
BLACKBURN, By Bathgate,
West Lothian EH47 7QS
01506 655221
• e-mail: cruachan.bb@virgin.net
• website: www.cruachan.co.uk

Guest House
International Guest House, 31 Mayfield
Gardens, EDINBURGH, Lothians EH9 2BX
0131 667 2511
• e-mail: intergh@easynet.co.uk
• website: www.accommodation-edinburgh.com

Guest House
Dorothy Vidler, Kenvie Guest House,
16 Kilmaurs Road, EDINBURGH,
Lothians EH16 5DA
0131 668 1964
• e-mail: dorothy@kenvie.co.uk
• website: www.kenvie.co.uk

B & B
McCrae's B&B, 44 East Claremont Street,
EDINBURGH, Lothians EH7 4JR
0131 556 2610
• e-mail: mccraes.bandb@lineone.net
• website:
  http://website.lineone.net/~mccraes.bandb

Guest House
D. Green, Ivy House, 7 Mayfield Gardens,
Newington, EDINBURGH, Lothians EH9 2AX
0131 667 3411
• e-mail: don@ivyguesthouse.com
• website: www.ivyguesthouse.com

B & B
Mrs Mary Chase, Jadini Garden, Goose
Green, GULLANE, East Lothian EH31 2BA
01620 843343
• e-mail: marychase@jadini.com
• website: www.jadini.com

•FIFE

B & B
Mrs A. Duncan, Spinkstown Farmhouse,
ST ANDREWS, Fife KY16 8PN
01334 473475
• e-mail: anne@spinkstown.com
• website: www.spinkstown.com

•HIGHLANDS

Self-Catering / Guest House
Mr A. Allan, Torguish Self-Catering & B&B,
DAVIOT, Inverness-shire IV2 5XQ
01463 772208
• e-mail: torguish@torguish.com
• website: www.torguish.com

Guest House B & B
Mrs Sandra Silke, Westwood,
Lower Balmacaan, DRUMNADROCHIT,
Inverness-shire IV63 6WU
01456 450826
• e-mail: sandra@westwoodbb.freeserve.co.uk
• website: www.westwoodbb.freeserve.co.uk

Hotel
Allt-Nan-Ros Hotel, Onich, FORT WILLIAM,
Inverness-shire PH33 6RY
01855 821210
• e-mail: fhg@allt-nan-ros.co.uk
• website: www.allt-nan-ros.co.uk

Guest House
Mrs M. Matheson, Thistle Cottage, Torlundy,
FORT WILLIAM, Inverness-shire PH33 6SN
01397 702428
• e-mail: m.a.matheson@amserve.net
• website: www.thistlescotland.co.uk

Hotel
Clan Macduff Hotel, Achintore Road,
FORT WILLIAM, Inverness-shire PH33 6RW
01397 702341
• e-mail: reception@clanmacduff.co.uk
• website: www.clanmacduff.co.uk

Guest House
Mr & Mrs McQueen, Stronchreggan View
Guest House, Achintore Road, FORT
WILLIAM, Inverness-shire PH33 6RW
01397 704644
• e-mail: patricia@apmac.freeserve.co.uk
• website: www.stronchreggan.co.uk

Guest House
Norma E. McCallum, The Neuk, Corpach,
FORT WILLIAM, Inverness-shire PH33 7LR
01397 772244
• e-mail:
normamccallum@theneuk10.fsbusiness.co.uk
• www.theneuk@fortwilliamguesthouse.com

Guest House
Gary Clulow, Sunset Guest House, MORAR,
by Mallaig, Inverness-shire PH40 4PA
01687 462259
• e-mail: sunsetgh@aol.com
• website: www.sunsetguesthouse.co.uk

Self-Catering Chalets / B & B
D.J. Mordaunt, Mondhuie, NETHY BRIDGE,
Inverness-shire PH25 3DF
01479 821062
• e-mail: david@mondhuie.com
• website: www.mondhuie.com

Hotel
Loch Leven Hotel, ONICH, By Fort William,
Inverness-shire PH33 6SA
01855 821236
• e-mail: reception@lochlevenhotel.co.uk
• website: www.lochlevenhotel.co.uk

Self-Catering
Mr A. Urquhart, Crofters Cottages,
15 Croft, POOLEWE, Ross-shire IV22 2SY
01445 781268
• e-mail: croftcottages@btopenworld.com
• website: www.scotia-sc.com/335a.htm

Hotel
Mrs Campbell, Rhiconich Hotel,
RHICONICH, by Lairg, Sutherland IV27 4RN
01971 521224
• e-mail: rhiconichhotel@aol.com
• website: www.rhiconichhotel.co.uk

B & B
Jean Wilson, Tirindrish House, SPEAN
BRIDGE, Inverness-shire PH34 4EU
01397 712398
• e-mail: wpeterwilson@aol.com
• website: www.tirindrish.com

Hotel
Borgie Lodge Hotel, Skerray, TONGUE,
Sutherland KW14 7TH
01641 521332
• e-mail: peter@borgielodgehotel.co.uk
• website: www.borgielodgehotel.co.uk

Self-Catering
Wildside Highland Lodges, By Loch Ness,
WHITEBRIDGE, Inverness-shire IV2 6UN
01456 486373
• e-mail: info@wildsidelodges.com
• website: www.wildsidelodges.com

•LANARKSHIRE

Self-Catering
Carmichael Country Cottages, Carmichael
Estate Office, Westmains, Carmichael,
BIGGAR, Lanarkshire ML12 6PG
01899 308336
• e-mail: chiefcarm@aol.com
• website: www.carmichael.co.uk/cottages

•PERTH & KINROSS

Self-Catering
Loch Tay Lodges, Acharn,
by ABERFELDY, Perthshire
01887 830209
• e-mail: remony@btinternet.com
• website: www.lochtaylodges.co.uk

Hotel / Self-Catering
Dalmunzie House Hotel, Spittal of Glenshee,
BLAIRGOWRIE, Perthshire PH10 7QG
01250 885224
• e-mail: dalmunzie@aol.com
• website: www.dalmunzie.com

Hotel
Atholl Arms Hotel, Bridgehead,
DUNKELD, Perthshire PH8 0AQ
01350 727219
• e-mail: enquiries@athollarmshotel.com
• website: www.athollarmshotel.com

Self-Catering
Laighwood Holidays, Laighwood,
Butterstone, By DUNKELD,
Perthshire PH8 0HB
01350 724241
• e-mail: holidays@laighwood.co.uk
• website: www.laighwood.co.uk

Self Catering
Mrs Hunt, Wester Lix Holiday Cottages,
Wester Lix, KILLIN, Perthshire FK21 8RD
01567 820990
• e-mail: gill@westerlix.co.uk
• website: www.westerlix.co.uk

B & B
Mrs P. Honeyman, Auld Manse Guest House,
Pitcullen Crescent, PERTH, Perthshire PH2 7HT
01738 629187
• e-mail: trishaatauldmanse@hotmail.com
• website: www.guesthouseperth.com

Hotel
Balrobin Hotel, Higher Oakfield,
PITLOCHRY, Pethshire PH16 5HT
01796 472901
• e-mail: info@balrobin.co.uk
• website: www.balrobin.co.uk

Guest House
Jacky Catterall, Tulloch Enochdhu,
by PITLOCHRY, Perthshire PH10 7PW
01250 881404
• e-mail: maljac@tulloch83.freeserve.co.uk
• website: www.econet.org.uk/tulloch

B & B / Camping (wigwam)
Mrs Ann Guthrie, Newmill Farm, STANLEY,
Perth, Perthshire PH1 4QD
01738 828281
• e-mail: guthrienewmill@sol.co.uk
• website: www.newmillfarm.co.uk

•STIRLING & TROSSACHS

B & B
Mrs Judith Bennett, Mossgiel, Doune Road,
DUNBLANE, Stirlingshire
01786 824325
• e-mail: mossgeil2000@yahoo.co.uk
• website: www.mossgiel.com

•ISLE OF SKYE

Self-Catering
Cottage in HARLOSH, c/o Mrs I. MacDiarmid,
21 Dunrobin Avenue, ELDERSLIE,
Renfrewshire PA5 9NW
01505 324460
• e-mail: irenemacdairmid@yahoo.co.uk
• website: www.skyecroft.co.uk

Guest House / B & B
Fiona Scott, Blairdhu House, Old Kyle Farm
Road, KYLEAKIN, Isle of Skye IV41 8PR
01599 534760
• e-mail: blairdhuskye@compuserve.com
• website: www.blairdhuhouse.co.uk

•WALES

Self-Catering
Quality Cottages, Cerbid, Solva,
HAVERFORDWEST,
Pembrokeshire SA62 6YE
01348 837871
• website: www.qualitycottages.co.uk

•ANGLESEY & GWYNEDD

B & B
Mrs M. Billingham, Preswylfa, ABERDOVEY,
Gwynedd LL35 0LE
01654 767239
• e-mail: info@preswylfa.co.uk
• website: www.preswylfa.co.uk

B & B
Mrs J. Bown, Drws-y-Coed,
Llannerch-y-medd, ANGLESEY LL71 8AD
01248 470473
• e-mail: drws.ycoed@virgin.net
• website:
www.SmoothHound.co.uk/hotels/drwsycoed.html

Self-Catering / Caravan
Plas y Bryn Chalet Park, Bontnewydd,
CAERNARFON, Gwynedd LL54 7YE
01286 672811
• e-mail: philplasybryn@aol.com
• website:
www.plasybrynholidayscaernarfon.co.uk

*Please mention
Self Catering
Holidays in Britain
when enquiring
about
accommodation*

Self-Catering within a Castle
Bryn Bras Castle, Llanrug,
near CAERNARFON Gwynedd LL55 4RE
01286 870210
• e-mail: holidays@brynbrascastle.co.uk
• website: www.brynbrascastle.co.uk

Guest House
Mrs Manya Ann Parker, Seaspray,
4 Marine Terrace, CRICCIETH,
Gwynedd LL52 0EF
01766 522373
• website: www.seasprayguesthouse.co.uk

Self-Catering
Anwen Jones, Rhos Country Cottages,
Betws Bach, Ynys, CRICCIETH, Gwynedd
LL52 0PB
01758 720047
• e-mail: cottages@rhos.freeserve.co.uk
• website: www.rhos-cottages.co.uk

B & B
Mrs G. McCreadie, Deri Isaf,
DULAS BAY, Anglesey LL70 9DX
01248 410536
• e-mail: mccreadie@deriisaf.freeserve.co.uk
• website: www.deriisaf.freeserve.co.uk

Farm B & B
Judy Hutchings, Tal y Foel, DWYRAN,
Anglesey, Gwynedd LL61 6LQ
01248 430377
• e-mail: hutchings@talyfoel.u-net.com
• website: www.tal-y-foel.co.uk

Caravan & Chalet Park
Catherine Jones, Wernol Caravan & Chalet
Park, Chwilog, PWLLHELI, Gwynedd LL53 6SW
01766 810506
• website: www.wernol.com

•NORTH WALES

Guest House
Mr M. Wilkie, Bryn Bella Guest House,
Llanrwst Road, BETWS-Y-COED,
Gwynedd LL24 0HD
01690 710627
• e-mail: brynbella@clara.net
• website: www.bryn-bella.co.uk

Guest House / Self-Catering
Jim & Lilian Boughton, Bron Celyn Guest
House, Lôn Muriau, Llanrwst Road,
BETWS-Y-COED North Wales LL24 0HD
01690 710333
• e-mail: welcome@broncelyn.co.uk
• website: www.broncelyn.co.uk

Hotel
Fairy Glen Hotel, Dolwyddelan Road,
BETWS-Y-COED, Conwy,
North Wales LL24 0SH
01690 710269
• e-mail: fairyglenhotel@amserve.net
• website: www.fairyglenhotel.co.uk

B & B
Christine Whale, Brookside House,
Brookside Lane, Northop Hall,
near CHESTER CH7 4HN
01244 821146
• e-mail: christine@brooksidehouse.fsnet.co.uk
• website: www.brooksidehouse.fsnet.co.uk/

Hotel
Caerlyr Hall Hotel, Conwy Old Road,
Dwygfylchi, CONWY,
North Wales LL34 6SW
01492 623518
• website: www.caerlyrhallhotel.co.uk

Hotel
Castle Bank Hotel & Licensed Restaurant,
Mount Pleasant, CONWY,
North Wales LL32 2NY
01492 593888
• e-mail: contact@castle-bank.co.uk
• website: www.castle-bank.co.uk

Hotel
Golden Pheasant Hotel, Glyn Ceiriog,
near LLANGOLLEN, North Wales LL20 7BB
01691 718281
• e-mail: goldenpheasant@micro-plus
• website: www.goldenpheasanthotel.co.uk

B & B
Pen-Y-Drffryn Country House Hotel,
near Rhydycroesau, OSWESTRY,
North Wales SY10 7JD
01691 653700
• e-mail: stay@peny.co.uk
• website: www.peny.co.uk

Hotel
Hafod Country Hotel, TREFRIW,
North Wales LL27 0RQ
01492 640029
• e-mail: hafod@breathemail.net
• website: www.hafodhouse.co.uk

•CARMARTHENSHIRE

B & B
Miss S Czerniewicz, Pant y Bas, Pentrefelin,
LLANDEILO, Carmarthenshire, SA19 6SD
01558 822809
• e-mail: anna@pantybas.fsnet.co.uk
• website: www.southwestwalesbandb.co.uk

•CEREDIGION

Self-Catering
Mr Tucker, Penffynnon, ABERPORTH,
Ceredigion SA43 2DA
01239 810387
• e-mail: tt@lineone.net
  or: jann@aberporth.com
• website: www.aberporth.com

• PEMBROKESHIRE

Self-Catering
John Lloyd, East Llanteg Farm Holiday
Cottages, Llanteg, near AMROTH,
Pembrokeshire SA67 8QA
01834 831336
• e-mail: john@pembrokeshireholiday.co.uk
• website: www.pembrokeshireholiday.co.uk

B & B
Sandra Davies, Barley Villa, Walwyns
Castle, near BROADHAVEN, Haverfordwest,
Pembrokeshire SA62 3EB
01437 781254
• e-mail: sandra.barleyvilla@btinternet.com
• website: www.barleyvilla.co.uk

Farm B & B
Mrs Margaret Williams, Skerryback, Sandy
Haven, St Ishmaels, HAVERFORDWEST,
Pembrokeshire SA62 3DN
01646 636598
• e-mail: williams@farmersweekly.net
• website: www.pfh.co.uk/skerryback

Guest House
Mrs Sandra J. Thompson, Ramsey House,
Lower Moor, ST DAVIDS,
Pembrokeshire SA62 6RP
01437 720321
• e-mail: info@ramseyhouse.co.uk
• website: www.ramseyhouse.co.uk

Self-Catering
Lower Moor Cottages, c/o Thelma M
Hardman, High View, Catherine Street,
ST DAVID'S, Pembrokeshire SA62 6RJ
01437 720616
• e-mail: enquiries@lowermoorcottages.co.uk
• website: www.lowermoorcottages.co.uk

Farm Guest House
Mrs Morfydd Jones, Lochmeyler Farm
Guest House, Llandeloy, Pen-y-Cwm,
near SOLVA, St David's,
Pembrokeshire SA62 6LL
01348 837724
• e-mail: stay@lochmeyler.co.uk
• website: www.lochmeyler.co.uk

B & B
Mrs J. S Rees, Pen Mar Hotel, New Hedges,
TENBY, Pembrokeshire SA70 8TL
01834 842435
• e-mail: penmarhotel@jhurton.freeserve.co.uk

•POWYS

B & B / Self-Catering
Laura Kostoris, Erw yr Danty,
Talybont-on-Usk, BRECON,
Powys LD3 7YN
01874 676498
• e-mail: kosto@ukonline.co.uk
• website: www.wiz.to/lifestyle/

Farm
Mrs Ann Phillips, Tylebrythos Farm, Cantref,
BRECON, Powys LD3 8LR
01874 665329
• e-mail: sa.phillips@ukonline.co.uk

Motel / Caravans
The Park Motel, Crossgates,
LLANDRINDOD WELLS, Powys LD1 6RF
01597 851201
• e-mail: lisa@theparkmotel.freeserve.co.uk
• website: www.theparkmotel.freeserve.co.uk

•SOUTH WALES

Self-Catering
John & Sue Llewellyn, Cwrt-y-Gaer,
Wolvesnewton, CHEPSTOW,
Monmouthshire NP16 6PR
01291 650700
• e-mail: john.ll@talk21.com
• website: www.cwrt-y-gaer.co.uk

Hotel
Mark Cottell, Culver House Hotel,
Port Eynon, GOWER, Swansea,
South Wales SA3 1NN
01792 390755
• e-mail: info@culverhousehotel.co.uk
• website: www.culverhousehotel.co.uk

Guest House
Green Lanterns Guest House, Hawdref
Ganol Farm, Cimla, NEATH,
South Wales SA12 9SL
01639 631884
• e-mail: caren.jones@btinternet.com
• website: www.thegreenlanterns.co.uk

Hotel & Inn
Michael J. Thomas, The Inn at the Elm Tree,
St Brides, Wentlooge, NEWPORT,
South Wales
01633 680225
• e-mail: inn@the-elm-tree.co.uk
• website: www.the-elm-tree.co.uk

•IRELAND

Co. Donegal

B & B / Guest House
Nuala Duddy, Pennsylvania House B & B,
Curraghleas, Mountain Top, LETTERKENNY,
Co Donegal
00-353-74-26808
• e-mail: pennsylvania.house@indigo.ie
• website: www.accommodationdonegal.com

Index of towns and counties
Please also refer to Contents pages 44 – 45

The FHG Directory of Website Addresses
on pages 243 – 272 is a useful quick reference guide for
holiday accommodation with e-mail and/or website details

When making enquiries or bookings, a stamped addressed envelope is always appreciated

THE FHG DIPLOMA

HELP IMPROVE BRITISH TOURIST STANDARDS

You are choosing holiday accommodation from our very popular FHG Publications. Whether it be a hotel, guest house, farmhouse or self-catering accommodation, we think you will find it hospitable, comfortable and clean, and your host and hostess friendly and helpful. Why not write and tell us about it?

As a recognition of the generally well-run and excellent holiday accommodation reviewed in our publications, we at FHG Publications Ltd. present a diploma to proprietors who receive the highest recommendation from their guests who are also readers of our Guides. If you care to write to us praising the holiday you have booked through FHG Publications Ltd. – whether this be board, self-catering accommodation, a sporting or a caravan holiday, what you say will be evaluated and the proprietors who reach our final list will be contacted.

The winning proprietor will receive an attractive framed diploma to display on his premises as recognition of a high standard of comfort, amenity and hospitality. FHG Publications Ltd. offer this diploma as a contribution towards the improvement of standards in tourist accommodation in Britain. Help your excellent host or hostess to win it!

FHG DIPLOMA

We nominate ....

....

Because

Name ....

Address ....

....

Telephone No...

𝕱𝕳𝕲 Diploma Winners 2002

Each year we award a small number of diplomas to holiday proprietors whose services have been specially commended by our readers. The following were our FHG Diploma Winners for 2002.

England

DEVON

Woolacombe Bay Holiday Park,
Woolacombe, North Devon
EX34 7HW (01271 870343).

LANCASHIRE

Mrs Holdsworth,
Broadwater Hotel,
356 Marine Road, East Promenade
Morecambe, Lancashire LA4 5AQ
(01524 411333).

Peter & Susan Bicker,
Kelvin Private Hotel,
Reads Avenue, Blackpool,
Lancashire FY1 4JJ
(01253 620293).

LINCOLNSHIRE

Sue Phillips & John Lister,
Cawthorpe Farm, Cawthorpe
Bourne, Lincolnshire PE10 0AB
(01778 426697).

OXFORDSHIRE

Liz Roach, The Old Bakery,
Skirmett, Nr Henley on Thames
Oxfordshire RG9 6TD
(01491 638309).

SOMERSET

Pat & Sue Weir, Slipper Cottage,
41 Bishopston, Montacute,
Somerset TA15 6UX
(01935 823073)

Scotland

ARGYLL & BUTE

David Quibell,
Rosneath Castle Caravan Park
Near Helensburgh,
Argyll & Bute G84 0QS
(01436 831208)

DUNDEE & ANGUS

Carlogie House Hotel,
Carlogie Road, Carnoustie,
Dundee DD7 6LD
(01241 853185)

EDINBURGH & LOTHIANS

Geraldine Hamilton,
Crosswoodhill Farm, West Calder
Edinburgh & Lothians EH55 8LP
(01501 785205)

FIFE

Mr Alastair Clark,
Old Manor Country House Hotel,
Lundin Links, Nr St Andrews
Fife KY8 6AJ
(01333 320368)

HIGHLANDS

N & J McCallum, The Neuk
Corpach, Fort William PH33 7LE
(01397 772244)

HELP IMPROVE BRITISH TOURISM STANDARDS

Why not write and tell us about the holiday accommodation you have chosen from one of our popular publications? Complete a nomination form giving details of why you think YOUR host or hostess should win one of our attractive framed diplomas and send it to:

FHG Publications, Abbey Mill Business Centre, Seedhill, Paisley PA1 1TJ

OTHER FHG TITLES FOR 2003

FHG Publications have a large range of attractive holiday accommodation guides for all kinds of holiday opportunities throughout Britain. They also make useful gifts at any time of year. Our guides are available in most bookshops and larger newsagents but we will be happy to post you a copy direct if you have any difficulty. POST FREE for addresses in the UK. We will also post abroad but have to charge separately for post or freight.

The original
**Farm Holiday Guide to
COAST & COUNTRY
HOLIDAYS** in England,
Scotland, Wales and Channel
Islands. Board, Self-catering,
Caravans/Camping, Activity
Holidays.

**BED AND BREAKFAST
STOPS**
Over 1000 friendly and
comfortable overnight stops.
Non-smoking, Disabled and
Special Diets Supplements.

**BRITAIN'S BEST
HOLIDAYS**
A quick-reference general
guide for all kinds of holidays.

Recommended
**WAYSIDE AND
COUNTRY INNS** of Britain
Pubs, Inns and small hotels.

Recommended
**SHORT BREAK
HOLIDAYS IN BRITAIN**
"Approved" accommodation
for quality bargain breaks.

PETS WELCOME!
The original and unique guide
for holidays for pet owners and
their pets.